Praise for
Ashley's War

Named One of "10 Books for 2015" by *Military Times*

"Lemmon has done her homework. . . . She is a strong and capable guide. . . . With a fine eye for detail, she shows us what set this program apart."
—*Foreign Policy*

"*Ashley's War* quietly grips the reader with the untold story of a small group of women selected to serve in combat alongside the US's best soldiers. . . . Rich storytelling. . . . Compelling. . . . In battle as in life, these women refuse to quit."
—*Christian Science Monitor*

"[Y]oung women will be moved by this book which will teach them that they can do absolutely anything. *Ashley's War* is a remarkable war story (and one of the very few that showcases women on the battlefield)."
—*BuzzFeed* (picked as one of "29 Books You Should Definitely Bring to the Beach This Summer")

"The summer's must-read."
—Joanna Coles, *Cosmopolitan*

"Gripping. . . . After two years of assiduous research, in *Ashley's War* Lemmon tells the powerful story of an extraordinary group of women, and after knowing them, I was left cheering."
—*Daily Beast*

"Through meticulous research and hours of interviews, [Lemmon] gets inside the heads and hearts of these soldiers and deftly captures what it was like for the pioneering women to go through grueling training together and then deploy, as individuals, across Afghanistan."
—Janine Davidson, *Women in the World/NYT Live*

"Lemmon's depictions of these women are vivid, giving readers a textured understanding of who they are and what drove them to volunteer for an unprecedented program that would place them in incredibly dangerous situations."　　　　　—Military.com

"An unforgettable story of female soldiers breaking the brass ceiling. The women who answered America's call to serve show that our military is stronger when it engages both halves of the population. This book will inspire you and remind you of the power that comes with defying limits."

—Sheryl Sandberg, author of *Lean In*

"*Ashley's War* shares the remarkable stories of one of the first teams of women serving in the U.S. Army Special Operations Command. This team forged the path for American women who serve in harm's way all over the world and continue to make the ultimate sacrifice."　　　　　—Senator John McCain

"Fascinating and often moving, *Ashley's War* follows one of the early groups of women who volunteered to serve alongside special operations soldiers, vividly portraying their training, their early missions as they learn their jobs, their bonds of friendship, and their reckoning with the toll of war. Remarkable."

—Phil Klay, author of *Redeployment*

"Gayle Tzemach Lemmon expertly gives readers an inside look at what it takes to work alongside America's elite forces. The book is a gripping, moving, and well-told war story, but more importantly it offers the first glimpse into a historic program."

—Kevin Maurer, author of *Gentlemen Bastards*

ASHLEY'S WAR

Also by Gayle Tzemach Lemmon

The Dressmaker of Khair Khana

Ashley's War

★ ★ ★

The Untold Story of a Team of Women Soldiers
on the Special Ops Battlefield

Gayle Tzemach Lemmon

HARPER ● PERENNIAL

NEW YORK ● LONDON ● TORONTO ● SYDNEY ● NEW DELHI ● AUCKLAND

HARPER ● PERENNIAL

A hardcover edition of this book was published in 2015 by HarperCollins Publishers.

P.S.™ is a trademark of HarperCollins Publishers.

HarperCollins books may be purchased for educational, business, or sales promotional use. For information, please e-mail the Special Markets Department at SPsales@harpercollins.com.

FIRST HARPER PERENNIAL EDITION PUBLISHED 2016.

Photographs:

Part I: Cultural Support Team recruiting poster

Part II: 1st Lt. Ashley White in uniform (*Courtesy of the White family*)

Part III: Ashley White and Jason Stumpf on their wedding day (*Courtesy of the White family*)

Epilogue: The funeral of 1st Lt. Ashley White (*Courtesy of the White family*)

Designed by William Ruoto

Library of Congress Cataloging-in-Publication Data has been applied for.

ISBN 978-0-06-233382-7 (pbk.)

16 17 18 19 20 OV/RRD 10 9 8 7 6 5 4 3 2 1

To all the unsung warriors. That you may never be forgotten.

To Rhoda Spielman Tzemach and Frances Spielman.

And to JL, who believed from the start.

Contents

Author's Note

This book is the product of twenty months of travel, hundreds of hours of interviews conducted in a dozen states across America, a review of primary research and documents, and an illuminating set of conversations with some of America's most seasoned military leaders.

It also has been a puzzle to assemble, a privilege to tell, and a humbling responsibility to bring to life.

What follows is a ground-level view of the women who answered the call to serve with Special Operations Forces, soldiers who raised their hands right away when they heard of the chance to volunteer with the best in battle. Readers seeking to learn more about military tactics, decision making, and the formulation of military strategy will find several suggestions in the select bibliography that follows these pages.

Most names have been changed to protect those involved and those still connected to the special operations community. Some details have been omitted for the sake of security.

I had the privilege of meeting many men and women not mentioned in these pages. Each one had a story worth telling.

The soldiers who spoke with me shared their war stories not because they wish to be known—they do not—but because they want their friend and teammate to be remembered.

The stories are theirs. Any errors are mine.

At a time when the divide between those who volunteer to fight America's wars and those who never served is wide and growing, it is more important than ever to know who these soldiers are and why they sign up to fight for the sake of the rest of us.

Author's Note

Whatever any of these soldiers do in the future, this past year has convinced me that nothing, ever, will come close to the year they spent serving on the battlefield alongside the men of America's Special Operations Forces.

And no passage of years will lessen their sense of belonging to CST-2.

Acronyms

DFAC   Dining facility

JOC   Joint Operations Center

JSOC   Joint Special Operations Command, based in Fayetteville, North Carolina

KAF   Kandahar Airfield

MP   Military Police

MREs   Meals, Ready to Eat

SF   Special Forces: the Green Berets

SOCOM   Special Operations Command, based in Tampa, Florida

SOF   Special Operations Forces, this includes Delta Force, Green Berets, Navy SEALs, 75th Ranger Regiment, Air Force Special Operations Command, Marine Corps Forces Special Operations Command

TOC   Tactical Operations Center

XO   Executive officer, the second in command in certain military units

Preface: Kandahar

Second Lieutenant White entered the "ready room" and began preparing for the night of battle.

Kandahar, August 2011, 2200 hours: a narrow room just off a main hallway, lined with plywood shelves and plastic drawers stuffed with rolls of Velcro, electrical cables, and heavy-duty packing tape. The smell of gun oil clung to the air. White had written down the long list of gear, and now calmly grabbed items the mission required:

> *Helmet and night vision goggles. Check.*
> *Headset for communicating with platoon leader. Check.*
> *M4 rifle. Check.*
> *M9 pistol. Check.*
> *Ammunition for both. Check, check.*
> *Eye protection to keep dust and dirt from causing sudden*
>   *blindness. Check.*
> *Notecards and pens to document everything that was said and*
>   *found. Check.*
> *Clif Bars in case the mission went long. Check.*
> *Jolly Ranchers and Tootsie Rolls for village kids. Check.*
> *Tourniquets to stop the bleeding of a fellow soldier. Check.*
> *Medical gloves.*
> *Zip ties.*
> *Water.*

Check. Check. Check.

White felt the fear rising, but more seasoned soldiers had provided plenty of advice for the special brand of trepidation that accompanies a soldier on their first night mission. "It gets easier after the first time," they assured the newbies during training. "Don't indulge it, just pass through it."

Ready now, White stepped into the briefing room and took in the scene. Dozens of battle-hardened men from one of the Army's fittest and finest teams, the elite special operations 75th Ranger Regiment, crowded in to watch a PowerPoint presentation in a large conference room. Many had Purple Hearts and deployments that reached into the double digits. Around them was the staff that supports soldiers in the field with intelligence, communications, and explosives disposal capabilities. Everyone was studying a diagram of the target compound as the commanders ticked through the mission plan in their own vernacular, a mix of Army shorthand and abbreviations that, to the uninitiated, sounded like a foreign language. But every person in the room knew precisely where they needed to be, what their role was, and how they would help accomplish the night's mission.

White had the feeling of being in a Hollywood war movie. Standing nearby was a noncommissioned officer (NCO) and Iraq War veteran whom the second lieutenant had trained with.

"Are we supposed to say something?" White asked

Staff Sergeant Mason, also out for the first time, scooted closer and whispered back. Neither new arrival wanted to stand out any more than they already did.

"No, I don't think so, not tonight. The last group will speak for us."

That was a relief. White had no desire to draw attention in a room filled with soldiers who clearly felt at home in combat. Like a cast of actors who had performed the same play for a decade, they knew each other's lines and moves, and offstage they knew each other's backstories. It was an unexpected revelation for White, gleaned during a fifteen-minute mission review in a makeshift conference room in the middle of one of Afghanistan's most dangerous provinces: this was a family unit. A brotherhood.

The briefing ended, the commanding officer approached the front of the room and the soldiers suddenly shouted as one:

"Rangers Lead the Way!"

They saluted in a finely choreographed sweep and filed out.

The rookie second lieutenant did the same, hoping the gesture didn't look too awkward for a first-timer, then followed the others, trailed by Sergeant Mason. They stepped into their office—a broom closet, actually—and exhaled for the first time.

"Whew," White allowed.

"That shit is serious," Mason said. "This is the real deal."

Then, without another word, they began a systems check, testing the frequency of their radios to make sure they operated properly. This would be their lifeline while on mission. They triple-checked their night-vision goggles, which clipped onto the top of their helmets, and made sure they had batteries for all the electronics they carried: headsets, radios, and a red laser that allowed them to silently point things out to one another. By the time they exited the barracks each was carrying close to fifty pounds of gear.

In one of the many Velcroed pockets of White's uniform was information about the insurgent they were after and a list of crimes he was suspected of committing. In another pocket was a medal of St. Joseph and a prayer card. White stepped out of the barracks and worked to conceal any trace of the intense emotions this moment conjured up: pride in being part of a team hunting a terrorist who was killing American soldiers and his own countrymen; trepidation at the thought that after a short ride on the bird they would all end up in his living room. But it was exactly what White had wanted and trained for: to serve with fellow soldiers in this long war and do something that mattered.

The fighters lined up by last name and marched into the yawning darkness of the Kandahar night. Unlike the American cities they came from, whose skies were often clouded by the pollution of industry, traffic, and the millions of lights that power a modern, twenty-four-hour-a-day society, Kandahar's blackness stretched on forever with constellations you only read about at home. The sky was glorious, and for just an instant White slowed and wondered at the sparkling celestial recital that was on display up above. But then a powerful stench yanked the young officer back into the moment. As heavenly as the skies were, just so earthly was the smell of human excrement that hovered over and seemed to surround the Kandahar camp. In a city whose sewage system had been all but destroyed by war, the smell of feces attacked with ferocity anytime a soldier was downwind.

But White was focused on something even more mundane: staying upright while marching along the unpaved, rock-strewn tarmac for the first time in total darkness. "Focus on the next step," White silently commanded. "No mistakes. Do your job. Don't mess up."

Here and there came the sound of fellow soldiers ribbing one another, swapping jokes and gallows humor. But White also detected, in the orange ember of one Ranger's dying cigarette, hints of the stress they all shared. They wore their exhaustion well, but it was there.

White and Mason fell in alongside their fellow special operations "enablers," a group that included the explosive ordnance disposal guys who became famous in the Hollywood blockbuster *The Hurt Locker.* (Even if all the guys didn't love the movie, every one of them could appreciate the scene at the end in the grocery store where a soldier who has just returned stateside scans the cereal aisle in all its overfed glory and wonders why any country needs so many choices.) Close behind was their interpreter, an Afghan-American now entering year four in Afghanistan. Language expertise notwithstanding, the interpreter's gear looked like it came from the Eisenhower era. They all guessed some soldier had worn that helmet back in

Vietnam; it barely held the clips for night-vision goggles and was seriously dinged.

Entering the cramped helicopter, White and Mason were determined not to make a beginner mistake by taking the wrong seat, so they fell in behind a first sergeant, who had taken the new arrivals under his wing. After he sat, they followed his example, snapping a bungee cord that hung from a metal hook on their belt into hooks beneath a narrow metal bench. In theory, these cords would keep them from flying across—or *out* of—the helicopter while it was airborne. The soldiers took root, and with a sudden whirr the bird was off. The only thing Lieutenant White could see through the green haze of the night-vision goggles was a flash from the helicopter's lights as it left the ground.

Here we go, White thought. Outwardly the picture of calm, inside the young officer felt a rush of adrenaline and fear. Everything— the selection process, the training, the deployment—had happened so quickly. Now, suddenly, it was real. For the next nine months this is what every night would look like.

But enough nightdreaming.

Focus, White commanded. Get back to the work at hand. What is the protocol for next steps?

> *Brace for landing.*
> *Unhook.*
> *Evacuate the bird.*
> *Run like hell.*
> *Take a knee.*

Over the booming engine noise the first sergeant barked out the time stamp in hand signals.

"Six minutes."

"Three minutes."

White turned to Mason and gave the thumbs-up with a smile that was full of unfelt confidence.

"One minute."

Showtime.

The bird landed and the door flew open, like the maw of some huge, wild reptile that had descended from the sky. White followed the others and ran a short distance before taking a knee, managing to avoid the worst of the brownout, that swirling mix of dust, stones, and God-only-knows what else that flies upward in the wake of a departing helicopter.

Choking on a batter of dirt and mud, White mumbled inaudibly, *Welcome to Afghanistan*, before rising up to adjust the awkward night-vision goggles that now provided the only lens to the outside world. With barely a word exchanged, the Rangers fell in line and began marching toward the target compound.

The ground crunched beneath their feet as they pressed forward through vineyards and wadis, southern Afghanistan's ubiquitous ditches and dry riverbeds. They marched quickly, and even though the night goggles made depth perception a nearly impossible challenge White managed not to trip over the many vines that snaked along and across the rutted landscape. No one made a sound. Even a muffled cough could ricochet across the silence and bring unwanted noise into the operation. Every soldier on target knows that surprise is the key to staying alive. And silence is the key to surprise.

Fifteen minutes on they reached their objective, though to White it felt like only a minute had passed. An interpreter's voice could be heard addressing the men of the house in Pashto, urging them to come outside. A few minutes later the American and Afghan soldiers entered the compound to search for the insurgent and any explosives or weapons he might have hidden inside.

And then Second Lieutenant Ashley White heard the summons that had led her from the warmth of her North Carolina home to one of the world's most remote—and dangerous—pockets.

"CST, get up here," called a voice on the radio.

The Rangers were ready for White and her team to get to work.

The trio of female soldiers—White, Mason, and their civilian interpreter, Nadia—strode toward the compound that was bathed in the green haze of their goggles. It was dead in the middle of the night, but for White, the day was just beginning.

Her war story had just begun. It was time for the women to go to work.

ASHLEY'S WAR

I

The Call to Serve

1

Uncle Sam Needs **You**

★ ★ ★

Two years before Ashley White ran off the helicopter in Kandahar, Afghanistan, U.S. Special Operations Commander Eric Olson had an idea.

Working from a second-floor office in the headquarters of the U.S. Special Operations Command (SOCOM) at MacDill Air Force Base in Tampa, Florida, Admiral Olson had spent years studying the ever-changing battlefield in what had become the longest war in American history. Twenty-first-century technology, advanced weaponry, and instant communications radically altered the modern battleground, offering fighters more real-time information than ever before. But specific pockets of what Olson called "micro-knowledge"—meaningful, detailed intelligence about a region's people, culture, language, and social mores—remained out of reach to American forces. He wanted to change that.

Olson was a groundbreaker in his own right. The first Navy SEAL to be appointed a three-star, then a four-star admiral, he was also the first Navy officer to lead the Special Operations Command. It was a position widely considered to be among the most important—and least-known—jobs in America's fight against terrorism.

SOCOM's creation in 1987 ended a bruising Washington brawl that pitted special ops supporters in Congress and the special operations community against senior military and civilian Pentagon leaders. The military leadership viewed the command as a needless drain of resources from America's armed forces, of which special ops formed just a very small part, less than 5 percent of America's military men and women. As a distinct culture that favors small units over large forces and independent problem solving over the formal, traditional military hierarchy, they were viewed with deep suspicion by much of the Army, Navy, Marines, and Air Force. America's first special operations teams were created in World War II for missions that rely on the kind of nimble, secret, surgical actions for which large-scale, conventional forces are ill-suited. Their portfolio was always intended to be utterly different from that of traditional ground forces. In his 1962 speech to West Point's graduates, President John F. Kennedy reflected on the new geopolitical landscape that gave rise to special operations forces:

> *This is another type of war, new in its intensity, ancient in its origins—war by guerrillas, subversives, insurgents, assassins; war by ambush instead of combat; by infiltration instead of aggression, seeking victory by eroding and exhausting the enemy instead of engaging him. It requires—in those situations where we must encounter it—a whole new kind of strategy, a wholly different kind of force, and therefore, a new and wholly different kind of military training.*

Over the years, special ops forces were subject to boom-and-bust cycles as conflicts escalated and ended. They played a heroic and prominent role in World War II, when special operations teams parachuted into German strongholds, scaled the cliffs at Pointe du Hoc in Normandy to destroy enemy gun positions, and dropped behind enemy lines to liberate American prisoners of war from a Japanese prisoner of war camp. In Korea special ops units ran raids and ambushes, but soon afterward saw their budgets and their numbers shrink. They once again bulked up to join the fight in Vietnam, running small-unit reconnaissance missions far behind enemy lines and working with and training local South Vietnamese fighters, but by the late 1970s, the force had again been whittled down to near extinction. In the era of Cold War confrontations, their style of fighting was seen as a mismatch against the Soviets, who were rapidly building up conventional forces.

Everything changed in the 1990s with the successful use of special operations forces in Operation Desert Storm and the rise of modern terrorism by non-state actors like Hezbollah and, toward the end of the twentieth century, al-Qaeda. After the attacks of 9/11, the subterfuge, speed, and surprise that were the hallmark of special operations moved its forces front and center in the war against terror. By 2010 SOCOM could draw upon people, technology, dollars, and equipment that its founders wouldn't have dared imagine twenty years earlier. During that period, in the latter half of the post-9/11 war in Afghanistan, Eric Olson's Special Operations Command demanded a great deal more of its fighting men and women than ever before.

Olson was the quintessential special ops man. Slight in build and large in presence, he is the model "quiet professional" that Special Operations Forces style themselves after. Those under his command described him as "a cerebral officer," unusual for his tendency to listen more than he speaks. He had seen plenty of combat in his long career; a highly decorated Navy SEAL, he received a Silver Star for leading a team through Mogadishu's streets to rescue injured soldiers overcome by Somali fighters in the battle popularly known as "Black Hawk Down."

From the start of the war, Olson believed that America was never going to kill its way to victory in Afghanistan. "We have to learn to think our way through this fight," he would say. To do that, "we have to understand it better." For some time, Olson had been thinking about "the whole yin and yang of modern warfare capabilities." As he saw it, "concepts that may at first appear to be opposed to each other may in fact be parts of the same whole," and he had come to believe that the United States was out of balance, too tilted toward the hard side of war and not devoted enough to what he viewed as its softer side: the knowledge-based war.

Part of the problem, Olson felt, was that the military's incentives—its systems, programs, personnel policies, promotion paths—all rewarded hard skills over deep knowledge. He believed that even the most knowledgeable members of the military's elite special operations teams in Afghanistan—experts who had studied the geography, history, and language of the region and had become comfortable in the environment—even *they* were missing a huge chunk of intel about the enemy they were fighting and the people they were there to protect. Some of the most crucial information, Olson believed, was hiding within a population to which special ops forces, nearly a decade into the war, had virtually no access: the women.

For centuries Afghan culture has enshrined women as vessels of family honor. In some regions, particularly in the more conservative and rural Pashtun belt, from which most of the Taliban fighters come, women are kept separate from any man unrelated by marriage or blood. Pashtunwali, an unwritten tribal code governing all aspects of community life, delineates the laws and behaviors of the Pashtun people. At the heart of the system is the principle of *namus*, which defines the relationship between men and women, and establishes the primacy of chastity and sexual integrity of women within a family. *Namus* commands men to respect—and more fundamentally, to preserve—what it holds to be the honor of Afghan women. An essential part of preserving that honor means keeping women separate from men from the time they near adolescence until their marriage. When a woman does venture out from her family's walled compound, she must be accompanied by a male family member or a group of other women led by a male chaperone. When in public women wear the *chadri*, or burqa, which covers their face completely.

While much has changed for the millions of Afghans now living in many of Afghanistan's increasingly crowded cities, where girls go to school and women work outside the home, in the most remote reaches of rural provinces where the Americans have been fighting their toughest battles, women's lives often look very different.

The ancient practice of *purdah*, or the seclusion of women from public view, makes women in these regions nearly invisible to the foreign men fighting in their country. And it means that foreign troops cause a serious affront to Afghan families when a male soldier even catches sight of a woman's face. Searching a woman is an even graver offense. By engaging with Afghan women the male soldiers are disrespecting them as well as the men in their family charged with protecting them. The act violates a code of honor that lies at the very foundation of their society.

This form of cultural trespass was also in direct opposition to counterinsurgency, a newly revived military doctrine based on a commitment to protect the local population while stopping insurgents and helping build a government that could provide basic services to its people. Fresh from its prominent role in the Iraq troop surge of 2007, counterinsurgency was at the center of the 2009 addition of thirty thousand U.S. forces into Afghanistan. In counterinsurgency theory the "population is the prize." Winning hearts and minds and protecting civilians now played a key role in America's military strategy, but both would be undermined if American men searched Afghan women.

And there was another important cultural reality in play. In a communal society such as Afghanistan, in which family is central, the role of women is critical. Afghan women saw, overheard, and understood much of what was happening in the households they ran, and they exchanged information with one another every day. In rural Afghanistan, information travels faster via the network of extended families than it does via instant messaging in most other parts of the world, and the women often have an idea of what their sons, husbands, brothers, and in-laws are up to.

What Admiral Olson was coming to understand was that from a strategic point of view, not having access to Afghan women meant that U.S. soldiers were entirely blind to half the country's population, and all the information and social influence it held. Even more: whatever may have been hidden in the women's quarters—everything from enemy combatants to weapons and nuggets of critical intelligence—would remain unfound. This reality signaled a dangerous security gap, for no soldier had ever truly cleared a house when even a single room went unchecked. The only question that remained was: could the military actually do anything about it?

In Iraq, a similar question had been asked and answered years earlier with the creation of the "Lioness" program within the Marine Corps. In 2003 and 2004, as the budding insurgency grew bolder in the city of Ramadi, commanders gathered an ad hoc group of twenty female soldiers and female Marines—most of them drivers or mechanics certified on the .50-caliber machine gun—to join male Marines and Army soldiers on raids, security patrols, and at the increasing number of security checkpoints designed to stop suicide bombers. Much of the Lionesses' work consisted of searching Iraqi women for hidden weapons and explosives vests, and confirming they were indeed women, not men who had disguised themselves beneath the veil.

A similar story played out later in Afghanistan, and once again it was the Marines out in front. It was early 2009, and a unit was planning an operation in Farah Province to capture the men responsible for planting improvised explosive devices (IEDs) that had killed several fellow Marines.

One of the planners was Lieutenant Matt Pottinger, a Marine who traveled an unlikely path to Afghanistan. Before arriving there, Pottinger spent five years covering China for the *Wall Street Journal*'s Beijing bureau, where his aggressive reporting got him detained for a piece about political corruption. He watched from Beijing with growing concern as his *Journal* colleague Daniel Pearl was abducted and killed by al-Qaeda and the war in Iraq descended into chaos. Then, in 2004, the *Journal* sent him to cover the Asian tsunami that killed a quarter of a million people. The only first responders who impressed him on a personal and professional level were the U.S. Marines and sailors who landed there en route from Iraq. While local and international charities fumbled in disorganized chaos, the servicemen and women methodically tackled problems and found ways around the countless obstacles to get actual relief to the people in need. Witnessing them in action profoundly affected Pottinger, and he thought if he were ever going to serve his country, he should do it now, with this caliber of people, at this time of severe national crisis. So in 2005, at the age of thirty-two, he entered Marines' Officer Candidates School. A year and a half later he deployed to Iraq.

By the time Matt Pottinger reached Farah Province, the battlefield acumen of a trained Marine and Iraq veteran now complemented a reporter's instincts for navigating the cultural fault lines that shape the country. He soon realized that, given Afghanistan's social customs and traditions, it would be nearly impossible for the military to raid homes filled with women without alienating everyone in the village. After months of study he reached a surprising conclusion: in order to achieve success, *the missions needed women*.

It was a counterintuitive idea, one Pottinger himself initially mistrusted, so with the help of a satellite phone he tracked down a few U.S.-based Afghanistan experts, including Sarah Chayes, an American journalist who had lived on her own in Kandahar for several years. Chayes confirmed what Pottinger had hypothesized: having U.S. female soldiers on hand would not ratchet up tensions with Afghan men, but instead was likely to defuse them and make the whole operation run more smoothly. And if the experts were right, far from violating social codes, it would, on the contrary, help build trust. With his commander's approval, Pottinger assembled a group of seven female Marines and one female interpreter, and over a period of several days led impromptu lessons on Afghan culture, proper search techniques, and how to conduct tactical questioning.

The experiment worked. With the help of local village women who had been questioned by members of the female engagement team—soon to be known by the acronym FET, coined by Pottinger and logistics officer Lieutenant Johannah Shaffer—the Marines located the insurgents responsible for killing their brothers-in-arms. As significant: village elders expressed approval that neither Afghan nor American men had interacted with their women. Having the female Marines on-site had proven to be a boon both culturally and tactically.

This point was driven home during a failed mission a few months later in southern Helmand Province that became notorious when male insurgents literally, and brazenly, walked past a team of Marines who had cordoned off their compound. They simply donned burqas and filed right by the Marines, who had called for the women to leave the compound so they would be protected from the fighting that would inevitably follow. Only later did the Marines realize what had happened.

Word of Pottinger's work spread. And soon former Marine 1st Lt. Claire Russo, who was determined to formalize for the Army the kind of female engagement teams Pottinger was developing for the Marines, reached out to him for advice. Russo arrived in Afghanistan in 2009, the same year as Pottinger, as part of a civilian team created to help the Army better understand the cultural terrain. The C-130 transport plane had no sooner dropped her off in eastern Afghanistan than the colonel in charge of the region enlisted Russo for a very specific mission—one for which this female former Marine was particularly well suited.

The Army colonel had been hearing from battalions and companies across the region that certain units were using ad hoc, informal teams of women soldiers to help achieve their missions. He wanted to understand what female soldiers were being asked to do, why commanders thought they were uniquely suited to these assignments, and whether it was legal, given the military's official ban on women in ground combat. Russo's task was to investigate and to come back with answers.

Russo's fact-finding mission took her to bases all around eastern Afghanistan, where she surveyed Army units from Provincial Reconstruction Teams to infantry units. She found they all were using women in different ways: some started livelihood projects for local Afghan women while others had women soldiers "going outside the wire" to learn what was happening in their community.

But what alarmed Russo was the clear lack of tactical training the female soldiers received. These women, mostly medics, sometimes civil affairs officers, were now operating in close quarters in areas heavy with insurgents and other enemies in the middle of a war zone. Competent at their jobs and brave though they were, basically they all were improvising. It was clear to Russo that there was a need for female engagement among Army units, and commanders told her they were getting valuable intel and a stronger understanding of local dynamics from the teams of soldiers. But there was still a persistent belief among some senior Army leaders that women in Afghanistan had no power or influence. Russo's direct observations had led to the opposite conclusion: Afghan women sat at the center of a complex web of family relationships and had a significant effect on the population.

Buoyed by this conviction, and encouraged by senior Army officers who wanted this capability in their units, Russo was determined to press the case. She had always been nearly impossible to deter once she put her mind to something, and personal tragedy had only hardened her resolve. In 2004, Russo was a newly minted intel officer who had fulfilled her childhood dream of becoming a Marine, which had been sparked by the movie *A Few Good Men*. A few months into her first assignment, a fellow Marine raped her at a Marine Corps ball. She reported the assault, but the Marine Corps refused to press charges. Eventually, with the help of a Navy criminal investigator, Russo's case landed on the desk of the San Diego district attorney, whose investigation revealed that her accused had done the same thing to another servicewoman. For her refusal to be silenced, Russo eventually received a "Citizen of Courage" award from the San Diego district attorney.

Now in Afghanistan five years later, working as a civilian for the Army and still passionate about serving, Russo was searching for someone with experience in building these all-female teams—and Pottinger's name immediately came up. Borrowing some of Pottinger's FET materials after tracking him down in Kabul, Russo began the process of training Army FETs for a commander in northeast Afghanistan.

Later, with a trove of knowledge they had gathered about women and both the cultural and actual battlefields, Pottinger, Russo, and an influential Afghan-American cultural advisor named Hali Jilani teamed up to publicly address the persistent myths surrounding the FETs. The title of the report, published in 2010 in a military journal, spoke for itself: "Half-Hearted: Trying to Win Afghanistan without Afghan Women."

The article began by explaining that Afghan men tend to see foreign women as a third gender: not threatening, like American men or subject to the cultural restrictions of Afghan women, but a third group with whom they could interact in a respectful and forthright manner. Noting that "our reluctance to employ all but a few allied servicewomen in tactical counterinsurgency operations mirror-images the Taliban," the authors pointed out that in 2009 "so few U.S. servicewomen had meaningful contact with Afghan women that, statistically speaking, they literally had a higher chance of getting pregnant than of meeting an Afghan woman outside the wire."

"Who," they asked in conclusion, "is shielding their women from Afghan society more: Pashtun men or U.S. commanders?"

At around the same time, back in Tampa, Admiral Olson was working on his own concept of the all-female teams. Though he found the Marines' FET model interesting, he believed it was too structured for special operations. While movies portray these men as Olympian athletes and tactical geniuses, Olson often described the best of the SEALs and other special operations teams—including the Army Special Forces and the 75th Ranger Regiment, Navy SEALs, Air Force and Marine special operations forces—in much more earthbound language: "physically fit problem solvers."

Olson knew that any proposal to put women in direct combat zones would guarantee heavy resistance from within the military. Although special operations had long deployed women to hostile zones in a number of roles, including psychological operations and intelligence, the direct ground combat exclusion prohibition—the official ban, formalized in a 1994 memo, that prohibits women from serving on the front lines—was, for Olson, the "bridge that we had to cross." And it was clear that the time to cross it was *now*.

Since 1948 women's military service had been governed by the Women's Armed Services Integration Act. Among other limits, women were barred from serving aboard any navy ship other than hospitals and transports and from aircraft that could have a combat mission. No mention was made back then of women in ground combat. By the 1980s things were slowly changing: women formed part of non-combat air crews and served aboard some Navy ships. More roles opened up after more than 40,000 servicewomen deployed in 1990 and 1991 as part of Operation Desert Shield and Operation Desert Storm. By the mid-1990s women could serve in aviation and naval combat. But assignment to units "whose primary mission is to engage in direct combat on the ground" remained off-limits for women.

Around headquarters Olson began to raise the issue of getting women into battle roles to support special operations teams, and again and again he met with the same, unenthusiastic reception. Olson understood the limits of his power, for while the role of SO-COM commander carried a great deal of clout, in actual fact he was a "force provider," not the commander of all Special Operations Forces operating around the world. This made him effectively the CEO of Special Operations Inc. with a mission to provide a product—readiness, options, and capabilities—that commanders on the ground could choose to use. Or not. Olson couldn't *make* commanders use these teams; he could only imagine and then develop the ideas so they would be there if and when they were wanted.

Officials around SOCOM listened politely enough to Olson's idea, then they slow-rolled him. Most gave him the clear impression they couldn't wait for his time as commander to end so he could take his idea about these new all-female teams with him. It was the same thing that had happened in the Pentagon twenty years earlier, when Congress demanded the creation of SOCOM.

A few months later, however, the landscape changed. By April 2010, a new wave of U.S. troops was entering Afghanistan as part of a force surge announced the previous December, and the fight against the insurgency was accelerating. Olson's idea was about to get a second chance, and from a most unlikely source, a group of the Army's most grizzled infantry fighters: the U.S. Army's 75th Ranger Regiment, the night-raiding special operations ground-pounders whose history dates back to colonial times.

In April 2010 Admiral William McRaven, the highly regarded head of the Joint Special Operations Command, submitted a formal request to Olson at SOCOM that *women soldiers* be made available to join the Rangers on missions. It was based on a radical premise from a forward-thinking leader: that women enablers could make Ranger missions more successful. The idea was that the best female soldiers in the Army would join the 75th Ranger Regiment's elite strike forces as they went out on nightly direct action raids to get terrorists and insurgents.

JSOC, McRaven's command, came to life in the early 1980s following the humiliation of the failed attempt to free American hostages in Iran. In the aftermath of the disastrous aborted mission that ended with eight American servicemen dead, the Pentagon created a commission to figure out how so much had gone so wrong. One of the panel's recommendations was the creation of a "joint" command that would create a cohesive team of special operators from the toughest units in the service: Navy SEALs, the Air Force's special operations pilots, Army's Delta Force and Green Berets, and, eventually, the Army's 75th Ranger Regiment.

In 2003 General Stanley McChrystal took command of JSOC and over five years oversaw its evolution into a speed-sensitive, data-driven, high-value targeting machine. Insurgents would be targeted, then targeted again, until they were captured. Each raid yielded new information that produced the next set of targets. The results were astounding. Raids on terrorist homes, weapons depots, and safe houses that had taken days to plan in 2003 required, by 2010, mere minutes. In August 2004, JSOC had overseen 18 night raids in Iraq over the course of a single month. By August 2006, it was 300.

McChrystal uses a civilian analogy to describe the JSOC evolution from specialized force into an organization directed and shaped by the power of its network: "We started the war as the greatest booksellers in the world and ended as Amazon.com." America's premier raid force had morphed into a ferociously organized, streamlined organization powered by data from across the United States government and had fought to become as adaptable as its formidable enemy, the al-Qaeda network.

Responsibility for the tactics and planning of missions moved downward to ground-level commanders as the pace of raids surged. No longer could Delta, Green Berets, and SEALs—the most "special" guys of special ops—handle all the workload. As McChrystal put it in 2014, "when we started going at a faster and faster pace, it just wasn't sustainable to have some guys that weren't hitting targets, so suddenly they said, 'Rangers, you take this target, Army Special Forces, you take that target,' which caused everybody to be hitting targets on their own."

Rangers, who began the wars in Afghanistan and Iraq as the "little brothers" of special ops—the typically younger guys who supported more seasoned, elite units on big operations—now became central to their success. The Rangers matured in their assignments; their competence, sophistication, and confidence grew in turn.

McRaven succeeded McChrystal at JSOC in June 2008, and he built on the ever-increasing agility and nonstop operational tempo his predecessor and mentor had instituted. But like Admiral Olson, Admiral McRaven, the author of *Spec Ops*, a book filled with case studies in special operations warfare, felt certain they weren't getting the whole job done if half the population remained out of reach.

For his part McChrystal, now in charge of the whole American war effort in Afghanistan, still felt stung by a review years earlier of an operation that had cost hearts, minds, and allies. His men had raided a compound and followed what they thought were strict, careful, and culturally sensitive procedures: they hadn't searched the women and instead had ushered them into a different part of the compound before moving through the house searching everything—including the women's quarters. "We got the feedback later that said 'you dishonored the women,'" McChrystal remembers. "How?" he and his men had asked. They had never even come close to them. The answer that came back stunned McChrystal: It doesn't matter, he was told. You went through their things and you touched their clothing.

"That was the level of ignorance we still had. And this was pretty late in the war," McChrystal observes today, noting that while U.S. forces increasingly understood the broad outlines of Afghan culture, the nuances often remained out of reach.

By 2010, the fight in Afghanistan was going badly enough that all anyone wanted was a solution that worked. For the past decade women had been serving in combat, McChrystal notes—regardless of official policy—as intel analysts, combat pilots, and in Delta Force. Women had won Purple Hearts and Bronze Star Medals for

Valor, and had been killed and grievously wounded alongside their male colleagues. McRaven was a practical problem-solver. What would have been unthinkable just five years earlier because of preconceptions about American servicewomen in combat as well as ignorance about the role of women in Afghan culture now became unavoidable. McRaven made a decision: female soldiers would now *officially* accompany the Rangers on target. Ideology be damned.

That it was the "knuckle-dragging" Rangers who first asked for the female "enablers" held irony for many. (McChrystal notes that the old joke was that the *n* in *Rangers* stood for "knowledge.") These were not touchy-feely men; they were the "blunt instrument" of special operations, guys whose idea of fun was guzzling a Rip It energy drink, working out for two hours, and then getting into a gunfight against bad guys. Nor did they bother with building foreign forces or forging relationships with locals, which was the specialty of the storied Green Berets. The Rangers had a pure and easily quantifiable mandate: you either got the insurgent you wanted or you didn't. And by now McRaven was ready to employ any smart strategy that would make his men and their mission more effective.

So when McRaven's official Request for Forces landed on his desk, Olson viewed it as an immediate call to action. This was no longer about his ideas of the "yin and yang of warfare," Olson told the men who worked for him: this was a hard requirement from a JSOC commander in the field. And everyone knew that what JSOC requested, JSOC received. Olson immediately began putting the wheels in motion, beginning with a request to the Army Special Operations Command to start training the new teams of female soldiers at its Fort Bragg headquarters. Olson divided the teams into two groups: the "direct action" side would go with counterterrorism-focused units, alongside the Rangers. The second group would accompany the more "indirect action" teams out in the hinterland where Green Berets forged relationships with local people and their leaders. These women would be part of VSOs, or Village Stability Operations.

In the meantime, Olson consulted his lawyers about the ban on women in ground combat and learned that as long as he "attached" rather than "assigned" women to these special operations units, he could put them almost anywhere. Including on missions with Rangers.

Finally there was the issue of the team's name. Everyone agreed that the word *female* should be avoided, since that would make acceptance all the harder among the all-male units. Since the concept of teamwork was so fundamental to special operations and its distinctive sense of community, they all agreed that it should be a "team." Another carefully selected word would help blunt the argument of those who thought the program was just a backdoor way for women to become frontline operators: *support*. Finally, they needed a term that would express the idea that these American female soldiers would make inroads into Afghanistan's social fabric to reach places and people that men couldn't: *cultural*.

The Cultural Support Teams were born.

And so it was that from Olson's kernel of an idea about what female service members could do that men could not; from McChrystal's desire to win and his experience on the ground; and from McRaven's request for women to support his men, there grew a series of conversations that matured into plans that took unexpected twists and eventually produced a program that led Second Lieutenant Ashley White and her female comrades onto the battlefield in Kandahar, Afghanistan, late one night in August 2011.

2

Hearing the Call to Serve

★ ★ ★

Lane Mason heard the ding of an incoming email and gazed down at her aging laptop. Tall, with ice-blue eyes, walnut brown hair, and tattooed arms, she looked like a Harley-Davidson model. A twenty-three-year-old Iraq War veteran from a small town in northeast Nevada, Lane worked for the local National Guard shepherding new recruits and transitioning them into the Guard.

Despite motherhood Lane's body still possessed the taut strength of the track star she had been. In high school she had led her team to the state championships year after year, but didn't realize until it was too late that she could have ridden her athletic talent all the way to a college scholarship. Instead she signed up for the National Guard because she knew her parents could never afford her tuition. The Guard would pay for college.

From childhood she had fended for herself. Her mother's life collapsed after her dad walked out on them when Lane was fourteen. After that, track and field raised her and kept her out of trouble. Together she and her older brother ran the household, cared for the pigs and cows on their small farm, and pushed each other every night to at least try to finish some portion of their homework.

At the moment the email sounded she was thinking about her Guard unit, trying to figure out when it would deploy and how she would prepare her two-year-old daughter for her absence. Her unit had served in Iraq early in that war and she had led supply convoys

in the south through some seriously heavy fighting. She was prepared to deploy again; with two wars on, most every Guard member
had to go to Iraq or Afghanistan at least once, often more. But she
did not want to go to war again with her particular unit, which she
felt was not well disciplined—or prepared to protect its members.

Now a friend from the Wisconsin National Guard was forward-
ing an email about a new job on something called a "Cultural Support Team."

"Hey, Lane, this sounds just up your alley," she wrote.

The subject line of the email read: "Female Volunteers for the
US Army Special Operations Command Female Engagement Team
Program."

Females in Special Ops? Lane was intrigued. Everyone knew
that women couldn't officially serve in any unit that engaged in direct ground combat, and Special Operations was among the most
combat-focused parts of the American military machine. But the
email made it clear the women would not be operators themselves:
they would be *supporting* Army special ops. It went on:

> *Currently, the US Special Operations Community has very
> few trained soldiers which limits Army Special Operations
> Forces' ability to connect and collaborate with this critical
> part of the Afghanistan society. As mitigation, US Army Spe-
> cial Operations Command has begun a Female Engagement
> Training program at Ft. Bragg, NC, to meet this critical mis-
> sion requirement.*

Lane's heart beat faster as she continued reading. She saw another benefit: the deployment was already scheduled and would last
only six to eight months instead of the usual year. She would finish
training by July and be back home with her daughter well before
summer vacation began. Plus, anything beat driving convoys and
sitting in a truck for up to twelve hours while people shot at you.

Lane had mastered the art of peeing in a bottle, a skill that had yet to prove useful back at home. She was eager to do—and learn—something more.

But Lane had another, more urgent reason for wanting to leave her Guard unit and do the CST mission. Back in Iraq, a fellow soldier in another unit had raped her. Not knowing where to turn, she had said nothing to anyone. Her marriage was already on the rocks, and she worried this might tip the fragile balance. But the experience had haunted her, and changed her. After returning home to Nevada she enrolled in college, only to find she couldn't focus on her studies and kept suffering flashbacks. A doctor at the local veterans' hospital told her it couldn't be post-traumatic stress: that could only come from combat injuries, not from trauma caused by rape.

A year after returning stateside Lane's Guard unit played a video about rape in the military, in which experts counseled soldiers on how to spot the "predators" among them and introduced the concept of "acquaintance rape," which put a name to Lane's personal nightmare. Watching the video unleashed a tsunami of horrific memories Lane had been trying to suppress. She ran out of the room desperate for fresh air, eyes watering, leaving her fellow Guard members whispering to one another, trying to figure out what the hell had just happened. When she returned, she sat down with her team and finally, for the first time, shared her story about Iraq. She assured them that what they were watching on that video was very real. They needed to watch out for their fellow soldiers—and not just on the battlefield.

Talking about what happened to her left Lane feeling suddenly lighter. Her fellow Guard members wrote letters to tell her how much her admission had meant to them and taught them. She vowed that from that moment on she would not let the rape define who she was or what kind of person—and soldier—she would be. When the email announcing the CST program arrived, Lane felt a door opening; she believed it would offer her a rare opportunity to both serve alongside the Army's finest fighting units and confront her demons in the open, on the battlefield. She would put herself in the most challenging combat situation possible with the most elite fighters possible, and prove to herself she was no victim. Lane knew she was tough enough.

"If I get to Bragg," she vowed, "there is no way I am letting them turn me down." She felt her old intensity return for the first time in years. "No one is keeping me out of this."

Two thousand miles away, in Columbia, South Carolina, another soldier received an email from a fellow sister-in-arms. Amber Tread-mont, a twenty-eight-year-old first lieutenant, had enlisted just as soon as she could, at the age of seventeen. Now a message arrived announcing that the Army was seeking exceptional females to support special operations. She read the cover note from her company commander:

> *If I weren't about to become a major I would absolutely do this. You should go for it.*

Amber had wanted to be in the Army for as long as she could remember. With blond hair and blue eyes, everyone thought she looked like Heidi in the popular children's movie, a fact that made her passion to be out shooting guns all the more surprising to those who didn't know her. In high school in rural Pennsylvania she spent hours every week shooting targets and dreaming of the day when she could aim her weapon at a real enemy, not a piece of paper or a Coke can. But Amber was a girl, and women could not serve in the infantry. So she joined the Army's intelligence teams, training at Fort Huachuca, a dozen miles north of the Mexican border in Arizona. Her first deployment, at the age of nineteen, was to Bosnia, where she analyzed terror networks for a task force hunting war criminals and terrorists transiting through the region. Her skills as an analyst became known, and the FBI brought her on for three years to help with counternarcotics operations in Pennsylvania. Her team's efforts led to the indictment of thirteen members of the infamous Bloods gang.

By the early 2000s the Afghanistan war was well under way, and Amber decided to build upon what she had learned and become an interrogator. As part of her training the Army sent her to learn Farsi at the Defense Language Institute in Monterey, California. The idea of being an interrogator appealed to Amber; she liked using her brains to keep other soldiers safe. If she couldn't join them on the front lines she could at least give tactical support and find out about terrorists and insurgents before they had a chance to put their plans into action.

After seven years as an enlisted soldier and following graduation from college and the birth of her son, Amber decided to head to Officer Candidate School. She became a rarity in the Army: someone who has been both an enlisted soldier and an officer.

Amber was serving as an officer at South Carolina's Fort Jackson Army base, doing a job she hated: overseeing paperwork and processing awards for returning soldiers. She was far from the action, bored by the work and stuck in a marriage that was all but over. She was just sitting around, waiting to see when her next deployment would come.

And then the CST email arrived. The timing couldn't have been better. This was the best chance she was going to get to go out on missions with special operators, and she was fully prepared to embrace the rigor of CST selection.

It took Amber less than a minute to print out the application form and get to work.

Kate Raimann first learned of the CST program from a flyer she spotted on a crowded poster board just outside a drab building where she worked at Fort Benning, Georgia. It featured a large photograph of a female officer crouching with an M4 assault rifle in her hands. The headline blasted its invitation in bold block letters: FEMALE SOLDIERS: BECOME A PART OF HISTORY.

Approaching the poster Kate felt a surge of adrenaline and curiosity. "Join the US Army Special Operations Command," it announced. She was already reaching into her backpack for a pen, scribbling down the website address, and hoping the ad wasn't too good to be true. As she wrote, Kate felt something she hadn't experienced since returning home from her deployment to southern Iraq: a sense of purpose.

Kate was an MP—military police officer—and had been home from war for just five months. Even with the twin burdens of Iraq and Afghanistan, the Army gave its soldiers time at home between tours, and Kate still had several months before she had to start preparing for her next rotation. But already she yearned to get back to the fight. She missed the sense of direction, the focus, the shared mission that she felt while deployed. Here, who needed her? Her time was wasted, and so were her skills.

Kate had never contemplated another career, though occasionally she wondered why God hadn't made her taller than five feet, since He knew she was going to be a soldier. Or male, since He knew she wanted to be infantry. Petite and blond she may have been, but Kate's compact body was ripped with muscles. Since she was a kid people had called her a tomboy, but Kate didn't care; all she knew was that she liked running and competing, playing soccer, basketball, and softball with her brother and sisters. A child of Title IX, she played high school football all four years at her western Massachusetts high school. Local newspapers wrote about "the girl who liked to tackle," but secretly Kate hated football with all its concussions and endless practices. But the fact that guys in her school believed a girl couldn't play football guaranteed Kate would never quit. Ever. No way would she give in to their doubts. Concussions be damned.

The Army was in Kate's genes and wrapped around her family

tree. Her father had spent twenty-three years as an Army pilot and he inspired all his children to follow his path. Kate and her younger siblings all headed to the U.S. Military Academy at West Point when it came time for college.

After graduation, Kate became an MP because it was the closest she could get to the infantry. MPs overseas perform the whole range of law enforcement functions for the military, from searching homes and suspects to running patrols, doing reconnaissance, and joining search operations. Now a poster on the wall was pointing the way right into the heart of the action, offering a chance to return to the purity and clarity of life at war. Kate wanted to get to Afghanistan, she wanted a mission that mattered, and she wanted to be as near to the front as possible. Here was a groundbreaking team that would let her do all three.

All across the country in the first months of 2011 this same story played out as friends of soldiers, commanding officers, and fellow warriors spread the news about a program that would match America's toughest fighting men with a special team of women who could fill a gap that no other force could. From Florida to Alaska, North Carolina to South Korea, women answered the call. Most of them had been itching all their lives to go to war—not as nurses or typists or machinists or any of the other jobs that gradually, over decades of struggle, came to admit women, but as special operations soldiers. Or as close as they could get to them. As one CST put it: "All my life, all I ever wanted was to belong to a group of ass-kickers battling on the front lines."

When Ashley White heard about the CST program she was running drills at the local armory in Goldsboro, North Carolina, where she was serving with the National Guard. Ashley had come to the Tar Heel State two years earlier to be with her fiancé, Jason Stumpf, a lieutenant stationed at the Fort Bragg Army base. Ashley had met

Jason during her first months at Kent State University, less than an hour's drive from her small Ohio hometown of Marlboro, at a pizza party in the offices of the school's ROTC program. It was love at first sight, though neither did anything about it for more than a year.

It surprised everyone in Ashley's tight-knit family when she signed up for ROTC. She had never offered the slightest hint that she wanted to serve. Her grandfather had been a Marine as a young man and a great-uncle had won a Purple Heart as a Navy corpsman in the Korean War, but the military tradition did not otherwise run through her family. Yet there was a deeply ingrained sense of duty in the White family when it came to work, along with spirited—and intense—competition among her siblings: twin sister Brittany and older brother Josh.

The Whites formed complementary and opposing forces. Debbie, Ashley's mom, was warm and caring, a nurturer who loved swimming and diving and hiking. She worked as a school bus driver and teacher's aide so she could arrange her days around her most important job: being a mom to her three children. The house was always filled with young people: classmates of Josh and gymnastic teammates and cousins of Ashley and Brittany. Known as "Mama Whitie" to Josh's high school football teammates, Debbie traveled to every game in her minivan stocked with snacks for the kids. At pregame dinners Debbie always made room at her table for boys whose parents couldn't make it.

Bob White was as tough-minded as his high school sweetheart wife was kind. He had had to be: his parents operated on the premise that children "made money, not cost money," and put him to work as a kid in his family's toolmaking business in Akron. He would stand on milk crates to reach the machines he was responsible for operating. Extracurriculars were discouraged; when Bob wanted to play basketball, his dad said he would have to find his own way home. That meant walking more than five miles each way, even in the dead of winter. But all that work did pay off: he bought a candy-apple-red 1973 SS Nova—his high school's "car of the month" eight times—and won the heart of a leggy blonde named Debbie, whose parents owned a pizza shop.

Right after they were married, Bob made a promise to his wife that he would be a dedicated and engaged father. They both wanted a family. Doctors said that Debbie couldn't have children, but after ten years of marriage Josh arrived. Three years later the twins followed. Shock greeted the September arrival of the two baby girls; the doctors had told the Whites all along to expect boys. So certain had they been that Bob and Debbie hadn't even considered girls' names. Bob, then working the overnight shift at his family business, sometimes caught the soap opera *The Young and the Restless* during the day before heading to bed. Thinking quickly he named his first beautiful baby girl after the show's stunning fictional character Ashley Abbott. Bob kept his promise to his wife: though he would work ten-, twelve-, even sixteen-hour days to provide for his family, he made sure that he knew every detail of his children's lives—who their friends were, how they were faring academically and in sports. Bob believed in teaching his children the value of hard work and vowed that each would have the college opportunities he hadn't, no matter how hard he had to toil. If the kids weren't at school, they were studying, and if they weren't studying, they were either training for sports or working at White Tool. Nearly every weekend from the time they were teenagers, Ashley, Brittany, and Josh logged a full day on the toolmaking assembly line, helping their dad and earning money for themselves. They complained constantly, but the truth was they loved it, even as their fingernails collected a distinct type of dirt—oily and noxious—that they nicknamed "White Tool grunge." Quiet Ashley made a name for herself as one of the White Tool "chucker chicks"—despite being left-handed, a hindrance in factory processes, she could produce 1,000 metal clips in an hour when most of the guys who ran the machines could barely reach 700. Bob attributed her success to her work ethic: when she ran the machines Ashley didn't leave for the bathroom, for a soda break, or for a chat with her siblings.

The White family was intense with competition, from the basketball court to the football field and gymnastics meets. "If you're not first you're last," Bob regularly reminded his kids. "You can't settle for second." "Don't start what you can't finish," he would add. He wanted them to see early on how tough factory work was and how excellence could be both its own reward and a path to an easier life built on education. He was constantly telling his children that "actions trump words." His mantra: "Don't tell people what you're going to do, or what kind of person you are. Just show them."

Josh and Brittany both had natural athletic talent that propelled them into local headlines and won them medals and trophies—a whole room in the Whites' basement was dedicated to their glittering awards. During his senior year Josh was thrilled to break his high school record for pull-ups, logging 35 straight from a dead hang, but his pride was short-lived; his freshman sister Brittany trumped his achievement with 45 pull-ups that very same afternoon.

Despite the competition, the siblings were one another's greatest supporters and best friends. To motivate Ashley before her cross-country training runs in high school, Josh would blare Metallica's "Seek & Destroy" as they drove to school. At night, Ashley and Brittany would creep across the hall into one another's rooms and swap problems, daydreams, and plans for the future.

Bob taught Ashley to push herself beyond her limits and to always do what she thought was right. But he never meant for his daughter to learn his lessons so well. When she first came to him during her freshman year at Kent State and said she wanted to join ROTC, his answer was "absolutely not." Nothing in his own upbringing prepared him to believe that military service was the right path for his children: not the fact that ROTC would pay her tuition; or that her fellow cadets shared a camaraderie and a value system based on integrity; or that she thrived amid the intense physical challenges;

or even that the discipline and high standards reminded her of the same high bar he had set for her for as long as she could remember.

When he put his foot down and said no to her first request for support, she came back with two ROTC recruiters to help make her case. They too failed to win him over.

"Ash," he said sharply, ignoring the men who sat in his living room, "nothing is free. They are not just paying for school; you will be paying for that education with your life. There's no guarantee you won't have to go to Afghanistan or Iraq. And I don't want to lose my daughter."

But Ashley was determined. She told him she was only seeking his blessing because she respected him so deeply; she was of legal age and could sign her own paperwork to join the program without her parents' approval. Debbie, who had once put aside her own ambitions to serve, would not stand in her daughter's way. "I won't stop her," Debbie answered Bob's entreaty. "I always regretted not joining the Navy and I don't want her to do the same." Eventually he relented. On the issue of ROTC he and Ashley came to see they would not agree, but would respect one another's views.

By February 2011, Ashley was working as an athletic trainer at a local college and a medic in the North Carolina National Guard, living in a cozy starter home with Jason. But she felt something was missing. Surrounded by fellow Guardsmen who had done at least one deployment in Iraq or Afghanistan, she felt guilty about wearing the uniform without having served in at least one of the two wars America was fighting. Accepting a check and school tuition without completing the work to deserve it felt like freeloading. And that was *not* Ashley. Already some of the guys she commanded had jeered at her, claiming they didn't have to take orders from some green, young officer who hadn't ever deployed. It burned Ashley to see herself the way they did.

It was Ashley's commander who handed her the CST flyer one Saturday afternoon after the daily drills were over. "I can't do this,

Ashley," she said, "but maybe it's for you." It was the same poster Kate had seen in Georgia and hundreds of other potential young recruits had received by email from their friends and fellow soldiers. "Looks pretty interesting. And it would get your deployment out of the way."

The timing couldn't have been better, and Ashley, studying the photo of the intimidating soldier kneeling with her M4, was intrigued. It wasn't long before she was determined to apply.

Now she just had to convince Jason.

Jason had always supported her. He had pushed her throughout her time at ROTC, urging her to take on the toughest challenges and to speak up when she disagreed with what she saw or experienced. Debbie said it was Jason who had made Ashley "sparkle." For proof, she pointed to her family photo albums, which showed that until she met Jason, Ashley rarely smiled in pictures, too self-conscious to let her real self show. But with Jason she would grin with abandon come photo time.

By the time she rang Jason that Saturday from Guard drills, Ashley had not only prevailed against her formidable father, she felt ready to compete with the best women the Army had to offer no matter that she was just a second lieutenant in the National Guard. Her husband had made it possible.

"Hey, I want to tell you about this new program," she said when he picked up the phone in their bright yellow kitchen that Saturday morning.

From the sound of his voice she had a feeling that persuading "Mr. Sexypants," as she lovingly called him, was going to be an even bigger challenge than getting her father to agree to ROTC.

3

The Landmark Inn

★ ★ ★

Four weeks later, Ashley was filling her cup from a hotel coffee urn, about to begin the first day of the very first all-Army "Assessment and Selection" for the new CST program. She pulled a lever on an industrial-size milk machine and watched the white stuff pour into her coffee. She would definitely need caffeine to begin this day. It was March 2011, and this was the initial round of what would be two separate selections: the Guard and Reserves first, then, two months later, active-duty soldiers.

Gripping her cup she leaned against the Formica counter and watched as a swarm of high-octane women assembled in the breakfast room of the Landmark Inn, a hotel located on the grounds of Fort Bragg dedicated to serving soldiers, their families, and civilian guests. It was quite a sight: dozens of sweat-suit-clad Army Guard and Reservists, many of them with flushed cheeks and disheveled ponytails fresh from working out, were milling around the dining room. The high-backed chairs at the large, round tables were covered in a durable fabric designed to disguise spills of everything from maple syrup to ketchup. An arrangement of bright orange silk flowers sat at the center of each table, the only burst of cheer in an otherwise drab setting. Ashley grabbed an apple—part of a limited offering of healthy fare in this land of waffles and pancakes—and quietly observed the scene.

The women came from every region of the country, from cities, farms, and suburbs, and they came in a variety of heights and builds: some were lanky and lean, others were squat, compact, and broad across the shoulders. These girls look like they lift some serious weight, Ashley thought. They also ranged in age: some, like Ashley, had barely crossed into their twenties. Others looked nearly two decades older, but, amazingly, were no less fit. An uninformed observer would have thought he had stumbled across either a championship softball team or a women's soccer league. But it was unusual for another reason: rarely did Army women gather in large groups. Aside from the Army Nurse Corps—none of whom were permitted to participate in that CST selection—there usually weren't enough women in the same place at the same time to fill a conference table, let alone a hotel dining room. Women may have been serving in most Army roles by 2011, but they still accounted for just around 15 percent of all active-duty soldiers and a bit more for National Guard and Reservists. Those small numbers meant that women rarely found themselves surrounded by other women.

And then there was the alpha thing. The female soldiers who had come to take part in this CST selection had genuine swagger. Ashley spotted a trim woman whose sculpted muscles were bulging beneath a gray Army T-shirt. Thick veins lined her strong arms. Another had a book propped up against her oatmeal bowl: *Get Selected for Special Forces: How to Successfully Train for and Complete Special Forces Assessment & Selection.*

A buzz filled the room, even as the women tried to hide their amazement at seeing so many people just like themselves. Ashley had never before seen anything like it. She guessed that neither had anyone else who was there that morning.

Ashley didn't know what to expect at the Landmark Inn, but she knew she would be doing a lot of paperwork—"in-processing," in Army terms. Then at some point they would move to Camp Mackall, the World War II–era site nearby used for Special Forces selection and training. This was where the real test of the soldiers would begin. In the meantime, the CST hopefuls talked loudly and acted tough over their morning coffee. Gazing around the room, it occurred to Ashley that not a single person here looked like she had ever endured a moment of self-doubt in her entire life. More than the muscles, shoulders, and popping veins, this thought intimidated her. Ashley knew how to put on a game face—childhood gymnastics and then ROTC had taught her that—but she wondered whether she really fit in with these women, some of whom looked like they could bench-press five times their body weight and strode around like female John Waynes.

Hey, she commanded herself. Get your mind in it, Ashley. Focus.

To do that, she took herself back four years to Ranger Challenge, where teams of the best ROTC cadets from each school competed against other colleges in the region. For years prior to Ashley's arrival at Kent State, the Ranger Challenge team had consisted solely of men. They trained at a facility with a long military history, the Ravenna Arsenal, where more than fourteen thousand Ohioans had produced weapons during World War II. Most of the men were surprised to learn that this quiet blonde who didn't even reach five foot three wanted to join the big boys in the competition. They couldn't believe that "Little White" could keep up with their long strides, and throughout the training sessions they waited for Ashley to fall out of formation. But every morning the determined sophomore cadet showed up at the Arsenal to march the morning's miles, and every morning she kept up, even when they moved the start time to 5 a.m. They were required to add first twenty, then thirty pounds of gear to weigh down their rucksacks in preparation for the actual competition. Every time team leader Jason Stumpf turned around, he expected to see Ashley way back in the rear, but there she was, right behind him in the formation, keeping pace with the guys.

The biggest test aside from rucking was the rope bridge. Cadets would string a line of knotted rope between two wooden posts and clamber across it upside down, belly up, legs straddling the rope and propelling the body to the other end. Arm over arm they raced, with fully packed rucksacks and rifles slung across their backs. Time was critical—and so was teamwork. Small and fast, Ashley had learned as a girl on the uneven parallel bars to use her stomach muscles to force her body into one line and make her weight lighter on her arms. That training meant she could zip across the rope faster than anyone could imagine.

It was Jason, then a senior and already her boyfriend, who had put her on the Ranger Challenge team, with support from Sergeant First Class Stewart McGeahy, the NCO who oversaw the ROTC cadets. McGeahy was a veteran of the Army's bloody fight in Fallujah, an armored cavalry guy who had seen combat close and fierce in Iraq. He recognized warriors when he saw them, even if this one— the quiet little blonde—didn't look like any he had ever met before.

It was Jason's job to make the final selection for the Ranger Challenge team, and he sought out McGeahy's advice. "You don't see that kind of heart very often," the older veteran observed. "I'd like to see you take her."

During the Ranger Challenge competition, Ashley had proven to be a real asset to the team with her physical endurance, her land navigation and rope bridge skills, and her ability to keep cool under pressure. The sweetest moment came toward the end of the final event, a ruck march with more than thirty pounds of gear. Ashley stayed in the middle of her team's pack, not setting the pace, but not slowing it, either. And then her group passed their bigger and better-funded rival, Ohio State.

"Oh, fuck," one guy bellowed as Kent State passed. "We're screwed. Pick it up!" And then, a moment later: "Holy shit, they got a *female*. And they are fucking passing us. *Pick it up!*"

"I'm trying, dude, I can't go any faster," one guy huffed to his teammate. "Man, I'm hurting all over."

"What the fuck? Are you kidding me?" the first cadet answered. "That girl's not complaining. Step it up. *Now!*"

Jason laughed. "See you at the finish line, boys!"

Ashley slogged along and remained expressionless. One foot after the other. Eyes straight ahead. No way she was reacting to that nonsense. As she had learned from her father as a girl, she would let her actions show what she was made of. Forget them, just focus and move on. Ashley had mastered the art of silently pushing herself onward, and she was tougher on herself than anyone else could be.

Now, as the much more competitive CST selection process was set to begin, Ashley would channel that dedication. She had fought hard to be here, not only against the wishes of her beloved father and role model, but initially against Jason, too. Ever since her first year in ROTC he had been her biggest champion and most devoted ally. Sitting in the motel dining room surrounded by some of the Army's toughest female warriors, she reflected back on the conversation that Saturday night after she first learned about the CST program. It was one of the most heated they had ever had.

Over a dinner of broiled chicken she had prepared after returning home from Guard drills at the armory, Ashley gently pressed her case. Ten years of war meant that nearly everyone who served in the Guard had done at least one tour in Iraq or Afghanistan. Young officers like her who had no "combat stripes"—the gold "Overseas Service Bars" on their uniforms indicating they had served at least six months at war overseas—were noticed by others. And not in a positive way.

"I have to do this," Ashley said. "People at the Guard unit are making fun of me—you know I have to get this deployment out of the way. My regular unit won't be deploying for Kuwait until 2013, and that will be a whole year of us apart. If I do this CST program, it's just six or seven months, and it's *now*. We can begin a family all the sooner."

Jason listened, stone-faced.

"Listen, Jason, this is *special operations*," Ashley said. "You're the one who said they're the best of all the guys you saw in Afghanistan.

You know I'll be working with a top-notch, professional community. I'll knock the deployment out and come home and then we can move forward with our lives."

Jason reminded himself to breathe. He had just returned from a year as a field artillery officer in eastern Afghanistan, where he had seen firsthand the war's dangers—what it was like on the battlefield and what it did to the people who made it back home. The absolute last thing he wanted was Ashley going over there. It was only now—two months after his own tour ended—that he had finally gotten used to normal life again, and that was because of Ashley. She hadn't pressured him to talk about Afghanistan or smothered him with attention once he got home; instead, she gave him space and let him get accustomed once more to life's daily rhythms.

Jason had served at a particularly grueling time in the long war. The surge that was announced in December 2009 was in full swing, and he provided artillery support to both conventional and special operations units operating in the field. Insurgents regularly attacked his NATO base, lovingly referred to as "Rocket City" by the soldiers who lived there. Enemy fighters even managed to breach the base's wire one night, sending him running to his position ready to shoot artillery if needed. Fortunately the attack ended in short order with no one on his side dead or injured, but the enemy had literally brought the fight to him, and it was sobering.

For Jason the rules of engagement were frustrating. He understood that protecting civilians was critical to the war effort, but he knew the enemy followed no such rules and that counterinsurgency's reluctance to use artillery firepower—for fear of civilian casualties—meant that American soldiers now had to fight without the full arsenal of the United States Army at their side. He also witnessed internal turf wars and political battles he hadn't expected to see in wartime play out before his eyes. He still loved the Army and his men, and he remained committed to serving his country. But he returned home questioning America's chances of success given the years of commitment the mission would require.

Worse, he was unable to forget what he had seen in the southeastern province of Khost: one of his men twitching in a morphine coma, his leg torn apart by rocket fire, another soldier severely injured, with a pint of Jason's blood helping keep him alive. He relived it every night when he first returned home and he sure as hell didn't want that for Ashley. Afghanistan changed everyone it touched, and his wife would be no different. He couldn't bear to think of the nightmares that would accompany her back to North Carolina from whatever remote outpost would be her home for the better part of a year. Right before he deployed they had a secret wedding in a minister's office, sealing the ceremony with a temporary ring from Walmart. This way Jason could be certain that Ashley would get his survivor benefits if something happened to him overseas. Their "real" nuptials—the big, white dress, huge party, proper Catholic mass—were planned for May, just two months away.

And now that Jason had made it back safely *she* wanted to go to Afghanistan and upend their lives once more? He struggled to get his mind around this.

"Ash, this is Afghanistan," he finally replied. He wrapped his hands around a glass of Jack Daniel's and Coke and worked to keep his voice steady. "These are the people who successfully fought Alexander the Great, the British, the Russians, and now they are fighting us. This is no joke. People are getting hit all the time now. Do you have *any* idea what you'd be getting yourself into? You don't need to deploy now—I just got back. Let's think about this for a while, find you a good medical deployment you can do another time, once we've had our wedding and honeymoon and some actual time together." Ashley had studied sports medicine in college—often with Jason serving as her test patient—and trained as a medic at Fort Sam Houston during her ROTC years. Jason saw no reason why she couldn't deploy as a medical officer—and one who stayed on base.

It was Ashley's turn to sit quietly and listen. She heard him out, but it was clear she was unmoved by his entreaties.

"I promise," he continued, "I'll help you find another tour. Why do you want to go looking for trouble?"

"I want to do this, Jason, I think this program is important and I want to go for it. I am not going to train all of these years and then not serve when my country is at war." As she pressed her argument to the one person who had always encouraged her to speak her mind, Ashley's eyes were now watering. "What if I wait for another deployment and then the war is over? I can get this out of the way and do something I'll be really proud of when I'm a grandma and rocking on our porch.

"Besides," she added, moving next to her big husky dog, Gunner, on the couch where she and Jason snuggled and watched movies on weekends, "who knows if I'll even make the team? We don't have to decide anything yet."

She motioned for Jason to join her, but he sat silently in his recliner, trying to put himself in her place. He knew his wife was tough and talented. If she wanted something she would get it. He wasn't worried she wouldn't be selected; what worried him was he was certain she *would*.

He saw in her eyes that same look of determination, that total indifference to everything around her that had been so evident in Ranger Challenge. If she really thought this was something she had to try for, how could he do otherwise, when he loved her so much and she had done exactly the same thing for him a year earlier?

"All right, Ash, if you want to go for this, let's do it," he finally said. It was long past midnight, and he was exhausted, both physically and emotionally. "But you better dig in. You're going to have a tough fight at selection. You don't quit. If you call me and say you need me to come pick you up because you didn't make the cut, it had better be because you broke a bone and couldn't walk yourself out of there. You want this? We're going at it full throttle. No half steps."

This is what Ashley was thinking about at the Landmark Inn as she grabbed a yogurt and set off to find a seat with the other girls. She had promised then to give it her all, and she was ready.

No half steps, Ashley thought. Time to dig in.

She sat down and began introducing herself to her tablemates.

Anne Jeremy was one of the first people Ashley met that morning. Tall, fit, and blond, she looked more like a television anchor than a soldier, but her temperament was serious, no-nonsense. She had proven herself on the battlefield at just twenty-three after Taliban rocket fire blew up and sliced through a caravan of vehicles in the supply convoy she was leading. She never felt she deserved the awards she received for her bravery and thought only of her soldiers killed in the battle, but her commanders felt otherwise after seeing her composure in leading her convoy through more than twenty-four hours of intermittent heavy arms fire and hours of prolonged enemy contact. Back at her base she went on to become her combat engineer company's first female executive officer, or XO. Officially the role was off-limits to women, because the Army had coded the job for men only in its personnel system. But the colonel she served under in Afghanistan thought she was one of his most promising officers, so he simply left that entry in her personnel file empty while she served in the role. Her records could be corrected later.

It was another senior officer Anne worked with in her new role who told her about the CST program. He was a tough-talking Yankee and a true professional; she credited his leadership with her success in the position. "Hey, Anne, I hear they're letting chicks go to Q Course now." He was referring to the Special Forces' qualification course, a direct line to the Green Berets that had always been open only to men. "You gotta check this out, you would be great."

Anne was an engineer by training. She had completed the highly competitive Sapper Leader Course, a body-numbing, twenty-eight-day program that teaches combat leadership skills and small unit fighting, and had earned the right to wear the prestigious Sapper patch on her left shoulder. Sappers are trained to clear mines, deploy field defenses, and fight in close quarters. Women account for barely 3 percent of all Sapper Course students, and only 2 percent of its graduates. Not that Anne had ever thought of herself as being a "groundbreaker" or a feminist; in fact, she paid little attention to the fact that she was one of only three females in the course. She preferred to focus on her grit, not her gender, and wanted others to do the same. It was the difficulty of the Sapper Course—both mental and physical—that motivated her, and she finished strong among her male peers.

Special operations had been a dream for her. Having seen bloody attacks in Afghanistan and lost soldiers in battle left Anne with a powerful feeling of unfinished business. She wanted back in the fight, and the Cultural Support Team was the perfect way to get there.

Her colonel gave Anne a phone number for a civilian who was involved with the nascent CST program, Claire Russo, Matt Pottinger's old pal from Afghanistan, who by then had been sent to Fort Bragg to help prepare candidates for the new teams. In February 2011 Russo had been quoted in a *Foreign Policy* article written by Paula Broadwell describing the new all-female unit headlined "CST: Afghanistan." Within days the former Marine was fielding a barrage of calls and emails to her personal Gmail account from female soldiers who wanted to know more about this chance to work with special operations and exactly what they needed to qualify for it. Anne was among them.

"You should come to Assessment and Selection," Russo told her when they spoke in early 2011. "Sounds like you'd be terrific for it." Not long afterward, Anne was sitting next to Ashley White over a bowl of cereal at the Landmark Inn.

She looked around the motel and was astonished. Wow, all these girls could form their own little company of soldiers, she thought.

She laughed as a serviceman who was staying at the motel wandered in to grab some breakfast, only to stop in his tracks, visibly startled, at the sight of thirty buff women dominating the room. He quickly turned and hurried out.

Anne was ready. CST selection couldn't be *that* much more of a mental and physical test than Sapper school, but whatever it was she felt prepared. War had changed her; most significantly, it had made nearly everything else seem easier by comparison. She welcomed whatever the week would bring.

Leda Reston was also at the Landmark Inn that morning. She had known about the CST program before the other women, having learned about it from colleagues in the special operations unit she was working with just then. There was only one problem: the cutoff level was captain, and Leda had just been promoted to major. She was too senior for the program.

Reston had served in the storied 82nd Airborne Division in Iraq as a civil affairs officer. Among her responsibilities was accompanying and advising the local U.S. Provincial Reconstruction Team as they opened women's centers and vocational training schools, which were designed to build goodwill among Iraqis. In addition, her brigade commander had made her the direct liaison to all key Iraqi officials with whom they worked, including the local governor and deputy governor. No woman had ever served in this role, and Leda was determined to live up to the faith her colonel had placed in her by picking this young captain to replace a battle-seasoned major. She may have been the sole female on the colonel's staff, but, like Anne, she thought little about it. She considered herself first and foremost a soldier entrusted with a job that could further America's mission and keep soldiers alive if she did it well, and she was determined to succeed.

She did that by developing solid working relationships built on mutual respect with Iraqi officials. They would call her cell phone directly at all hours of the day and night, often to warn her when ambushes lay in wait for U.S. military convoys on the most well-traveled roads. She also received valuable intel from the Iraqis about how the American forces could track down certain insurgents. This was the height of the surge in Iraq and the fight was escalating. During her service with them, the 82nd's deployment was extended from twelve to fifteen months, a blow for many, especially those who had previously deployed and had now logged a series of holidays away from their families. Leda carefully studied her commanding officer as he led his soldiers, and absorbed everything she could about leadership and about the new rules of counterinsurgency.

Leda was one of the few females serving in the military who fully appreciated the advantage their gender difference could bring to the fight at hand. Being a female had proven handy in Iraq; like her compatriots in Afghanistan, she inhabited that "third gender" Pottinger and Russo had identified (neither American male or Iraqi female). This enabled her to be taken seriously without being viewed as a threat. She loved being outside the wire, mingling in Iraqi communities and developing relationships with military men and civilians alike. She also loved working with the special operations guys, whom she saw as embodying the integrity and high standards she had always hoped to find in the Army.

Leda's experience in Iraq had cemented her determination to deploy again, and she especially wanted to work with special ops. Already her career had taken her on a circuitous path from cross-country star—she attended a small college in Florida—to Army reservist to high school teacher and, finally, back to the military after 9/11. When she learned the Army was looking for women willing to go out on dangerous missions with special operations teams, there was no way she was going to miss out on this one-of-a-kind opportunity because of some technicality.

Eventually she won approval from Lieutenant General John Mulholland, the decorated Special Forces commander who led his men into Afghanistan following the attacks of September 11, 2001. Mulholland now headed the Army's entire Special Operations Command. If he would sign off on her application, no one would overrule him.

There was only one caveat: the more senior Major Reston would have to serve as the officer in charge and handle all the team's administrative demands as well. She agreed immediately. For a workaholic like Leda, with little need for sleep and few outlets aside from running marathons and working out at the gym, the twin jobs were hardly an issue.

She couldn't wait to get started, but the scene at the Landmark Inn threw her off kilter, just as it had Ashley. First: There were dozens of tough, strong, women roaming around the room, cautiously sizing each other up. Each knew that the program had a limited number of spots, so they would naturally be in fierce competition with one another. But the vibe in the room went well beyond competitiveness. Here was a group of women who cared more about being the best they could, not besting the girl next to them. A sense prevailed that this was a unique Fort Bragg event.

"Let's kick this thing's ass!" *That* was the attitude of the moment.

On her way to work out at the gym across from the Landmark, Leda ran into Ashley, who was heading to the same place. Both of these women were gym junkies; neither would go a day without hard-core exercise. Each started her morning with a dawn workout that included CrossFit routines and a several-mile run.

CrossFit for most of these women was a way of life. Many of them did at least one workout a day, and sometimes two. This results-oriented fitness regimen was stacked with movements such as squats, jumps, sit-ups, handstands, and pull-ups, and reflected influences from gymnastics to rope climbing, rowing, and weight lifting. In CrossFit every exercise is measured and the routine is constantly varied, so the body gets stronger while always being forced to adapt to a new set of strength tests. The program started in California, then spread to gyms around the country, and it particularly attracted members of law enforcement, and special operations—men and women alike. Virtually all the CST hopefuls were CrossFit devotees who tracked their workouts meticulously in their quest to be stronger, faster, fitter, and tougher.

Leda had spotted Ashley earlier that day standing by herself in the Landmark's lobby. While most of the other women were buzzing around and talking a big game about their physical readiness for the upcoming selection, Ashley seemed content to quietly take it all in while she waited in line at the front desk for her room key. It takes a great deal of self-possession to look so at ease in that sea of type A women, Leda thought.

Now working out next to Ashley in the gym, Leda was impressed with her raw strength, to say nothing of the ridiculously high number of dead-hang pull-ups she could bust out. Most men couldn't make it to twenty-five as Ashley was doing now, Leda thought. She looked forward to getting to know this girl.

She had no idea then just how intertwined their paths would become.

The second group of fifty applicants, the active-duty soldiers, gathered at the Landmark Inn two weeks later, and included Amber Treadmont and Kate Raimann. Also there was Kristen Fisher, a military intelligence officer just months out of liberal arts college in Pennsylvania. Kristen's father was an Air Force veteran who had impressed upon her the importance—as well as the fun and camaraderie—of serving. Like Ashley, she had turned to ROTC to pay for school. Somehow the four years of college snuck by her and before she knew it she was in the Army. She and a fellow intel officer, Rigby Allen, had both spotted the "Become a Part of History" poster at Fort Huachuca in Cochise County, Arizona, where they were training, and decided to take on the CST application process together. Polar opposites—Kristen was a bubbly former NFL cheerleader and Rigby was a self-described "roughneck" who played rugby in college—the two were just three months into their intel officer training before they arrived at the same gloomy assessment: their future held endless desk jobs, not the excitement of the front lines they had had in mind when they signed up.

All Rigby had ever wanted was to be a soldier. She grew up in Michigan playing "army" in the woods with her older brother and sister, and dreamed of leading a real maneuver one day. Her grandfather had served in the 82nd Airborne Division and her dad was a Navy photographer for three years during Vietnam. Without them ever explicitly pushing the children to serve, both men had made it clear that being in the military and serving your country was the most important and patriotic work an American could do. After the Navy, Rigby's father took a job as an engineer at the defense contractor Northrop Grumman. On "Take Your Kids to Work" day she and her siblings would scamper through the helicopters he designed. When she finally landed in ROTC at Western Michigan University, she felt more focused than she did in any classroom; the program trained cadets to be infantry platoon leaders, which was exactly what she had always wanted to do in life. But soon reality set in. "Then," as Rigby later put it, "you realize you are a woman. And women can't be infantry platoon leaders." Stuck to a desk in Arizona, she spent so much time staring at a computer that she finally had to see a doctor about her eyestrain. That was the last straw. Rigby decided she was going to find a way to get as close to the front row as she could, and the minute she spotted that female with an M4 on the poster taped to the bathroom wall at Fort Huachuca, she knew this special operations program was her ticket out.

When she first met Kristen at officer school, Rigby was surprised that the ebullient cheerleader wanted to pursue the CST program, too. She seemed unserious, a "stereotypical" Army female more focused on her marital status than her military record. But then they went on a six-mile ruck march together and the beauty queen kicked her ass. Kristen made the hike look virtually effortless despite the thirty pounds of gear she carried on her back, and instead of passing Rigby and letting her stay behind, she marched right next to her and encouraged her fellow soldier to push harder. The rugby player who thought she was so tough finished the outing with an entirely new respect for her far fitter classmate—and made a harsh rebuke to herself for falling prey to such easy prejudice.

Rigby and Kristen had called the CST recruiter every week to plead with him to let them apply for the program despite how young and how new to the Army they both were. In the end both got the green light to attend the selection process. They made the long drive together from Arizona to North Carolina full of excitement and self-confidence. And then they walked into the motel, took one look around them, and realized they had just landed in the big leagues. "Kristen, these women are *specimens*," Rigby whispered. She had just overheard one of the women in the lobby talking about the Ironman competition she had just finished.

Rigby checked in, made her way upstairs, opened the door to her room, and was immediately confronted by a vile smell. She thought there must be a body decaying somewhere inside.

She stepped tentatively into the room and discovered instead a smiling brunette with sparkling blue eyes sitting on one of the beds. She was decked out head to toe in running gear and was still sweating from what must have been a very long workout.

The woman leapt to her feet and extended a hand. "Hi, how're you doing? I'm Tristan Marsden," she said. The breezy, peppy tone was as grating as the stench.

"*Why* does it smell like that in here?" Rigby asked. She couldn't believe the assault on her senses.

"Oh, I am so sorry, I tried to open the window to air it out, but they're sealed shut," Tristan said, smiling. "I just went for a run—and it's my sneakers. . . . I never wear socks when I run or ruck, and well, you know what happens inside the shoes . . ."

Rigby looked at the Nikes in question and picked them up by their shoestrings.

"These are going in the bathroom," she said. She grabbed the plastic bag that lined the trash can, dropped the damp shoes inside, and dumped them in the bathtub. She was utterly indifferent to any offense caused by her actions.

"I'm Rigby, by the way," she said, now returning to the work of making an acquaintance of her roommate.

Like Rigby, the military was in Tristan's blood; the second oldest of five children in a tight-knit, conservative, New England Catholic family, she had grown up with her father's Marines flag hanging in the basement weight room. By the time she was five she and her older sister could sing the Marines' Hymn together, by heart:

> From the Halls of Montezuma,
> To the Shores of Tripoli;
> We fight our country's battles
> In the air, on land, and sea. . . .

Tristan had been an elite runner—an all-state standout in high school—and had her choice of colleges offering her full athletic scholarships. But while touring college campuses she felt wooed by the siren call of West Point, with its rugged beauty and history nearly as old as America itself. She was drawn to both the physical and mental challenges that West Point offered, and went on to become one of the U.S. Military Academy's top track stars. But she was hardly a typical warrior-in-waiting. Each time a West Point graduate was killed in action the school made an announcement over the public address system, and the entire community observed a moment of silence in the mess hall over breakfast. By 2008 the booming announcements became so frequent that Tristan felt haunted by the pointlessness of it all. What did any of the athletic achievement or the years of study matter when they were all going to go off and die? How could these people just keep passing the eggs when one of their own would never return home? War had sounded a lot more glamorous before those who were killed were people she knew, fellow students who had sat at that very same breakfast table only a year earlier.

"It just seems like no one is even affected by it anymore," Tristan told her track coach one afternoon. "Everyone just goes about their business." Her coach tried to explain to her that that was the reality—and the risk—of being an officer in wartime. "You have to come to peace with that," she advised.

As time went on, Tristan did come to terms with her trepidation, and by the end of her studies she was ready to deploy. The desire only grew as she watched more and more of her classmates heading to Iraq and Afghanistan. What use was she here at home? At West Point she had chosen field artillery as her specialty because at that time, seven years into the Afghanistan war, she had heard the artillery branch was opening a lot of jobs to women and it meant she would get to shoot big weapons and be in the fight. She specialized in the Multiple Launch Rocket System, an armored rocket launcher that could hit critical targets at distances both short and far. When an infantry unit was in trouble the MLRS was one of the weapons they called in for precise—and lethal—backup. But Tristan soon was disappointed to learn that the most exciting jobs—the ones that would put her in combat next to the infantrymen who called in the artillery during critical battles—remained male-only.

By the time Tristan showed up to her first assignment out of West Point, she was already determined to find a way out of artillery. But her brigade commander had read her file along with all the other new officers and noted her mix of West Point experience and athletic fitness. Shortly after she arrived at Fort Sill, Oklahoma, he sent word that he wanted to formally interview her. "I want you to be a platoon leader," he told her. It was a job that officially only men could hold, but Tristan, like Anne Jeremy, was clearly worth betting on.

"I read your file and I think you're the best person for the job," the commander said. He made it clear he didn't care if it was "coded" male-only. Army policy or not, he offered it to her.

At first the noncommissioned officers and enlisted men Tristan led, most of them veterans of at least one war deployment, unleashed a pile of grief on her. They had never had a female platoon leader and had no intention of changing their ways for one now. Their behavior spanned from rude and crude to just plain silly, and they went out of their way to make sure Tristan overheard their colorful stories of sexual exploits and conquests. Tristan shrugged it all off and kept her focus on her work. She had heard a lot worse at West Point and had learned how to ignore it. A few weeks into her new role, after they realized she wasn't the stereotypical, shrinking female who would take offense from their rough talk, the men moved on. But just because the men supported her presence didn't mean the women in their lives did, and Tristan regularly received angry, sometimes drunken calls from wives ordering her to "stay away from my husband." Tristan patiently answered that she would be very happy to, just as soon as her time as their officer ended. In the end, Tristan's men became her biggest champions and most vocal backers, and they fully supported her when she became the battery's first female executive officer, the number-two position in her battery. It was another job that was officially open only to men.

And then, a little more than a year later, Tristan was walking back to her office from a brigade maintenance meeting when she saw the bold headline above the female soldier. BECOME A PART OF HIS-TORY, the poster beckoned. She stopped to take a closer look, and as she read the fine print a senior officer passed by and ribbed her. "Oh, yeah, Marsden, you going to go change the world? Going to go be 'part of history'?" Ten minutes later, back in her office staring at the small mountain of administrative paperwork on her desk, Tristan felt like she was in a version of the movie *Groundhog Day*. Every morning she came into her office and pored over reports, paperwork, and Excel spreadsheets with training schedules. One day the same as the next wasn't what she had hoped for when she chose West Point.

When she told her commander—the one who had kidded her about making history—that she wanted to apply for the program, he looked up from his desk with a quizzical expression. Seeing she was serious, his reply was immediate.

"Okay," he said, "you got it. Let me know what I can do to help."

Now, only a few months later, sitting in the Landmark Inn breakfast hall with several dozen like-minded women, she finally felt like she was close to reaching her goal. She had rarely had female friends, other than one or two of the girls she knew from the track team, but she instantly connected with the women at the Landmark. Part of the bond came from the intense athleticism they shared, but it was also about the unusual mix of intensity and femininity they had in common. They were all out to push their own limits and achieve as much as they could. Incredibly, they all looked as hungry as she was to venture into the unknown and tackle a special operations mission that meant more to them than any desk job ever could.

Back on her bed at the Landmark, trying to figure out what to make of her plainspoken new roommate, Tristan looked over at Rigby's overstuffed bag filled with uniforms, socks, military boots, T-shirts—all items she recognized from the long list of gear each soldier had been instructed to bring to selection. She asked herself if she had any idea what she had gotten herself into? Probably not, she thought. But I've gotten this far. No turning back.

Beyond the parade of Amazons, the first day of CST assessment and training was an otherwise dull affair, with nothing but paperwork on the agenda. By lunchtime, with all the candidates checked in, they were free to do whatever they liked until 0800 hours the next morning.

"Kristen," Rigby mischievously whispered to her friend as they filed out of the motel conference room. "Let's get some of the girls and watch *G.I. Jane*!" Rigby had already seen the movie five or six times and still felt inspired by the sight of Demi Moore as Lieutenant Jordan O'Neil, crew cut and all, fighting for a fair shot at joining the Navy SEALs. Like Rigby and Kristen, O'Neil was an intel officer who wanted only to be out in the field. Most war movies had no female characters—this one was different. It was Hollywood, for sure, and over the top, but Rigby was inspired by the heroine's unwillingness to quit. And they needed some inspiration right about now. The two CST candidates headed over to a sprawling Walmart near the base, and of course the movie was in stock.

That night a few of the women piled into Rigby and Tristan's room to enjoy Thai takeout and a double-feature: *G.I. Jane* and *Two Weeks in Hell*, a documentary about Green Beret selection. They laughed when Lillian DeHaven, the senator who arranges O'Neil's entry into SEAL selection, complained that one of the female candidates for the program looked "like the wife of a Russian beet farmer." And they all nodded in agreement when O'Neil announced, "I don't want to be some poster girl for women's rights." None of these women was looking "to make some kind of statement," as Ashley had told Jason. All they wanted was a shot at going to war on a mission they believed in with America's best fighters.

Tristan leaned back to rest her head on one of the extra-firm motel pillows as she watched Demi Moore bust out a row of free-hanging sit-ups on a Navy ship bound for the Middle East. Might as well enjoy a rest now, she thought. *Starting tomorrow we'll all be out there with old Jane getting our asses kicked.*

The next day, Tristan and the other women would find out if they would make the cut.

4

100 Hours of Hell

★ ★ ★

Get your bags into the vehicle. Now!"

A training instructor was standing on the sidewalk before a large military transport truck, its open bed facing the fifty soldiers who were lined up in formation holding giant rucksacks. He had come to transport the women to the real action: CST Assessment and Selection.

Or, as the officer who designed the program called it, "one hundred hours of hell."

"Finally," Amber said to herself, smiling in relief. She hoisted her pack onto one shoulder and strode toward the idling truck.

"All right, ladies, let's load 'er up!" she yelled to the others. Amber leapt into the open truck bed and began dragging bags toward the rear to make it easier for others to toss theirs in without creating a chaotic mess. Following her lead the soldiers formed a single line and began dropping their rucksacks in an orderly fashion. They all knew they would be graded in Assessment and Selection as individuals, but they also knew, as Admiral Olson had noted back when he put the word *team* in the name of their program, that collaboration was central to *everything* in special operations. Their instructors would be watching to see how they performed as a team and what kind of leaders they were, particularly at the most trying moments. But it all began here, at the loading area.

For her part, after forty-eight hours lingering around the Land-

mark Inn, Amber was damned ready to be back at work. The former
interrogator had been up since before dawn mentally readying herself for the test to come. By 7 a.m., according to her Timex wrist-
watch, she was done with breakfast and racing back up the stairs
to her room, taking them two at a time. She grabbed her gear and
jumped in the elevator, rucksack on her back and her mind in the
moment. Another group of soldiers boarded on the floor below. A
particularly fit young woman—one of the few African-American
soldiers at selection—eyed Amber without a word, offering instead a
nod of mutual respect. "Kimberly," she said, extending her hand to
introduce herself. Amber did the same. On Amber's other side stood
a six-foot-three woman who was built like a WWE wrestler. Amber
had to look twice to confirm she was actually female.

By 7:45 a.m. she stood cooling her heels in the now-crowded
lobby, where several dozen women were getting ready for what
many expected would be the biggest test of their lives. By 8 a.m.
the truck arrived to take them to Camp Mackall at Fort Bragg,
where the men's Special Forces Assessment and Selection (SFAS)
also takes place. The women, by contrast, would have a week of
selection. And, if they were lucky enough to make the team, six
weeks of training.

By late morning the would-be CSTs had reached their destination: a line of evenly spaced large canvas Army tents they would call
home for the next six days. They were arranged in a semicircle, and
Amber thought they looked like brown caterpillars waiting to become butterflies. She located her assigned tent and stepped through
the wooden door into a space large enough to fit five cots comfortably on each side, along with a few desks and some standard-issue
metal folding chairs. Lightbulbs dangled from wooden struts lining
either side of the tent. Power outlets could be found here and there
for computer work and writing exercises.

One of her tentmates, an officer who held the rank of major, Amber guessed was the most senior female trying for this new position.

Judging by her officer rank, age, and the fact that she had worked for Admiral Olson, she was clearly a star. Also in the room was a soldier she nicknamed "the Trucker," who chewed Copenhagen Long Cut tobacco, stashed her spit cup beneath her cot, and had a mouth that would put a sailor to shame.

The only distinguishing feature of the uniforms was a rectangle-shaped piece of tape with the candidate's ID number written upon it attached to their camouflaged arms and legs. No tabs or insignia displaying rank or any other outward sign distinguishing between enlisted person and officer was permitted. Everyone had an equal chance to shine or shrink in the course.

The first official test commenced right then and there at the tent. Of the many challenges that would come over the next several days, this should have been the easiest, since it judged not endurance or intelligence but organization. The Army special operations trainers had given the women a precise packing list in advance of their arrival, and now they wanted to see if the soldiers had followed instructions and brought everything on it.

Among the mandatory items:

Two pairs of standard Army-issue boots (or their commercial equivalent, since almost everyone found other brands more comfortable)
Two pairs white cotton socks
Five pairs green/black socks
Gore-Tex top, Gore-Tex bottom
100 mph tape (better known as duct tape to civilians)
Two reflective belts
Long underwear
Two towels
Shower shoes
Sewing kit
Three pens, three pencils

Eyeglasses if needed. (Contact lenses are prohibited.)
Poncho
Canteen
One rucksack with frame
One duffle
Sleeping bag
Officially issued laptop
One headlamp
One flashlight
One penlight

They were also provided with a list of the *only* additional items candidates were allowed to possess:

Pace count beads for tracking distance traveled
Pocketknife
Bungee cords
Foot powder
Insect repellent
Lip balm
Map case
Moleskin
Vaseline
Scissors
Parachute cord

One book (and one book only). It could be a Bible, the Ranger Handbook, or a novel. No magazines were permitted.

A stern-looking female instructor approached, and Amber suddenly felt queasy as she realized in horror that she had failed this first, most simple test. All her gear was neatly sitting there, on the gravel entryway in front of her tent, at perfect attention. Everything, except for one item.

"Where is your duffle bag?" the instructor asked in a monotone. She was maybe a decade older than Amber and had a similar no-nononsense demeanor.

"I didn't need it, ma'am," Amber answered. "I packed tightly enough that I fit all the other gear on the list in my rucksack." As she spoke, she realized the folly of her hubris. She had only just stepped off the truck and already was showing herself incapable of following simple instructions.

The instructor didn't allow a hint of emotion as she began her interrogation about the missing item.

"Was it on the packing list?" she asked.

"Yes, ma'am, it was," Amber answered. Her stomach roiled.

The instructor scribbled something in her notebook and moved on.

Dammit, Amber thought. Seriously, if my own cockiness is what keeps me out of this . . . She forced herself to buck up her crushed spirit and remain at attention as the instructor moved down the line of fellow CST hopefuls. It was hardly an auspicious start to the week. And it had begun so well.

As the instructors proceeded from tent to tent Amber learned that others had also left stuff behind: a notebook, a canteen cover, an extra pair of socks. She watched as other aspiring CSTs who had completed their checks ran the missing items over to their fellow soldiers. The spirit of solidarity and leadership surprised and impressed her. Sure, they all were competing against one another, but they understood that each had to succeed if anyone like them was ever going to get this chance again.

The first physical challenge came in the form of the Army's standard physical training (PT) test. Amber busted out push-up after push-up in the two minutes she had, careful to focus on form so that every one counted.

"All the way down," she commanded herself. Focus on making them count. Don't go for one hundred, just make sure a few dozen are picture-perfect. But she went ahead and pounded out a lot more than that, a benefit of her own intense CrossFit training and a heavy surge of adrenaline.

For Amber and many of the others, including Kate, the West Pointer MP who had played football in high school, and Tristan, the sockless track star, the PT test was largely a formality. Much to their consternation, the Army had different standards for male and female PT scores, and they yearned to be treated equally in every respect. In any case, most of them always performed so well they left the top score of the female scale in the dust, proving they could be measured against the male standard on any metric, from push-ups to two-milers.

Amber, like most of the others, had long ago dedicated herself to spending hours in the gym and out on the track each week. She was not a naturally gifted runner—lifting weights was a lot easier for her—but, like Ashley, what she lacked in talent she made up for in tenacity. As soon as she had heard about the CST program Amber began training in CrossFit with kettle bells, Olympic lifts, and lunges upon lunges. By the time she arrived at Bragg in May she was in better shape than she had ever been. Here, at the start of the most demanding program she had ever faced, Amber felt more alive than she had in years, and more confident.

That first road march for an "unknown distance" quickly separated the crowd of candidates. Ruck marching—walking a long distance with a heavy backpack packed tight with gear—is a physical and mental trial some soldiers love and others loathe. Every pound matters since the weight will be borne across hours and miles and hills that would test even the heartiest soldier. In this case the would-be CSTs carried around thirty-five pounds of gear from the detailed packing list, plus the weight of the water in their canteens; all of it would be measured on a scale to make certain no one was cutting corners—or ounces. For Amber, Ashley, and the fittest CST candidates, years of training and growing their endurance had accustomed them to the physical misery. Many had come to find a certain kind of solace in the lengthy treks through every kind of terrain, their mind and body focused on transcending the next step to reach that rush of endorphins that over time rewards hours of exertion. Amber had learned how to mentally approach the trudge ahead by measuring the distance in klicks, military slang for one kilometer—1,000 meters or .62 miles—and running calculations in her head to estimate at what point she would reach the correct stride and pace that would carry her through the remaining hours. Ruck snugly packed, weapon slung across her chest, hat firmly in place keeping sweat at bay and every strand of hair pinned: she found herself in love once more with the work of soldiering for her country. Traversing the soft earth up and down the hills in her trusted Altama boots on this mild May day, she felt there truly was no place she'd rather be.

Of course, it was not all inspirational and bucolic. Eyes straight ahead, feet pounding out the first few miles, Amber passed a fellow CST candidate who was crying. The soldier moved slowly, clearly hobbled by pain of some sort, maybe a turned ankle or an aching tendon. It was easy to trip on a rock or fall over some uneven terrain out here in the wilderness. As she passed the woman the hard-edge side of her won out over the compassionate team player. Come on, Amber thought to herself. Really? If you are crying you shouldn't be here. There are things you should shed tears about—death, severe illness—but a ruck march isn't one of them. She kept marching.

I got this, she promised herself. Just don't get cocky again. And for God's sake, don't screw up.

A few tents away from Amber, Kate rejoiced at having hit the selection group jackpot. Rigby was part of her team and her enthusiasm for the week ahead showed in the first emphatic handshake she offered when introducing herself. Given the ban on contact lenses, Rigby sported dark-framed glasses that gave her the air of an aspiring PhD candidate. Tristan was also in her tent, and as it turned out,

Tristan and Kate had been classmates at West Point. They hadn't been close in school, but since women made up only around 15 percent of their class—about the same percentage as in active-duty military—most of them knew one another by face if not by name. Tristan and Kate became instant friends.

Rigby, for her part, had not expected to bond with or even like any of the women she roomed with in this selection. She had grown up with a hippie mom and a Navy veteran dad who taught her that nothing in life was either easy or handed to you, a reality that was reinforced by her dad's job woes, her parents' eventual divorce, and years of financial precariousness. She had arrived at Assessment and Selection with something of a chip on her shoulder. The West Point women, she thought, were sure to be an uppity bunch; her lower-middle-class upbringing made her mistrust anything that suggested pedigree. But just as she had been forced to question her stereotypes after Kristen bested her back in Arizona, Tristan and Kate made her feel embarrassed about her prejudices. These West Point women weren't just tough as hell; they were smart and funny. And *nice*. She wanted to dislike the naturally perky Tristan with her ridiculous physical stamina born of decades of race running and track training, but she simply couldn't: her good nature and her self-deprecating humor had won her over during their time as roommates back at the Landmark.

Instructors informed the women about what would be required of them during selection week by using a system of postings on a whiteboard that were updated throughout the day. Instructions were sparse and by design omitted much critical information; it was up to the women to figure it out. This meant that the soldiers had to be ready to leave the (relative) comfort of their tent at any moment, including during their rare rest periods, to find out what was coming next and when. In a selection process designed to keep soldiers off balance at all times, staying abreast of information was critical to success.

Tristan volunteered to be their tent's messenger, and neither Kate nor Rigby objected. After all, from that first day she looked like she had been born on her feet. When the ten team members returned to the tent after the opening ruck march, they crashed on their beds, peeled sticky, aching feet out of damp socks, and gingerly nursed their new blisters. Everything hurt—standing *and* sitting—and the thought of rucking again in a few hours was daunting. But not for Tristan. She was perched on her cot, airing out her infamous smelly boots and breezily chatting with the others as if she had just returned from an afternoon of sunbathing on the beach. Years of running and marching barefoot in her sand-colored Nike military boots had hardened her feet against blisters. Her feet were so calloused and tough it would take far more than twenty miles of marching to faze them.

Tristan also had her own unique strategies and mental tricks for bearing up under the stress of no sleep. First and foremost: she stayed ready, 24/7. On one of the first nights of selection the candidates had to pull a near all-nighter working on a written assignment their instructors would judge early the following morning. When they finally finished they all slid into the comfort of their PT gear—a cotton tee and nylon shorts—to grab an hour or two of sleep. But not Tristan. When dawn arrived barely a few hours later and Kate yelled for everyone to get up, it was Tristan who leapt from her cot first.

"What, what? Okay, I am here, I am ready," she said, fighting through a haze of sleep. The sight caused Kate to laugh out loud.

"Tristan, how in the hell are you dressed already? Did you sleep in your uniform?"

Tristan was already reaching for a batch of Handi Wipes that would serve as her mobile shower.

"Yes, I slept in it, of course," she replied. "You don't know when they're going to come and tell us to get up and get moving. I want to be ready."

Rigby took one look at her teammate and, between laughs, asked how she had managed to keep her hat on all night.

Tristan just smiled.

"Laugh away, friends, but when we are the first team to know what's coming next because yours truly was dressed and ready to go before everyone else, you will all be seriously grateful," she said.

As the days stretched on the women realized that each member of their team brought a different set of skills and talents. For Kate the physical tests had been a real challenge. Running with a full box of dummy ammunition or lifting on her shoulders the weight of a huge wooden log during one of the obstacle courses was tough for her.

But her ability to problem-solve under duress made her a real asset to the team. Early in the week the women faced an obstacle course that interspersed physical trials—climbing thirty-foot wooden walls and hiking long distances—with the kind of mental agility tests for which special operations is famous. In one exam the women had to disarm a (fake) bomb while blindfolded. Another required the soldiers to devise a way to get everyone across a rushing river using only wooden planks and rope. Kate was often the first to offer up a plan—and to give ground if someone else's sounded more logical.

And she knew how to use her grit and courage to bolster the spirits of the other women. During one of the many long ruck marches Kate realized that a teammate was lagging. The ten women had started out in one line and were told to assume they were on their own, no talking allowed. An hour later Kate saw that her tentmate was injured; she was limping so badly she needed to lean on a tree for support. Without saying a word, the other women nodded their heads toward the young woman, making sure that each team member was aware she was in trouble. Then they took turns staying close to her so no one would finish much before the others.

The instructors were not pleased.

"Do not help her, do not touch her, this is an individual assessment," one of the sergeants yelled. He got up close, right in their faces, and shouted from a distance of only inches, nearly spitting his words at them. Kate had read about special operations selection processes and she knew that much of this was an act, that the instructors were testing the soldiers to see how they would deal with stress. They wanted to judge the candidates' ability to stay together as a team when something went wrong.

"They are just mind-fucking you, don't listen to them!" Kate yelled to the other women marching next to her. She had always been outspoken and she prided herself on being a good teammate as well as a good soldier. This may have been the all-important Assessment and Selection process, but she wasn't going to start holding back now, even if it harmed her career. "They're just testing you. Don't be a jerk and leave a fellow soldier in the field." The young woman limped alongside them, at times falling to her knees and proceeding in a crawl to give her ankle some relief, and sure enough the others stayed with her, offering encouragement and moral support.

"You are messing with the system, guys," the instructor warned. "This is an *individual* assessment."

Kate had no idea if this was just a part of the test or if he really meant it. And she didn't know whether men in the same situation would be praised for surging forward or lauded for staying back to make sure all the others made it to the end. But she would leave no woman behind.

A few minutes later she helped her teammates reach the finish line. All of them.

By day four the all-night work sessions and all-day marching, running, and obstacle testing were beginning to take their toll on the women, and Tristan's strategy of sleeping in full uniform was looking increasingly sensible. The instructors were testing their mental and physical mettle, and that meant some of the Ironman women weren't faring as well as they thought they would. This was a mental game as much as a physical challenge, designed to reinforce the fact that staying focused and motivated is absolutely critical to mission success and basic survival in war. For many aspiring CST members who soared through the athletic tests, it was the verbal jousting that proved tricky.

Even the relentlessly upbeat Tristan was bending under the pressures of the program. She returned to the tent exhausted and demoralized after a day at the Soldier Urban Reaction Facility, established to help soldiers better navigate the cultures in which they would be operating. Tristan had been thrown during a role-playing scenario that took place in a sparsely furnished room filled with dark carpets and floor pillows meant to resemble an Afghan living space. The test encounter had started fine, but went south quickly when "husbands" of the "Afghan women" she was supposed to be interviewing burst into the room and began hitting their wives and screaming at the American soldier. Tristan simply froze where she sat, unable to conjure up, in the shrill chaos of the moment, the words and actions needed to calm the situation. Eventually she muttered something to explain why she was there, but it was too late: she had lost control of the situation. As a field artillery officer sitting at a desk and doing math problems to figure out the exact coordinates needed to fire precisely on the right location, she was not used to dealing with interpersonal crises.

It hadn't gone much better for Tristan later that evening when the instructors interrogated her about how field artillery bears any relevance to counterinsurgency. They kept demanding increasingly specific examples. A dull film of exhaustion now coated every corner of her brain, suffocating her best thoughts. She was overwhelmed by frustration, convinced she had failed miserably and that the trainers had already found the one chink in her armor. She was 100 percent confident in her physical abilities and her endurance, but as a field artillery officer who had never deployed she hadn't had much daily contact with COIN, or counterinsurgency. And it showed.

"Guys, I don't know if I can do this," she confided late that night from her bed, her head in her hands. "I know I want it, but I think I just lost my chance."

Kate and Rigby came over to her small cot and put their arms around her shoulders. "Come on," Kate said, "you're doing great out there and you're going to be even greater after this. Stay in it. One lousy test doesn't take you off track."

Rigby had had a grueling day as well, having pushed herself as well as her teammates through their misery. At dinner she had to prod Kristen to finish eating her MRE, or Meals, Ready to Eat, after she threw up half of it. Her body simply could not take in as much food as she needed to get through the day's tests. "You gotta keep going," Rigby insisted, pushing the unappetizing meal of chicken-with-something back toward her after she vomited just beside her seat. "Keep eating it." Everyone in her tent was physically depleted from the marches and runs and mentally drained by the exams and the need to impress their assessors at every moment. But they were determined to stay in it regardless of what their bodies and their minds told them.

One night Rigby found inspiration in an unexpected place.

"Hey, you guys, check this out," she said, running back into the tent after her visit to one of the port-a-potties that stood in a row behind their sleeping quarters. "The John has a message for us!"

"You gotta be joking!" Kate shouted. "Are you really bringing us wisdom from the shitter?"

Tristan too was preparing for a few moments of rest, in full uniform, and let out a big laugh. It was the first smile her face had found in hours.

"Yes, I am indeed, ladies," Rigby said in her matter-of-fact tone, pushing back her glasses. "There is some *really* good stuff in there. I've been reading a lot of it. Think about who has sat on those toilets before us—every man who has ever gone on to join Special Forces. They know what they're talking about when they leave that wisdom behind."

The entire tent was listening.

"Seriously," she continued. "Listen to this. And take it to heart, girls, as the last day approaches."

She paused for effect.

"The mind is its own place. And itself can make a hell of heaven and a heaven of hell. Don't quit."

The room was pin-drop silent.

"Pretty good, isn't it? Going to have T-shirts made for us with it when this is all done," Rigby said. Then she jumped onto her cot. "It's my favorite one so far. Good night, my friends, see you before I want to."

The room went dark as someone turned off the main light.

Don't quit indeed, thought Kate. Just one more day . . .

Two hours later they were awake.

"Up, up, get moving!" one of the tentmates yelled. "Cadre are out there—time to get up!"

It did not count as predawn, Kate thought; it was maybe 2 or 3 a.m. Her blistered feet burned and her body ached. Her eyes were completely dried out; they felt like glass that was being sandblasted. Meanwhile, Tristan, now recovered from her brush with hopelessness of several hours earlier, was trying to rally her troops.

"Come on, guys, let's go," she said, bounding from cot to cot to make sure no one was still asleep. She checked to make sure Rigby had on fresh socks since her last pair was soaked through with blood from her blisters. "This is it—last day."

The night ruled quiet and crisp. North Carolina has the brightest stars I've ever seen, Tristan thought. She inhaled the air and psyched herself up for the march that was soon to come. The women carried rucksacks, canteens, and fake weapons, and were poised to begin the most grueling physical and mental tests they would face in their weeklong training cycle.

"It will be a suckfest," Kate promised the others. "Get ready!"

It started with a ruck that had no end. The women marched on long stretches of flat brown dirt, up rock-strewn hills and alongside murky, mud-filled creeks lined by trees on either side. For more than six hours they rucked, and as they did they watched as the pitch-black sky slowly faded and gave way to a few rays of sunlight that signaled the approaching dawn. Many suffered from bleeding feet through layers of moleskin and medical tape, but they marched on. For some, like Kate, it was tough but bearable, since the end was so near. Rigby found it hard in a way that thrilled her; she had wanted to be tested to the full extent of her physical and mental faculties, and so far the CST selection hadn't disappointed. For Tristan, after the horrendous night before, it was a relatively easy day: rugged but entirely manageable.

Occasionally the instructors stopped the marchers to ask them a riddle. Some of the women used the break to kneel on one knee and give their feet a rest. During one such pause, the instructor had no sooner gotten mid-sentence in his question about how to move an item across a gulch when Kate stopped to interrupt him with the answer.

"I got it," she blurted out. "Move this, move that, move that, you're done."

Her answer was correct.

"What the heck?" Rigby said. "How did you do that? That was amazing."

"It came to me like Jesus," Kate said, stepping back to take a bow before her team, and inspire a moment of laughter. Then it was back to the march.

By the time the march ended some of the women were dizzy with exhaustion. Others sat down for the first time in hours for their ten-minute break for mealtime—more MREs—and believed they had never eaten anything so delicious in their lives. But the break was not to last long. Another obstacle course required they scale a thirty-foot wall by hoisting one another up in the air using their cupped hands as ladders. By 3 p.m. they had been at it for close to twelve hours and there was no end in sight.

Next on the agenda: more running. Out of boots and into track shoes. Tristan took the lead for her team and once again motivated them all to keep pushing through their mental exhaustion and physical pain. "Keep going, guys," she urged them as they swapped footgear. "Just a little more to go." Kate marveled at her stamina. She's a beast, Kate thought, filled with respect for her fellow soldier's strength.

Finally, late in the day when some of the soldiers thought they might not be able to stay awake much longer, let alone stand up and perform yet another physical task, they reached the capstone of the Assessment and Selection training: a long run followed by a series of "buddy carries." In the Army every soldier has to be fit enough and perpetually ready to carry a fellow soldier off the field in case the worst happens and he is injured or dead. Over the past fifty years in America, one of the central questions raised in the endless debates about whether women could serve in ground combat—even in support roles—has always been: would a woman be able to carry a large man off the battlefield under fire?

Kate's male Army friends had always told her that while they thought she was a great soldier, they could never trust a woman to hoist them to safety if they got shot or hurt. "It's not personal," they would say. "It's just biology."

"But what about guys who are five-four and a hundred and thirty pounds?" Kate would respond. "Why are they okay and not girls who are the same size?" No one could ever give her a satisfactory answer to that question. Out there for CST Assessment and Selection that afternoon, Kate was determined to let her actions prove her worth. She would neither give in to her exhaustion nor fail to carry a single soldier—no matter how heavy—out of harm's way.

As the afternoon wore on the cadre took turns walking up to the soldiers in the field and pretending to shoot them. "You're dead," they'd say, and walk away. The soldier's job was to fall onto the ground and go completely limp.

In the buddy-carry, three or four soldiers encircle the fallen comrade. Depending on how she lay, one would get behind and underneath her body and grab her armpits while another took her legs.

Together they would hoist her over a third soldier's neck and that soldier would carry the "dead" soldier, forming a sort of P around her neck. Most of the women on Kate's team were on the small side, so carrying them presented no real challenge, but still she took inspiration from Amber, who had a bunch of weapons slung over her and was carrying one of the bigger girls on her shoulders as if she were light as a feather.

Kate now was fully motivated. Whoever she is, Kate thought, that girl knows what she's doing. Kate pressed ahead and picked up a teammate who had dropped right in front of her.

A half hour later it was Rigby's turn to "die." She had already carried several of her more petite teammates to safety and joked to herself that the real test would come when they had to carry her, for while she was hardly big, she was taller and thicker than most of the other women in their tent. Finally the instructor came by and "killed" her.

By that time the temperature had climbed well above eighty degrees and the soldiers had sweated through every inch of their camouflage uniforms. Rigby's blisters bled freely and she was soaked through with perspiration from top to bottom. It was almost a relief to lie quietly on the dirt lane, playing dead and gazing at the gray sky, waiting to get picked up by her teammates. And then she looked down and saw that her pants were soaked in blood from her waist to her knees. She felt a jolt of panic wondering if all their combat role-playing had started to play tricks on her mind. And then she burst out in laughter. She had been out there in the field for well over twelve hours and had somehow missed the fact that her period had started hours before.

Kate looked over, saw her "dead" buddy laughing, then followed Rigby's eyes to the source of the moment's absurdity. "Oh shit," she said, "this one's going to be interesting!" She was already hatching a strategy for how the team would carry her safely home.

But Rigby darted off in another direction, and behind the spare cover of a spindly North Carolina tree she dealt with her feminine hygiene.

"I just gotta take care of my business," she shouted back. "Be there in an instant . . ." Kate looked on, trying unsuccessfully to suppress her own laughter.

"The bears are going to have a field day!" Kate shouted to her teammates.

Along with a woman's inability to carry a comrade off the field, another reason soldiers frequently gave for keeping women out of the infantry was that their periods would attract bears out in the wild. Among Army women there was a long tradition of joking about the ridiculousness of this idea, as if a bear would find a menstrual cycle any more attractive than they did.

The male cadre was standing twenty feet from the women and watched without saying a word. His own training had taught him to be stoic at all times and to betray no spontaneous expression. This guy is good, the soldiers thought, but of course he had never dealt with an all-female selection before and this body stuff was entirely new terrain. His eyes grew large, full of what Kate later called "shock and awe," but he stood there and simply watched as the women arranged themselves like nothing at all had happened, then got on with the task at hand.

"Okay, let's go," Rigby called out a minute later. Another teammate hoisted her up with help from Kate and another soldier and heaved Rigby's torso behind her shoulders and on top of her rucksack. The fake-dead Rigby hung limp, as the team humped its way back to the staging area.

"One hundred hours of hell" had lived up to the promise of its name.

Ashley's preparation for the hours of hell had started six years earlier when she was a freshman at Kent State and became addicted to rucking. On school breaks she would pack rocks into her backpack and head out of her family's house in Marlboro for her own "unknown distance" road marches.

"What are you doing, Ashley?" Bob would ask. "Why would you make it heavier?"

"I'm training, Dad, trying to get stronger," she would call back to him as she walked out the door and began to set a pace for herself on the two-lane highway that ran alongside their ranch home.

Now her years of preparation were paying off. The scale that weighed everyone's gear before the first ruck started, tipped well above the minimum requirement when Ashley's pack was placed on it. No way she would get penalized because the instructors found her pack was too light—if it came in underweight at the end she would have to start all over again, and she wasn't *about* to let that happen. Ashley had prepared her body for the long ruck marches in very specific ways. Unlike running, which is nearly all cardio exertion, the rucks require abdominal and back strength. The thousands of sit-ups and crunches and hours of CrossFit she had performed in the months leading up to selection meant Ashley's core was strong enough to bear the load of her pack without buckling. Pull-ups had built up her shoulder muscles. She may not have been a Pegasus like Tristan, but she was an outstanding athlete.

From her first stride to her last, Ashley never let up. Some soldiers fell out of formation. Others were slowed by the creeping burn of played-out calf muscles that began to atrophy from overuse. The soldiers who weren't suffering from physical discomfort struggled with the ruck's "no talking" rule, and found relief in swapping daydreams about the foods they would eat when the week had finished (lasagna and ice cream won the day) or the jobs this suffering would lead to.

But Ashley pressed on—quiet, focused, always at the front, just as she had been from the first day of ROTC training. She relished the silence and the *clop-clop* of her Gore-Tex boots as her feet hit the ground. All around her the North Carolina fir trees stood tall, lush, and green, stretching their limbs toward the sky. They reminded her of the state park where she ran races with Josh and Brittany as kids. Her every sense was tuned in to the moment and remained there. She heard the flapping wings of birds flying above against the steady, in-and-out pattern of her own breath and the *tap-tap-tap* of her heart.

The road ahead stretched out before her as she tracked the klicks on her pace counter. Nearly everyone else was now marching behind her. Only her tentmates Leda and Anne, the engineer, hiked alongside her, sometimes in front, sometimes slightly behind. These fittest of soldiers challenged one another by wordless example to be the best they could be.

That night, nearly every soldier was struggling to stay in one piece.

Along the route medics stood by at first aid stations to monitor injuries and examine soldiers who looked hurt. Not wanting to quit the selection process and miss out on this unique opportunity, most of the CST candidates hurried past the medical teams, assuring them they were "just fine." Even if they were lying prone on the ground, they wouldn't admit to an injury. Those who acknowledged any pain simply vowed to defy it. But the medics checked the soldiers' feet each evening to make certain they didn't overlook any serious injuries.

Lane, the Guard soldier and track star from Nevada, had been in extreme pain that morphed into agony by day three. Her Achilles tendon, which she had injured during high school track and field, was on fire. As she rucked, she considered the possibility that each step she took could be her last, but still she marched on, refusing to seek out the medic. When he made his nightly rounds, however, what he saw alarmed him.

"Hey, you know that Achilles tendon could snap at any moment," he said. "If I were you I would quit. That is a *terrible* injury—it takes months to heal and if the damage is severe enough it might never fully recover. It's not a good idea to risk it."

He was holding a folder that contained all the paperwork necessary for a medical drop.

Lane gaped at him and yanked her foot away.

"Are you kidding me? I am *here*. I made it this far. I am totally fine.

"Seriously," she said, looking up at him as she laced her boots back up, "if it rips just glue it back together."

A few tents down from Lane, Ashley's team awaited their own medic check. One soldier's blisters had worn through four layers of skin, down to what she thought must have been the dermis. Ashley put her medical training to work.

"If anyone needs her feet taped up, the doctor is in," she announced, facing two folding chairs toward one another so her "patients" could elevate their feet while she examined their blisters and swaddled them in moleskin. Back at Kent State, Jason had often been Ashley's guinea pig in such situations, allowing her to tape up his uninjured knees, ankles, and wrists to perfect her technique. One day she even had him come to one of her physical therapy classes so she could demonstrate her knowledge of how to palpate an injured shoulder. He joked with her later that she had just wanted to show off her handsome, shirtless ROTC boyfriend to all the girls in her class. Now Ashley was considering pursuing a job as a physician's assistant once her Afghanistan deployment was behind her. She had confided this to Anne while helping one of their tentmates; there was something about this environment that felt inspiring to her. There in her bunk, taping her teammates' torn-up feet at a makeshift first aid station, Ashley realized she was starting to become genuinely attached to the women in her tent. Like Rigby, she felt they were facing a trial that almost no one else on earth ever could or would understand. Even their own families.

Ashley, Leda, and Anne had become a trio that first weekend at the Landmark Inn, and Ashley wanted to introduce her new friends to Jason. She knew that if he met these remarkable women he would better understand why giving her his blessing to go forward with the selection process was so important to her. When one of the girls suggested a group dinner on the "down" night before selection started, Ashley surprised herself by her own bold question:

"Is it okay if I invite my husband?"

"Oh, of course, I'd love to meet him," Leda replied. And it was true: ever since she met Ashley, Leda had been wondering what Jason was like. Military couples, in which both wife and husband served in uniform, were still exceptionally rare. Happy ones rarer still.

Jason was as curious as Leda. He wanted to learn more about the CST program and meet the soldiers his wife would be joining—and competing against—in the selection process.

That night, at a steak house not far from the Landmark, Leda recognized Jason from Ashley's photos.

"Hi there," she said, flashing a radiant, confident smile. "I'm Leda."

He stammered out a greeting in response, scanning the room for Ashley, and was about to tell her as politely as he could that he was a happily married man, when she continued.

"I've heard so much about you, I'm in selection with Ashley," she said. "She just went to the restroom, by the way. I have to tell you, your wife is amazing."

Jason relaxed. "Oh, great to meet you," he said, extending his hand. "And yes, she most definitely is."

Ashley arrived and gave her husband a big hug and kiss.

"Jason," Leda said as they sat down to eat. "You seriously are the coolest guy in the world to come out here to dinner with all these women."

"I consider myself lucky," he replied, and glanced at his wife, who was smiling back at him. She was genuinely thrilled to see him in the company of her new friends. She had heard stories at the Landmark of marriages that had fallen apart under the strain of deployments, and she felt luckier than ever to have him. They spent the hour away from the Landmark talking about war: Leda shared stories about the work she had done in Iraq, downplaying her own role throughout, and Jason mentioned he had just returned from Afghanistan. He made his way through his rib eye and mashed potatoes and was happy to see how comfortable Ashley looked around them and how ready she seemed for the assessment tests ahead.

Driving back to the hotel after meeting Jason and watching him with his wife, Leda felt even more impressed by—and fond of—Ashley. As they chatted about her upcoming wedding in Ohio, and the three-tiered white-icing, chocolate cake that her mom would be making, Leda couldn't resist sharing her thoughts.

"You and Jason really are remarkable. I so admire the way you respect and love one another. You really have something special, Ashley."

The bond between the two women only deepened in the days ahead as they fought their way through one bleary afternoon of ruck marching after another. On the final day of the assessment, guessing that the cadre were shuttered away somewhere in a classroom at the Special Warfare Center and School headquarters deciding their fates, the two shared a quiet moment in a remote part of the training camp.

Leda, always interested in leadership styles and what motivates people, especially someone as silently determined as Ashley, now felt comfortable asking her young friend directly some questions about herself.

"So, do you like your work there at the college?" she asked about Ashley's work back home as an athletic trainer.

"Oh, yeah," she said. "I love being around the athletes and helping them deal with all their injuries. I don't think I want to do it forever, but for now and for a first job it's a great experience." She paused, weighing whether or not she felt comfortable enough to share more, then continued.

"I know they'd understand if I had to take a leave to do this deployment," she continued. "But there is one thing about CST that worries me . . ."

They were once again at the front of the pack, engaged in a land navigation exercise in which they had to find their way from a drop-off point in unfamiliar territory to a final destination on the map. False turns and wrong paths dotted the landscape; following the map expertly was crucial to reaching the right location in the limited amount of time allotted. This kind of exercise measures what the military calls "orienteering": the ability to do spatial analysis under stressful conditions. For the CSTs the exercise was part of the final test of the Assessment and Selection program, but for Ashley, who had done hundreds of these exercises in ROTC, the test presented little challenge.

"I worry I'm a little bit too shy for this," Ashley admitted as they walked toward a squiggle on the map they had received for the exercise. "I mean, *I* know I can do it, but maybe those guys will think I'm not aggressive or outspoken enough to do the job?"

"Well," Leda asked, "how is it working with all those type A male athletes?" She had watched Ashley over the past four days and was certain she would be an asset to the team. Physically she was a beast, but she had excelled in the puzzles and obstacle courses, too. Her thoughtful nature and tendency to analyze a problem before speaking made her stand out on her team.

"Do you ever find it intimidating working with those guys?"

"Oh, no, the guys are great, they come to me to take care of their injuries, and it doesn't matter that I'm the only female they're working with. To them I'm just the trainer. That's it. They never have any issues coming to see me."

Leda switched into coaching mode.

"Ashley, you have exactly what it takes for this mission. The CST role is a special mix of technical, problem-solving, and emotional intelligence skills. It's not something that just anyone can do, but it's also something at which more than one type of person can excel. You don't have to be outgoing to be good at it. I know the special ops community from other work I've done and you are exactly the kind of 'quiet professional' they're looking for. Your physical skills are obvious, anyone can see that, but you have a quiet confidence that they will respect and that they require out there in the field. That's all you need. Believe in that, and don't let anyone tell you otherwise."

Ashley looked back at her and, true to form, said nothing. Leda had a decade of experience in the military, served in the much more senior rank of major, and had far greater experience with the special operations community than any of her teammates. This was a woman who knew what she was talking about. That fact gave Ashley some comfort, even if it didn't silence all of her doubts.

Now she made another promise, not unlike the vow she had made to Jason late that night in the kitchen of their ranch house, to go at CST selection hard and never quit. "Okay," she said. "I won't; I promise. Now let's get this done and find out whether we made it!"

5

Making the Cut

* * *

The next morning, aching but hopeful, the women boarded a bus for the JFK Special Warfare Center and School at Fort Bragg to learn their fate. They may have been limping, sore, and exhausted, but a nervous adrenaline buzz kept them all at attention.

The soldiers filed into the Bank Hall auditorium, named after Army special operations pioneer Colonel Aaron Bank, known as the "father of the Green Berets." It was an appropriate setting for the young female trailblazers, all of whom knew the legend of Colonel Bank, a former OSS officer who helped train and equip the French Resistance in World War II and afterward led Operation Iron Cross, a daring mission to train German opposition members to capture high-ranking Nazis, including Adolf Hitler. (That mission was aborted before it launched.) Bank had always thought the base an ideal location for a special warfare school, writing in his memoirs that "everything we required was available at Fort Bragg," and had battled the Pentagon to get the center opened in 1952. This innovator of unconventional warfare had died several years earlier at the age of 101.

The theater's subdued blue-green hues belied the special warfare combat experiences that were usually shared from its stage. With nothing to do but wait, Ashley settled her nerves by trying to figure out the order in which the CST hopefuls would be called into a nearby classroom to learn how they had done in the Assessment and Selection. She knew she had finished all the physical tests at the head of the class, and had reason to be optimistic. But despite Leda's assurances to the contrary, she still worried that her less forceful personality would somehow count against her.

Strangely, no one who went into the room came back out; they just disappeared. "They must be leaving from doors we can't see," Ashley guessed, "so no one can ask them how it went." In fact, she reflected, the whole assessment cycle had been a journey through the unknown, with instructors simply commanding them about their tasks and scratching notes on their pads. There was no feedback at any time, and there had been no yelling, screaming, or intimidation tactics. It was nothing like what she had expected. It was just a cold, sterile assessment of whether she had what it took to join this mission. Or not, she worried. The minutes ticked by.

"Lieutenant White!" she suddenly heard from across the room. At long last it was her turn. Heart pounding, she struggled to keep her face expressionless and entered the large classroom where her "lane walker," the instructor who had observed her throughout the last day, sat with a stack of papers on a desk in front of him, one of which had her name on it. From the corner of her eye Ashley spotted fellow soldiers she had met during the week sitting at desks sprinkled throughout the room, but the space was so big it was impossible to hear what was being said. In any case, Ashley's eyes stayed glued to those of the instructor who sat across from her.

The cadre began with a positive observation about her performance—"outstanding strength and physical stamina in marches and runs; strong PT score"—before launching into a catalog of her weaknesses: "Need to exert more vocal leadership; be more forceful when leading group." The perfectionist in Ashley heard every fault he mentioned, loud and clear, and missed the achievements.

"You rated top ten percent of all the candidates, Lieutenant White," he finished. "Congratulations."

And that was it. Two arduous months of winning Jason over,

preparing her packet, readying herself physically and mentally, then working her ass off in the field, and it had ended in an instant. Fighting through a heady cocktail of excitement and fatigue she thanked the cadre, and proceeded toward the side door he had pointed her to. She quickly glanced back and watched as several candidates headed toward another exit. Ashley's path led to the main entrance of Bank Hall, where she stepped out the front door into the brisk March sunshine. She was holding a folder embossed with the image of *Bronze Bruce*, a twenty-two-foot statue of a Special Forces soldier that was the first memorial in the United States to the Vietnam War. The real statue towered over the Army Special Operations Command's Memorial Plaza and its wall listing the names of special operations soldiers killed in action. At the top of the folder was printed:

"2nd Lt. White Ashley I." for her middle name, Irene. Inside sat a certificate.

> *United States Army*
> *John F. Kennedy Special Warfare Center and School*
> *To All Who Shall See These Presents Greeting*
> *Be it known that 2nd Lt. Ashley I. White*
> *Completed*
> *Cultural Support Team Assessment & Selection Phase 1*

Ashley was in. Holding the papers made it all seem real.

She finally let out a big, magnetic smile, the kind that reaches from cheek to cheek and dares others not to return it. It was the first thing Jason had noticed about her at that ROTC pizza party all those years ago during her freshman year at Kent State.

As soon as she pushed through the front door she heard the cheers exploding. All the women who had been selected now stood milling about in an ever-larger cluster on the grass. Lane, the Guard soldier and Iraq veteran from Nevada, was there, though they didn't know one another yet. It was no surprise that Leda and Anne were there as well. Each time the door opened and a new teammate who had survived the grueling week emerged, the growing crowd shouted out its congratulations.

Leda rushed over to embrace Ashley.

"I knew you were in," she congratulated her tentmate. "See? I told you you have what it takes." Ashley only smiled. She hoped that someday she would get the opportunity to let Leda know how much her encouragement had meant to her.

The fact that the young lieutenant from the National Guard had finished so successfully spoke for itself. Of course, being Ashley and a White, she still wished she had come in first in everything, but given the caliber of the competition she would take it. And now she would focus on making herself stronger, faster, and fitter before the more formal CST training started the following month.

But there was just one problem. The training course was scheduled to begin around the same time as her wedding, and she and Jason had already postponed their church ceremony once. She had no intention of doing so again. Besides, she had her dream strapless white wedding dress picked out, and at that very moment a seamstress back in Ohio was busy tailoring the beaded gown.

I'll figure it out, she promised herself. For now, she would enjoy the day. She couldn't wait to call Jason and tell him her good news. She had indeed done him—and herself—proud.

The same set of nerve-racking evaluations played out two months later at the same Bank Hall theater on Fort Bragg. This time for the active-duty soldiers.

This group—including Kate, Tristan, Rigby, and Amber—had completed their Assessment and Selection in a separate program from the Guard and Reserves. Once all members of the CST team had been selected they would come together to train as one class, but for scheduling purposes the active-duty and Guard and Reserves troops tried out for the program separately.

Earlier that morning, the fifty or so active-duty CST aspirants had taken over an old barracks building they found on Fort Bragg, and spent an hour doing battle with the caked-on grime, mud, and sweat they had accumulated from a week in the field. When Kate heard one of the instructors shout from the doorway of the classroom, "Lieutenant Raimann!," she still felt the gleam that came from donning a fresh uniform after six days of rucking. Working to remain calm and expressionless, she took her seat across the desk from the cadre and waited.

"So," the young NCO said, and began to walk through her scores in each of the categories in which she had been tested. "You don't read well enough and you certainly don't write well enough. Officers are supposed to publish, you know, and you don't have the writing skills for that."

Kate was stung by his evaluation. She secretly harbored dreams of becoming a writer after she finished her service in the Army, and wondered who he was to question her ability. But she sat silently and betrayed no emotion, hands folded in her lap, waiting for him to continue.

"You are just average physically," he went on. "There are a lot of girls out here that are stronger than you are and a lot are fitter. You are definitely middle of the pack. At best."

He stared at her, then pushed the JFK Special Warfare Center folder toward her on the desk.

"Congratulations," he said, "you're accepted."

No longer able to suppress the pent-up emotion of the past few months, Kate let out a big sigh of relief and happiness. She scooped up the folder and ran out the door before the instructor could change his mind. On her way, she felt a pang of sadness as she looked over her shoulder at the women who were leaving through the other exit. They had tried as hard as she had but hadn't made it. Most of them she would never see again.

Outside, on the same patch of grass where Leda and Anne and

Ashley had stood not long before, Kate paced about waiting for her tentmates to emerge. She had been one of the first in her group to hear the good news.

Back in Bank Hall Tristan stood waiting her turn, trying to look cool and stoic. In truth, she was churning inside; she felt the stakes had only grown higher for her since the CST selection began.

I know in my bones this is what I'm supposed to do, she was thinking. And these are the people I'm supposed to be working with. The only other time she remembered feeling this certain about the rightness of her path was when she first visited West Point. But Tristan had grown accustomed to disappointment in her career, and from the moment she first spotted the CST poster back in Oklahoma, she hadn't let herself believe that the mission was even a possibility. Now that she had seen who and what the program had to offer, she couldn't hold back her enthusiasm. She had finally found her people; she wanted this opportunity so badly she feared she would crash if they turned her away. I am so close, she said to herself. They can't say no.

Now, sitting at the instructor's desk in the giant classroom, she was about to find out.

The cadre never looked up from his papers as he ticked through the different events. "You didn't take charge on the obstacle course," he began, clearing his throat to make certain she was listening. Tristan vividly remembered that test: the soldiers had to dig their way underneath a silver barbed-wire fence using a tool, and ensure that everyone else on the team made it through the makeshift tunnel. "People needed leadership and you just froze." She had been team leader at that point and when one of her fellow trainees got stuck in the mud beneath the coiled barbed wire she hadn't moved fast enough to develop an alternate plan.

"And you did well on the ruck march," he continued, "but at the end, when *you* were doing so great, leading at the front of the pack, so many soldiers were dragging behind you. You should have motivated your team more." That final, deadly ruck march in which they carried around forty pounds of gear all day included a portion where the women marched not as a team but at their own pace. Tristan had broken into a run every time she was on her own, blasting past nearly everyone while they slogged along in her wake. By the end of the march of twenty or so miles the cadre ordered the women to finish as a team. Some women limped and others were struggling to put one foot in front of the other. Tristan felt uncomfortable yelling at them to push through their agony and fatigue when they clearly were motivated and trying their best. She didn't want to make them feel any worse than she knew they already did; she felt it would sound like bragging.

But she remained silent, not daring to protest the cadre's account of her leadership skills.

She waited calmly for him to deliver the verdict.

"Okay, well, that's it," he said. "Congratulations, you're in."

Seconds later Tristan was running down the hall and pushing the front door open. For the first time since leaving college she felt she was finally on the right path.

For the duration of Assessment and Selection the soldiers had had to shed every digital or electronic device—watches, phones, personal computers—that linked them to the world outside, a challenge that for many was equal to the physical tests of the selection process. Now they had their gadgets back and everyone was busily phoning moms, dads, husbands, boyfriends, and friends to let them know they had made it.

Kate, Rigby, Kristen, and a half dozen others were already gathered on the lawn, and to cries of "TRIS-TAN!" they tackled their new colleague and fell into an impromptu group hug. Seven of their tent's ten candidates counted among the twenty-five or so soldiers who made the cut. It had been a fine showing.

The mind is its own place, Tristan thought, remembering Rigby's port-a-potty inspiration. Don't quit indeed.

Within a half hour the cadre led the active-duty group of twenty-five CST selectees onto a chartered bus bound for Fort Benning, Georgia. They were headed to what was officially called the CONUS Replacement Center, which everyone knew as CRC. The week promised a few days of medical and dental screening, weapons familiarization and qualification, and the issuance of uniforms and other equipment. No heavy lifting, just a lot of signing out gear and more paperwork. But they were on their way, headed into an experience that few, if any, women had ever had in the American military.

Kate found a seat toward the middle of the bus, basking in the jubilant ease that comes from having bested a life test whose outcome was uncertain. Amber, the interrogator and Bosnia veteran, was just across the aisle, and was savoring one of the most important moments of her life. She guessed that many of the other newly named CSTs were feeling the same sense of triumph and exhilaration, knowing they were on the verge of getting the best shot they would ever have to serve in war with Rangers and Special Forces, even if they still couldn't officially *be* either. Not far from her was Kimberly Blake, the fit soldier she had met briefly in the Landmark's elevator. Kimberly, an MP who had deployed to Afghanistan in 2005 and volunteered then to go out with Marines to search Afghan women on a three-day mission, had arrived at Camp Mackall certain she would be selected. Then she had a reality check: these girls ran two miles in thirteen minutes, marched without tiring, and, just like Kimberly, were accustomed to being number one. She felt compelled to step up her game, and by the time she reached Bank Hall that afternoon she genuinely didn't know whether she would be chosen. Now she leaned into the headrest and tried to ignore all the noise on the bus so she could finally, after a week of high stress and sleep deprivation, get some much-needed rest.

As the charter bus, plush by military standards, began the seven-hour trip to Georgia, a movie began to roll on little flip-down screens that ran the length of the bus.

"Seriously?" Kate called out to Cassie Spaulding, a fellow MP she had met in the breakfast room at the Landmark Inn. She shook her head and began to laugh. "*Black Hawk Down* is what they play for us? I love it."

Every woman on the bus had already seen the film at least once, but in this setting it felt more powerful than ever. Based on a book about the ill-fated mission to capture a Somali warlord in Mogadishu, the movie followed teams from Delta Force and SEALs leading the charge through the Somali capital while Rangers, who had been assigned to pull security for the mission, bravely fought their way through, block by block, after finding themselves pinned down on the city's streets. The operation may have been a disaster, but the fight was valiant.

These were the guys they'd soon be going to war to support. The men with whom they'd be going out on mission. This was the caliber of soldiers and SEALs they'd be going into battle with each day. Or night.

Kate settled comfortably into her seat to watch Eric Bana one more time. For now her view of Rangers at war remained on a movie screen. Soon enough it would be real life.

Cassie, Kate's fellow MP, was sitting just two rows away. She had come to North Carolina from an Army base in the middle of nowhere, deep in Alaska, about as far as one could go and still be in the United States.

A year earlier Cassie had returned home from Iraq, where her unit was charged with running security checkpoints and doing searches. She had joined the Army eager to find her own brothers- and sisters-in-arms, but for Cassie it had been the loneliest year of her life. Being female was a special burden in war. "Perception was reality," went the adage, and she found that *all* socializing between men and women was discouraged by commanders to avoid even the hint of a compromising situation. She couldn't even talk to a fellow officer about the food they were eating at the dining facility without arousing the suspicion of her commanding officer. He paid attention to every conversation she had with soldiers from other units, almost all of whom were, of course, men, and asked her afterward about the topics of their discussions. So every night Cassie sat by herself, cross-legged on the floor, for hours, filling up paperback books of crossword puzzles that her father sent in care packages.

It was an unnatural and solitary habitat for a creature as social as she, but in a way Cassie always had been an outsider. She was a child of privilege, a comfortable American girl born to an apolitical and decidedly nonmilitary Canadian mother and a bullishly entrepreneurial American father, a Reagan Republican who sold sports cars and gave her a Chevy Silverado on her sixteenth birthday. (He offered a Ford Mustang, but she assured him she preferred the pickup.) She had grown up in Canada, Mexico, and the United States as her parents chased the American dream across North America. She excelled in competitive tennis as a teenager, taking to the court whenever she wasn't in the woods behind her house playing Manhunt long past nightfall with a bunch of neighborhood boys. At first she had been deeply afraid of waiting for hours, alone in the dark, creepy woods, trying to avoid capture by the others, but she was certain the boys would look down on her and label her "a girl" if she admitted to any fear. So she trained herself to show no weakness, ever. She would stay hidden, come what may. No way would she allow the boys to think they were tougher than she was.

Later, in high school in Florida, Cassie felt jealous of her boyfriend, a star quarterback who was showered with fanfare and glory on the field each week. Being a girl sucks, she thought. Everything fun and daring and noble sat beyond her grasp, and at the age of nineteen, she found out that that included her dream of becoming an infantry soldier. Nor could she go to Ranger School. It made her crazy that her gender, a simple accident of biology, put her dream job out of reach. Why wasn't I just born a boy, she often thought to herself, so I can do what I really want to do? Seeing guys in her ROTC class who didn't even *want* to join the infantry get assigned to the branch only heightened her sense of the unfairness of it all. It felt like a slap in the face that the Army would choose men who wanted to become medics over her, who had been chosen as ROTC battalion commander and hungered only to fight as a foot soldier.

Eventually, after graduating from the University of Central Florida, the sorority sister and women's studies major joined the Army's Military Police Corps thinking it would be as close as she would get to actual combat. When she heard about the CST program three years later, she knew immediately she would do anything needed to win a spot on the new team. She called everyone she thought could help her, filled out the application the same day she received it, and then wrote an extra, unsolicited essay explaining all the reasons why she had exactly the right background for this new assignment. She had MP training, combat experience in Iraq, and had studied the role of women in Afghanistan. No one would work harder in this job, she promised.

All through the selection process Cassie felt certain she would make it. The first morning at the Landmark when a fellow candidate asked if she was nervous, Cassie tersely responded, "No, I am not going to let myself be nervous and neither should you." The expression in her tablemate's eyes suggested that her answer had only made the soldier more anxious. Too bad, Cassie thought. This is the only place anyone should want to be right now.

Confidence had never been her issue; if anything, a surplus of it was usually her downfall, and she knew it. But she didn't care. Nor did she apologize for knowing what she wanted, or for possessing ambition equal to an entire class of Harvard MBAs. It was in her DNA: from girlhood, her father had taught her to pursue what she wanted. His determined, stubborn-as-hell daughter was clearly *his* child, the one whose travel to Europe he had funded; the one he had taught to read the *Wall Street Journal* every day so she would know what was happening in the world; the one he watched Fox News with every night after dinner before discussing the day's events.

Now, all these years later, she sat with her new teammates on a chartered bus headed to CRC, *Black Hawk Down* playing in the background. Cassie pulled out her phone and texted the person she considered her best friend in the entire world.

"Dad," she wrote, "I got selected. This is the proudest accomplishment of my life so far."

The reply came a minute later.

"I knew you were going to make it," he texted. "I had no doubt."

A couple of hours into the trip the bus stopped at a gas station along Interstate 95 South.

The women poured into the convenience store to pick up Subway sandwiches and enjoy the luxury of indoor plumbing. The sight of two dozen trim young women in uniform turned every head in the small store.

First Lieutenant Sarah Walden grabbed a Gatorade and a protein bar and stepped into the long, slow-moving checkout line behind her fellow soldiers. She had recently awakened from a catnap in which the sound of helicopter rotors in *Black Hawk Down* had blended into a fuzzy battlefield dream. Now she heard a man from across the convenience store call out:

"Hey, you guys Army nurses?"

Sarah laughed. She predicted this wasn't the last time they'd get that question.

Sarah had joined ROTC and then the Army because she wanted to serve an organization whose values mirrored the ones her parents had etched in her soul from childhood: service to others, self-discipline, self-reliance, and a desire to be part of something greater than yourself. Every year, they taught Sarah and her brother to get by using only their own instincts and nature's wealth by spending half the summer completely off the grid in a cabin in upstate New York. Not only was it disconnected from TV, telephones, and the Internet, it also lacked central plumbing and water. They grew their own vegetables in the tough Adirondack soil and hiked for hours each day.

Sarah was a look-alike for a young Megan Follows, who starred in the film *Anne of Green Gables*. As a girl Sarah had loved, read, and memorized the books by Lucy Maud Montgomery on which the movie was based. Inspired by the feisty, independent Anne Shirley, Sarah originally wanted to be a nun, not only because of her religious faith but because she wanted to reform the church from the inside. One day she announced to her mother that she was planning to become the Catholic Church's first female priest. When she was a little older, Sarah dreamed of becoming a soldier and a doctor. By the time she reached her teens, she realized she couldn't manage all three—nun, soldier, and doctor—so she settled on the last two, and signed up for ROTC to help pave the way and pay for her medical studies. Her father, who spent four years in the Navy, used to amble around the house calling her "Colonel Doctor Walden."

To no one's surprise, Sarah excelled in ROTC. Pushing herself to the limit both physically and mentally came naturally, and was thrilling besides. As a sophomore she decided she didn't want to spend the summer in the Army's airborne school, which provided the traditional path for cadets. Instead she wanted to attend the more demanding air assault course. The colonel who led her ROTC program at first declined her request. He saw her as a promising leader and wanted her to succeed—and pass—whatever Army training course she signed up for that summer. Airborne school, he said, offered the best—and least risky—path forward. But the major serving beneath him saw she was serious and believed she had the grit to complete what she set out to undertake.

"If you really want to go," the major said when she made her appeal to him, "I'll do what I can to support you, but on one condition: you can't fail. Promise me that, and I'll talk to the colonel."

A few days later he pulled Sarah aside after a morning of PT.

"You're going to air assault school, Walden," he said. "Don't fuck up."

Once her wish had been granted, Sarah experienced a new sensation: the very real fear of failure. Immediately she began weeks of intensive research and preparation at an obstacle course on the nearby grounds of West Point. On Zero Day, the first of the ten-day course, she spotted only six other women among the hundred-plus soldiers reporting for classes. By the last day, despite going hyponatremic on a ruck march after drinking so much water that she flushed out all her electrolytes, Sarah became the only female to complete the course. She couldn't help but feel a twinge of satisfaction when the male soldier she overheard insisting to his buddies that women shouldn't even be allowed in the Army was evacuated during the final ruck march. Sarah returned to her ROTC posting with her head held high. Preparation had been its own reward, as her parents had always taught her; she had made it through.

Eventually, Sarah realized that Army doctors had little frontline exposure to the wars America was fighting, and increasingly that's where she wanted to be. She abandoned her med school dreams and, like Kate and Cassie, went to the division she believed would get her closest to the action: the military police. When she soon learned that her new unit, based in Europe, wouldn't deploy she felt utterly useless. This, she thought, is not why I joined the Army. Unlike some of her commanders and fellow soldiers, she didn't want to stay out of the two wars America was fighting. She signed up because she wanted *in*.

Now, finally, she had an assignment that might actually draw on some of her well-honed survival skills. With the CSTs, she had found her path to war, as her friends predicted. It may not have sounded appealing to the uninitiated, but Sarah was thrilled that Afghanistan would be her ticket out of Europe.

Three hours later the bus pulled into Fort Benning, "Home of the Infantry" and headquarters of the 75th Ranger Regiment. The 182,000-acre installation was home to nearly thirty thousand active-duty military, and the women were scheduled to be there for a week.

As the bus approached the main gate of the building where they were scheduled to stay, they found it unattended and locked tight. Clearly no one had anticipated the arrival of the CSTs.

Pacing around the building's fence, the weary soldiers realized that someone was going to have to do something if they were going to get any sleep that night. And they were desperate for rest.

"Looks like we're gonna have to storm the gates," someone said.

"I'll go under the fence!" Tristan shouted, and began shimmying her small frame under the wire with Kate coaching her through. Once in, the two opened the gate and ushered their teammates inside.

First night and already we're breaking the china, Kate thought, smiling to herself. I can only imagine the look on the faces of the folks in charge when they see who busted into their compound tonight.

6

Training Days

★ ★ ★

At the end of May the soldiers were back in Bank Hall, ready for the first day of Phase 2 training for missions that would start in less than three months. The room was humming.

"Okay, listen up," the cadre called out. He was standing in uniform at the front of the spacious classroom where sixty or so newly minted CST members, all-Army alpha females from around the globe, had taken their seats. Many recognized each other from Assessment and Selection and had exchanged hugs and high-fives. Soldiers who didn't know each other nodded and shook hands in introduction.

Sitting next to the still-open classroom door was Lane, the Guard soldier from Nevada; she could hear the voices of male soldiers passing by on their way to other classrooms down the hall. Having glimpsed the large gathering of female soldiers inside, a few paused to peek into the room for a better look.

"What's the deal with the bun brigade?" Lane overheard one soldier ask another.

They don't know the half of it, she thought.

Now the women were quietly sitting at attention, facing an American flag and a gigantic whiteboard. This opening morning at the Special Warfare Center and School marked the first time the entire class had gathered as one. It was also the first time that the best candidates from the active-duty Army, Guard, and Reserves had assembled as an all-female, special operations team to train for war.

But there was one piece of noncombat business on the agenda before the class would begin.

"Before we get under way," the instructor announced, "I want to congratulate Lieutenant White on her marriage this past weekend." The soldiers applauded and raucously cheered as Ashley turned red with embarrassment. Only a few days earlier she had stood before more than one hundred of her dearest friends and family in bright red high heels and her beaded white dress, and promised to love Captain Jason Stumpf "for better, for worse, for richer, for poorer, in sickness and in health, until death did they part." A rollicking party followed the ceremony and lasted well into the early morning hours. Now here she was, "honeymooning" among a bunch of soldiers headed to war. She had dreamed of a Jamaican getaway with her husband, but she and Jason had already postponed the trip once for his deployment to Afghanistan and now a second time for hers. As soon as she returned from war they were headed to the Caribbean, no more delays allowed.

The instructor then got down to business, explaining that this room in Bank Hall would be the CSTs' home for the next six weeks. Days would begin at 6:30 a.m. in the gym and end at 5 p.m. The first course would focus on "human dynamics," which included subjects like "cross-cultural communications," Afghan culture and language, the role of women in Afghanistan's history, and rural versus urban life. On deck: training in negotiation and mediation, tactical questioning and searching, and mental strategies to help manage combat stress. There would be psychological evaluations, peer evaluations, and a culminating exercise to finish the session. At the end of his introduction the cadre reminded the CSTs, almost as an afterthought, that making it to this point did not mean they were in the program. At any time soldiers could be asked to leave if instructors decided they didn't measure up.

It's like the first day of school all over again, Lane thought to herself. But after the last two months of preparation, she was ready for anything. Bring it, she said to herself, opening her notebook.

The instructor then launched into a description of "ARSOF," the labyrinthine and mysterious world of elite combat troops formally known as Army Special Operations Forces. The women were on the cusp of becoming on-the-ground enablers of some of the boldest, most sophisticated teams in the United States military. At the end of the course, the teacher went on to explain, they would be asked to choose between Special Forces—the Green Berets and their Village Stability Operations—and Ranger Regiment—the direct action raiders. Ultimately the course instructors and the special operations teams would make the final call about their assignments, but part of the CST training process was understanding the difference between the special ops forces and the CSTs' role in supporting them.

"VSOs," the cadre said, his voice carrying across the rows of neatly arranged gray desks, "are village-stability operations. They are the centerpiece of our counterinsurgency strategy." Counterinsurgency (COIN) was the hallmark of General McChrystal's tenure leading U.S. forces in Afghanistan and it continued to be part of America's strategy after he left in 2010. While counterinsurgency's feasibility had been questioned both publicly and in military circles by the summer of 2011, when the CSTs were preparing for their first missions, much of COIN strategy remained in place alongside counterterrorism, or CT, strategy, which called for finding the insurgents where they lived. That, of course, was the place where the CSTs would be headed: into the villages and compounds.

The teacher went on to explain how the VSO missions were designed to promote stability in strategically critical rural areas—often remote and usually hostile—that insurgents had come to dominate. These operations focused on "the center of gravity": the local population. The Green Berets leading VSO missions lived among Afghans and specialized in understanding the political and security terrain from the ground level in order to strengthen the work of local community leaders. To do this they partnered with village elders to get them the resources needed to deliver cash-for-work projects, agricultural training sessions, and medical services. And they equipped and trained men to form local police teams to protect the village from insurgent attacks. As security, local governance, and stability improved, the counterinsurgency theory went, citizens in a community would be more connected to one another and to their government, and therefore less likely to support the insurgency.

The Green Berets have long been known as "soldier-diplomats," since much of the work they do requires language skills and a cultural understanding of the war zone in which they fight. But they are also intensively trained in direct action and combat skills, earning them nicknames like "snake eaters" and "bearded bastards." Most CSTs would end up with these village-stability teams, where their work would consist of meeting and talking with local women in ways that men couldn't because of the cultural traditions that separate the genders. The female soldiers would help Special Forces to better understand local power and politics dynamics and community needs as they sought to win "hearts and minds."

But a small number of women would go to the other side of Army special operations and join the 75th Ranger Regiment in its direct action role. Rangers focus exclusively on the "clear" part of the "clear, hold, build" tenets of counterinsurgency—a shorthand first popularized in congressional testimony by then secretary of state Condoleezza Rice. They are not responsible for wooing and winning over local leaders; their job is to clear contested areas of men who support the insurgency and threaten a civilian population. The CSTs working with the Rangers would be responsible for building crucial relationships with women on the scene that would reveal the information needed to help capture insurgents. This work would be done inside the homes of Afghan women, and would take place in the midst of night raids aimed at capturing the weapons makers, fighters, organizers, funders, and insurgency leaders with whom the women lived as mothers, wives, sisters, daughters, and grandmothers. The idea behind the missions was to weaken the insurgency and give the military's "hold and build" work—the less "kinetic" aspects of warfare—a chance to succeed by creating the space to win over local populations through strengthening local services and reducing security threats. The men of Ranger Regiment had been deployed continuously since 9/11 and went out every night on these operations, as did other special operators, and over the years such raids had grown increasingly unpopular with both the Afghan government and its people. Even those who favored such raids as a critical tool to root out the most intransigent and dangerous insurgents worried they had the potential to create more terrorists than they eradicated. A major part of the CST role, then, was to be culturally sensitive at this tenuous and highly unpredictable moment, and be assertive and quick-thinking enough to find the information needed in the midst of this most dynamic and unpredictable kind of battle.

Every student was expected to keep a journal and to bring it to class every day to make notes about her responses to course activities, readings, and discussions. The journal would be graded at the end. Trainers provided a recommended reading list of popular titles such as *Half the Sky* by Nicholas Kristof and Sheryl WuDunn; *Kabul in Winter* by Ann Jones; *Three Cups of Tea* by Greg Mortenson; and Khaled Hosseini's bestselling novel *A Thousand Splendid Suns*.

Early in the course, the CSTs received training in Pashto, one of Afghanistan's two native languages (Dari being the other) and the one they would hear most often on their missions. They would of course be relying on interpreters to communicate with Afghan women, but being able to offer up some basic words would be a quick and powerful show of goodwill and respect. So they learned how to say "Salam Alaykum," the traditional greeting of peace, as well as the Pashto equivalents of "my name is"—*zamaa num*; "please"—*mehrabani*; "how are you"—*tsenga yast*; "thank you"—*manana*; and "woman"—*shedza*. An Afghan-American lecturer offered the women a primer on the code of Pashtunwali and a catalog of unacceptable behaviors:

- Do not eat in public during Ramadan.
- Don't rush or hurry an Afghan.
- Do not laugh loudly in public.
- Don't wag or point your finger.

As the course went on, one of the students began a collection of favorite quotes in her notebook. One characterized the brand-new CST program itself: "It's like building an airplane in flight."

The training program for the female enablers didn't come anywhere close to the formal preparation of Special Forces or Ranger Regiment men. To become a specialist in special operations and unconventional warfare requires training that is both extreme and extensive: for Green Berets, anywhere from 18 to 36 months and for the Regiment's elite strike force members, just under a year. After that lengthy preparation and selection process, only around one in four candidates make it through. But the reality was America was fighting a long, costly, and unpopular war in Afghanistan and leaders like Admiral McRaven wanted to find whatever edge, whatever useful tool they could to improve the prospects of that fight. Commanders were impatient for the skills the female soldiers could provide, and they wanted the women out doing their jobs *now*.

All the CSTs were aware that their training protocol was a work in progress, and they chalked it up to the program's newness. Aside from the language training and basic cultural education, much of the coursework struck one of the CSTs as "a whole lot of bookwork for people who were headed to war." Claire Russo, who had played a role in shaping the program from its start, expressed in a memo her own concerns about how the training program favored "culture classes" over ones that taught "hard skills such as tactical questioning, engagement, and basic tactical movements." Russo knew that culture varies significantly "from village to village, valley to valley and province to province" and she wanted the soldiers to have broad general knowledge. But she wanted them to be trained to defend their lives and protect their teammates, too. "It is critical that the students leave the CST class with the skills sets they need to execute the mission and survive while doing so," she had written.

But it wasn't only the Afghan community that the women needed to prepare for; they also had to win the acceptance of the American men they would be serving with. From the beginning, the instructors made clear that the CSTs would be wading into their own, female version of friendly fire when they deployed in August. Many of the male soldiers they supported would want nothing to do with them, the CSTs were warned. The trainers drilled the message home: "They are going to hate you, and you are going to have to be prepared for that." It wasn't just that they would have to "sell" their capabilities, as every enabler did, to a corps of battle-tested veterans, some now on their tenth or eleventh deployment in nearly as many years. As a constantly increasing share of responsibility for the fight in Afghanistan, Iraq, and other terrorism hotspots around the globe landed on their shoulders, Special Operations Forces now had within their reach nearly every flavor of weaponry and intel support possible. The dramatic capture one month earlier of Osama bin Laden, carried out by a team of Navy SEALS, had only added to the allure of special operators in the American imagination and the impression that special ops forces could accomplish any mission the conventional military and leaders in Washington tossed their way, no matter how wild the odds. CSTs were only the newest group among many "enablers" that served in a support role for these fighters; there were explosive ordnance disposal specialists, information support operations, weather experts, and communications specialists, to name only a few.

But the CSTs had one big difference: their gender, which rendered them both highly suspect and highly visible. One of the goals of the training course was to prepare the women for the internal hearts-and-minds campaign they would have to wage once they arrived in Afghanistan. The instructors devised a series of role-playing scenarios that would place the women in situations like the ones they could encounter in theater.

In one exercise, they were required to brief a Special Forces leader on the strengths and contributions the CST team brought to his mission. The idea was to get the women comfortable explaining their jobs and help them to develop a strategy for assimilating into their new teams.

"Who wants to volunteer for this one?" the instructor asked.

Amber's hand shot up.

She walked to the front of the room and held out her hand to the Special Forces soldier playing a reluctant team leader there to test her mettle. He had graying hair and light eyes and looked a few years older than Amber.

"Go ahead," he said, in his most uninviting tone. Amber took a seat at the small table in the front of the class.

"Given the current political climate in Afghanistan and the desire to respect the Afghan culture, the CST capability can be a real help," she began. "Right now you aren't able to access fifty percent of the population and so you can't get a well-rounded picture when it comes to what's happening in the community. You're also not getting some information you might want on the intel side."

The soldier sat stone-faced. He looked bored.

She inhaled, internally reloaded, and went on. "I know both intel and local knowledge are critical to the Special Forces mission, and we can really help to make a difference there because we can talk to women and children while being respectful of Afghan culture. We can help you learn more about what's happening on the ground, as well as the challenges local families are facing, and the kinds of services they need most. I also bring language experience from training at Monterey in Farsi, which is close to Dari, so I can act as an interpreter with Dari-speaking populations without taking any of your interpreter resources."

She waited for a response, but the soldier was unmoved. He let a few uncomfortable moments pass, then asked:

"Why should we give you resources that we need for ourselves? You aren't bringing anything to the table that we can't do without you, so why should we support you in this mission?"

Amber knew he was there to test her; that was the entire point of the exercise. She had promised herself she would stay calm no matter the provocation. But nothing she said was connecting, and her role-playing partner gave the impression that he had absolutely no interest in what she had to say, since he knew the world of Special Forces way, way better than she. His attitude was infuriating, and Amber could feel herself growing hotter.

She tried again.

"We are here to support the important work you are doing, and we want to further the mission," she said. "We think that talking to women and helping you have a window on what they see and do and know will be useful."

Nothing.

Then, finally, he said: "I'm not sure why you're here at all. We don't need this. What I *do* need is for every one of the precious spots I have on my team to go to people who are mission critical. This sounds like a lot of work for very little benefit. And besides, we are going to end up having to take care of you. You think you can hang with us? You aren't even going to be able to keep up out there. We're going to start marching and you're going to fall out of formation and then *we* are going to be the ones who will have to put aside our mission to take care of *you*."

Amber felt the anger rising from the pit of her stomach. Keep your cool, she cautioned herself. Do *not* lose it, you know that is *just* what they expect you to do.

"How about your fitness level?" he asked, almost taunting her.

"I just ran a marathon six months ago," she retorted. "I can run a mile in under six minutes. I do CrossFit every day, sometimes twice a day. Fitness is a cornerstone of serving in special operations, and I take that very, very seriously." She heard her voice rising and fought to rein it in.

"Listen, women are just built differently than men. It's a simple fact. You're just going to be a liability out there," he concluded.

That was it. Amber heard the word *liability* and it was like a switch flipped in her mind and unleashed a volcano of frustration she could no longer contain. Ever since she started in the Army more than a decade earlier men had thrown that word around in connection to female soldiers, regardless of how competent and fit the women actually were. Like many of her female colleagues, she had come to loathe these assumptions. But for Amber, it went beyond simple resentment.

As a nineteen-year-old private first class working as an intel analyst in Bosnia, she tried on numerous occasions to persuade the special ops guys to take her with them on missions to capture men indicted for war crimes. "I'll bring along an interpreter," she would say, "and we can talk to the women and help you find your guys." In essence, Amber had tried then to improvise her own version of a Cultural Support Team years before they were officially created. The soldiers, mature and intelligent men who were well into their thirties, received her entreaties patiently, but explained that she "would just be a liability" to their work. And Amber knew what they meant. It was nothing personal; the truth was that she simply *wasn't* strong enough to be out there. It was a wake-up call for her, and those words—"you'll just be a liability"—became her motivator. Ever since that tour she had devoted herself to becoming stronger, faster, and tougher than most men her size and age. She knew she had to be better than they were to be taken seriously, and she had spent the past ten years hardening her body and her mind so she would be ready for whatever challenge she could find that would take her out into the fight.

To have done all that and *still* be told she was a liability in this brand-new program was too much. Her frustration boiled over.

"You don't know me," she answered, quietly at first but her voice was rising. "You don't know what I am physically capable of."

For a fraction of a second she considered stopping there and shutting up before she really got herself into trouble, but Amber hurtled on. "I guarantee you that I can outscore you on a PT test."

Now she was leaning forward in her chair, getting in his face. "I guarantee that unless you run an eleven-minute two-mile, I can run faster than you. And I can guarantee that unless you can do one hundred push-ups in two minutes, I can do more push-ups than you."

The soldier stared back. The CST was doing exactly what he had expected.

"*And*: I bet I can do more sit-ups than you," Amber added.

Kate, watching from a few rows back, froze in her seat. She had the impression of watching a car smashing into a brick wall right before her very eyes, but in slow motion. Part of her felt that Amber should just pipe down, but another part was thankful and relieved that someone, finally, had decided to stop taking all that shit. She had grown tired of apologizing for the fact that she was a fit, battle-hungry patriot who wanted to serve her country, gender be damned. And right now, standing in front of the whole class, Amber was speaking for all of them. It may not have been an elegant performance, but it sure as hell was satisfying.

All the usual side conversations had stopped. The room was silent. For a half second Kate wondered if the Green Beret would accept the challenge and beat Amber into the ground with his fist.

"No, no, no, there is *no way* you can do that many push-ups. You girls don't even have to do that many in the girl version of the PT test," he said. "Come on. Be real."

"Oh yes, I can," Amber volleyed. "We can leave right now for a PT test. Let's do it."

She stood up and pushed her chair away from the small table, its legs scraping against the tile floor. She knew she was doing *just* what she shouldn't, but she couldn't stop. If someone is taunting you, telling you that you can't do something, and you *know* that you can, how can you just sit there and spew words, when you could let your actions prove you correct?

She stared at him, then pointed to the floor.

"Let's go, right now. Let's do push-ups here." Amber called out to the class, "Somebody get me a stopwatch, we are going to do push-ups."

The Green Beret stared back in disbelief.

"That is totally ridiculous, I am not doing push-ups right here in the middle of the class. You are way out of line, soldier."

"All right," Amber spat back. "But let's just be clear that that was *you* saying no."

The Green Beret offered nothing further beyond a searing look of disgust, and finally the instructors intervened.

"Well, okay," one of the female cadre announced in a softer tone than had been heard for the past ten minutes. "Why don't you go ahead and sit down."

The moment stretched on in all its awkward stillness as Amber made her way back to her seat.

"Do I have another volunteer?" the teacher asked.

As Amber sat quietly, sulking in anger and embarrassment, Lane passed her a note.

"Way to go," it said. "That was for all of us."

The sentiment wasn't universally shared, of course. Sarah, the MP who had served in Europe and abandoned her dreams of becoming an Army doctor so she could get closer to battle, understood Amber's frustrations but felt she should have been more tactful. Humility and tact, not tough-guy tactics, would win the day; going in aggressive with these guys would only alienate them further.

Even if some may have disagreed with Amber's tactics, they all knew what it was like to drown in frustration when other people place limits on you. In fact, the desire to bust through those limits was the reason most of them showed up for Assessment and Selection in the first place.

Later, during a water break on the firing range, where the women had been practicing on their Beretta M9s, a few of Amber's teammates and the trainers searched out a spot of shade from the North Carolina summer sun. Just then an older woman whom they had met earlier in the course approached the cluster of sweaty CSTs.

"I just want you girls to know how proud of you we are," the woman said. "In my opinion you deserve a Green Beret and you are going to be the first girls to get one."

Amber was too mortified to even look at her trainers. "This is why they don't want women here. These guys spend *years* getting trained to become Green Berets, they test themselves physically, mentally, and every place in between, and someone thinks that a couple weeks of training is any kind of equivalent—that we deserve anything close to the accolades that these guys get? We are no better than fresh-off-the-boat privates right now. No way in hell we are even *close* to what they do."

And that was the rub. Amber wanted to see special operations open to women and she believed they all should have a shot at going to Ranger School but only if there were no shortcuts, no dumbing down of any of the requirements, the same standards for everyone. And everyone would have the chance to meet them.

The month of accelerated training wore on, and by early July, four weeks into the class, it was getting close to decision time. The choice was essentially between the patient, persistent, creative work of building relationships—the Special Forces village-stability side— versus the aggressive, fast-paced, physically intense, and potentially far more dangerous task of being there when doors burst open—the Ranger Regiment side.

By this time, most everyone instinctively knew which "side of the house" she wanted. Most leaned toward Special Forces, but not all.

The more aggressive, outspoken personalities like Cassie felt they belonged with Ranger Regiment. She knew she would be inspired, not cowed, by these soldiers and was confident she would be able to hold her own with them in the field. Ever since the now-infamous role-playing exchange everyone assumed—correctly—that Amber wanted to go in that direction as well. Lane, too, was intrigued by the direct action side.

They all knew the Rangers tended to be a lot younger than the Green Berets and, consequently, sometimes less mature. The Rangers also had a strong identity; the roughly three thousand men of the 75th Ranger Regiment all wore a tan beret. The women would have to show they could fit in among these guys who lived for war. Fitness also was key. The Rangers marched toward their targets with anywhere from fifty to seventy pounds of gear on their backs usually in the dead of night, for miles on end and often on truly treacherous terrain. A serious misstep or the failure to keep up could quite literally cost a life—their own or, even worse in their own minds, a fellow soldier's. The only women the Rangers were willing to consider taking out with them were soldiers who tested off the charts in fitness levels and showed that they could keep pace and stay in formation. They also needed women who were aggressive enough to want to go on night raids, but likable enough to connect with Afghan women and children during some of the most difficult moments of their lives. And they had to be mature enough to understand that while they were there to help, their mission was not to run an election or open a women's center. Their job was to be the softer side of the hardest side of war.

Toward the end of the course, representatives from both mission sets came to brief the CSTs. The Ranger Regiment representative played a slick video shot in night-vision-goggle green that illustrated the direct action raids that were their specialty. "We are looking for the most outstanding soldiers," the sergeant major announced, "and we want you guys to come and work with us. We need the best people we can get." He was a stocky guy, brimming with energy. Standing at the front of the class he began to outline the traits they were seeking. "We're *really* excited to have you join this mission," he said, "because you can go places we can't and talk to people we can't. You are going to contribute a huge amount, and we need you to get the job done. And rest assured, if you belong with us, we will find you."

Sitting at a desk a few rows in front of the Ranger leader, Tristan couldn't believe what she was hearing. Oh my God, we are being recruited, she thought to herself. The burly Ranger was making Amber's argument that they actually did bring something to the mission, with a high-tech, multimedia assist to show them the intensity—and the adrenaline rush—of the fight they would be joining.

Tristan knew she belonged with the ass-kicking Rangers. Months earlier she had turned down a job training women at her base in Fort Sill because she saw no reason why she would be any better at it than a man. She was not a female soldier; she was a soldier who happened to be female, and all she wanted to do was go to work in a job—and in a place—that mattered to the mission. And that was *not* training women; it was with the Rangers tracking down insurgents in the hills of Afghanistan.

Her fellow West Pointer Kate's heart pounded throughout the recruiting pitch because she knew deep inside that that badass video was all her. Kate loved tactics, she loved fighting, and she wanted to wear her kit and get terrorists. She had even dreamed that evening in night-vision green about using her small frame to the Rangers' advantage by tunneling onto a target to get a bad guy.

Kimberly, the MP, had only one thought after watching that video.

I want to do this *now*. She, along with a handful of the others, was hooked.

Finally the day arrived when they learned their assignment, and there were few surprises. Among those who made the cut for the Rangers: Leda Reston, Tristan Marsden, Sarah Walden, Amber Treadmont, Kate Raimann, Lane Mason, Anne Jeremy, Kimberly Blake, and Ashley White.

When Ashley heard her name followed by the words "Ranger Regiment" she first felt surprised, then a strong sense of satisfaction, then trepidation. She had wanted this challenge, had even confided to her teammate Kristen that she hoped she would get the assignment, though she still had her concerns about her ability to fit in. Within minutes of the announcement the new team—the first-ever all-Army group of women to officially be joining Ranger Regiment on missions and in combat every night as enablers—made their way to a picnic table outside Bank Hall to discuss the details of their pre-mission training with Leda, their new officer in charge. From the original group of sixty, they were now just twenty. "The alphas of the alphas," someone joked.

There was one more challenge that Ashley faced after the past two months of Assessment and Selection and training, and she dreaded it. She had to share the news with Jason.

By the time Ashley arrived home, Jason was already in the living room waiting for her. He had received her text about Ranger Regiment, but when she walked through the door with a fellow CST and announced that a group of them assigned to Regiment would be heading over to Mash House for dinner, he knew that the longer discussion would have to wait. Her elation made it easy for him to hold his questions—for now. She was so happy and excited; he was left torn between feeling extreme pride in his ass-kicking wife and intense worry about what she was getting herself into.

At dinner that night Jason was again the only man, this time seated at a long table filled with more than a dozen buff female soldiers. Sitting at one end of the table next to Ashley, he found himself watching her intently. Something was different, and despite his anxieties about the reasons behind the dinner, he was feeling a deep sense of pride. Here she was, his typically reserved and quiet wife, with a group of women she hadn't even known two months earlier, and she was in the thick of the conversation, interjecting during other women's stories and cracking jokes with the other girls. He was surprised by how comfortable she was with her new teammates. And how popular. He heard stories from many of them about Ashley's performance over the past few months: how she had tried to help the other girls to learn to fast-rope in the gym, how her PT scores had impressed the trainers, who had rarely seen a woman score so high on the men's scale. And it wasn't just her physical prowess that inspired them; it was also her generosity. Girls told stories about her cookies and sandwiches, her loans of shoes and socks that Ashley brought for them without their ever having to ask. He realized that this CST thing was turning out to be a kind of sisterhood. It was something he never imagined women could have in the military, let alone a kinship his own wife would be part of.

Finally the couple found themselves alone, heading home in Jason's Chevy pickup, and the topic they had shoved to the sidelines came roaring back.

"So how are you feeling about it all?" Ashley asked.

Jason hesitated, chose his words carefully, and calibrated his tone in an effort to disguise his real feelings.

"I don't know, Ash, those guys are heavy hitters. I love those Rangers, and I truly admire what they do. You know I wanted to go to Ranger School. But it is guns-up for them. They are not hired to go give out hugs and be 'culturally sensitive.' Those guys are animals once they're in the field. That is what they're trained to do."

"I know," Ashley replied, "but these guys have a plan for us; they really want us there and they think we can make a difference."

The more she spoke, the more certain he was that she didn't fully understand what she was getting into. Jason felt his anxiety rising. By now they were home and had climbed out of the truck, but they got no farther than the entryway to the living room before the conversation turned hot and angry.

"Ash, these guys go looking for fights," Jason said. "That is what they do for a living. Do you understand? That's their job. Their body count is high—when I was in Afghanistan I saw their flag go to half-staff all the time because their guys were getting killed. You don't need to be there for that."

He was now pacing around the room. "What happened to the humanitarian stuff? When did you decide this direct action stuff was what you wanted to do? It just doesn't feel right."

Now it was her turn to give in to the anger.

"*You* are the one who always told me I can do anything," she said. "Is that only if it was a job you approved of? Why would you, *of all people*, want to hold me back now?"

"I had just finished school when you deployed. I never told you not to go to Afghanistan even though I sat, by myself here, in this house, for a year and I never complained to you. Now when I want to do *my* duty and get my deployment done you say, *it's too dangerous*?"

"You're just being selfish, Jason," she said. She wasn't quite shouting, but her voice had grown louder—and more filled with hurt. "And you know it."

Jason fought the urge to throw his fist into the living room wall. He felt even worse when he saw Ashley's tears start to fall.

She ran past her collection of Minnie Mouses and into the bedroom, then slammed the door behind her.

There, alone on the couch, he tried to calm himself. He watched the clock as the hours ticked by and the night passed. Never before, during all the years of their courtship or in their short and very happy marriage, had they slept in separate rooms.

As soon as the sun began to rise he called his father back home in Pittsburgh. He didn't give him all the details, but explained that Ashley wanted to deploy on some kind of special mission that made him exceedingly nervous. Jason's dad, who ran the family's grocery business, had always been his role model. His father was going through a difficult time, too, having started divorce proceedings from Jason's mother. This hadn't surprised Jason—their marriage had been a challenge for some time—but it did sadden him, and lately he had been thinking a great deal about lasting love and how to keep it.

"Jason, this is something you really don't want to do," Ralph Stumpf finally replied. "You don't want to hold your spouse back. Trust me on this. If you do that, if you hold someone back, they will eventually end up carrying a grudge. Let Ashley be what and who she is, and support her, the way she has supported you, even in those times when she was afraid that something would happen to you when you were off in Afghanistan.

"Look," he continued, "I've never experienced war, you know a lot more about it than I do, but in fifty years, do you want Ashley to look back at your kids and your grandkids and feel like she missed out on one of the most important opportunities she could have had because you didn't want her to go? Do you really want to take the risk that she might feel this sense of regret, wondering what things would have been like if she had had that experience? Everyone says 'no regrets,' but *everyone* has them, and if she gives this up for you, she will always look back on her life and there will always be something missing. And this program is always going to be the 'if only.'"

"Listen, Dad," Jason said, knowing he couldn't dispute the soundness of his father's argument and the deep personal experience it came from. But he was not yet ready to give in. "Here is the 'if.' If she doesn't do this program, she is still here. We start a family. We move forward with our lives."

"Come on, Jason," his dad answered. "You guys love each other so much—it's obvious. You all will have decades together and the children and the grandchildren will come. You'll have a happy wife and a happy life, as the saying goes. You'll see; it all will come in time."

Jason hung up the phone, put on his running clothes, and jogged out the front door and down the road. Even then he knew, in his heart, that she had to go, whether or not he wanted her to and even if he was right about it.

When he returned, she was still in the bedroom with the door closed. "Ash," he said, walking into the room, "look, I'm sorry, I know I was being selfish. I won't make you choose, it's just that . . ."

She interrupted him.

"Listen," she said, sitting up in the bed and looking like she hadn't slept, either. "I know you know a lot more about all of this than I do. I know you shot artillery for these guys and you know them and you know what they do. And if you want me to stop the program I will go in on Monday and tell them I'm out. That's it. I'll never bring it up again. I promise. I love you and respect you that much."

"No." Jason shook his head. "I thought about it all night and talked it through with my dad this morning. It's not about what I think. You want to work with those guys, that is who *you* are. You earned this chance. And I know if it were me going to work with Ranger Regiment you'd back me. I don't like it, you know that, but you have my unconditional support."

Ashley offered him her sideways smile.

"Just promise me you'll be careful, and you won't try to be a hero. That you won't take any more risks than you have to."

"I promise," she said. "I promise."

He prayed she would be able to keep that vow.

7

Diamonds Among Diamonds

★ ★ ★

Okay, soldiers, quit screwing around," Sergeant Scottie Marks bellowed. The twenty CSTs who had made the cut for Ranger Regiment were milling around classroom tables at a training facility sometimes used by the special operations command.

"Take your seats and hurry up!"

He flipped a switch and a screen rolled down from the ceiling. The room went quiet and on came a grainy video. Figures were moving across a dark field shrouded in the green haze of night-vision goggles. A group of Rangers were in the middle of a mission to capture an insurgent in an Afghan village. "This is what you will be doing," he told the women. "Night after night. And this is what the next eight days are about: preparing you for those missions."

The CSTs sat riveted as Marks talked about training their minds for the demands of the war they were about to join. All the while, he chewed on a hunk of tobacco lodged inside his left cheek. "Combat is the highest-stakes game on the face of the planet because in the end you either have winners or you have dead people," he said. "I don't want to die, and I know you don't, either. I want to be the killingest winner in the whole world. And you should, too."

It was the opening speech of Rangers' pre-mission training week—PMT for short—and no one moved an inch in her seat. It was so quiet, Lane thought her classmates might be able to hear the sound of her own breathing. She wondered if Tristan or Ashley was as frightened as she was. She stole a look a few seats over at Amber and was only mildly surprised that her gung-ho teammate looked happier and more fully engaged than she had in weeks.

Marks, a sandy-brown-haired veteran of more than twelve Ranger deployments in Iraq and Afghanistan, continued.

"You are CSTs and you have a very particular job to do on the battlefield. You have to deescalate whatever situation you are drawn into, and engage with the women and children." He was now moving through the room, Oprah-style, using his own considerable physical presence to drive home the urgency of his words and shake them out of their comfort zones.

"But we are not at war to pass out blankets and hugs. I need you to find out where the bad guys are, as quick as you can. It's my job to prepare you to sit within eighteen inches of a possible enemy every single night and do your job and stay alive. That means you need to be ready to pick up your gun and use it properly. You have to be prepared to pull the trigger and kill someone without hesitation. And you have to be ready to pick up a fellow soldier who has been shot or blown up while you are still taking fire and get him out of there."

He was speaking at a pace that sounded like a tape recorder playing at one and a half times its normal speed.

"War is chaos. That means you might be alone in a room with twenty women, one of whom is actually a heavily armed man in disguise. Nine times out of ten you will have other soldiers around you, pulling security. But there is a one percent chance you are going to be in that room by yourself. And you must be ready to react if that male belligerent tries to overpower you. You better be able, in that instant, to pull out your gun and shoot someone in the face without thinking about it.

"At the end of the day, our world lives and dies by a gun," he said. "That is the bottom line. Your job is not to be a Ranger and you are not a part of the Ranger assault team. You are not there to be a gunfighter. But we are going to put you in situations where you will have to flip that switch from 'CST' to killer in a heartbeat. No matter how nice and quiet and even safe the moment feels," he continued, "you are *always* in the middle of a fight. Any minute the world is going to turn to shit, and you have got to keep that in the forefront of your brain. You must maintain a security mindset at all times, day and night. That is also a part of the job."

As he paced and talked, Marks fixed his gaze on the eyes of his students. He was surprised, even inspired, by what he saw. He had given some variation of this speech on "combat mindset" hundreds of times as a Ranger trainer, but never before had he seen every single one of his students scoot to the edge of their chairs and stare at him so intensely, as if every muscle in their bodies was participating in the listening. He could *feel* the intensity of their attention; they gave the impression of being desert wanderers who had finally found water. These chicks give a shit, he marveled, as he scanned their eager faces. Now Scottie felt the burden of his task, as he realized he had just a little more than a week—a fraction of the time he normally had with his Ranger trainees—to get this group 100 percent ready for the community they were about to join.

"You will be going out at night with guys who have spent a good portion of their lives in war," he reminded them. "They know they are the best, and they know how important they are. If Rangers have been deployed to a combat theater, things are bad. If Rangers are in your living room, that means things are really fucking bad. And in case you hadn't noticed, we are not known for being the most subtle people in the world. We tend to tell you exactly what the fuck we are thinking about and we don't give a shit who you are, we are going to speak our mind. We also are not used to failure. We are used to working hard enough to be the very best at what we do. Period.

"My job is to prepare you to succeed. To have the mental armor that is required to do the job your country has asked you to do with the resilience you will need to get through the next eight months. You have got to find that switch that lets you know that you are at war. And then you're gonna have to flip it back the other way when your time on the battlefield is over."

Marks softened his tone slightly for the last part of his speech.

"You guys—each of you here in this room—are important to us. You are not some anonymous soldier. Look at the caliber of the CST sitting next to you, and then look around this room"—he gestured to the other Ranger trainers who were lined up against the wall. "You have got the best in Regiment standing in front of you. You were selected to go with Ranger Regiment because you are the best of the best. And all of us are excited to get you ready to go to war."

After weeks of being prepared for rejection and resentment from their fellow soldiers, not a woman in the room failed to notice that the tide was shifting. Holy shit, Lane thought, these guys are actually on our side.

Scottie Marks had seen plenty of combat before he left the battlefield and assumed the responsibility of helping train future Rangers for war.

As a young Army private first class he parachuted into Iraq as part of Operation Iraqi Freedom in 2003. He was among the last to leave the country seven years later, in the wake of Operation New Dawn, as a decorated sergeant first class. His baptism by fire had been the endlessly lethal, block-by-block fight for Fallujah in 2003 and 2004. Marks had seen every phase of the war and every shift in battlefield strategy during his nine deployments to Iraq, from the very chaotic start to the extremely controlled end. Working under General McChrystal for many of his years in Iraq, he and his buddies experienced firsthand how the occasional raids had become, under the new counterterror mandate, their normal nightly routine.

Soldiering was in Scottie's DNA; he decided to become a Marine at the age of six. He grew up in the yawning prairies of Katy, Texas, riding bikes and playing with guns. Wherever he went, trouble found him, and Scottie relished its irresistible charms. As a teenager, he would drink beer before school. Later he switched to Gentleman Jack, the favored drink of his grandpa, a self-described hard-ass who let it be known to Scottie that real men only drink whiskey. At night, young Scottie would camp out in his room watching *Night Court* and dipping Copenhagen snuff. He came from tough stock: his great-grandma was a chain-smoking old Cajun who, when her cigarette ash got too long, simply tapped the butt, let the ash fall, and then rubbed it into the carpet with her slippered foot.

His mother had Scottie when she was barely out of her teens. His father left when Scottie was a toddler. His mom hated guns and refused to let them in her house, a fact that only strengthened the boy's love for the forbidden weapons. One afternoon when he was twelve Scottie "borrowed" his dad's old pistol and took it out to the bayou behind his house. It was the beginning of a lifelong love affair with firearms. A year later, he and a buddy stole their friend's brother's gun and went down to a culvert to do some shooting. It was great fun, but what the boys didn't realize was that the cool, hissing sound coming from the weapon was actually the sound of a round coming back at them. Scottie got hit in his arm with a fragment of either a rock or a bullet—he never found out for sure—and started bleeding something fierce. Fear of his mother's wrath outweighed the pain he felt, so, instead of confessing his mischief and getting her help, he made his friend stick a spoon over an open flame and seal up his wound with the metal as it melted. His mother was never the wiser.

Scottie's role models were all Marines and war heroes. His grandfather, a veteran of the brutal campaign of Guadalcanal, led his fellow Marines both in World War II and Korea. He finished his career as a command sergeant major at Camp Lejeune. Scottie's uncle ran reconnaissance missions in Vietnam—a forerunner to the more elaborate raids that Special Operations Forces now undertake on a regular basis. For Scottie it was never a question that he would follow in their footsteps and join the Marine Corps.

But then a movie put him on a different course. In 1993 Scottie went to see the action film *Sniper*, in which a highly skilled master gunnery sergeant played by Tom Berenger saves the day with a perfect shot from his M4 sniper rifle. A new dream came into focus. When he was nearly old enough to enlist, he shared his plans with a close family friend, an Army soldier who was a member of Ranger Regiment. "They don't have any of that in the Marines," the older man told Scottie. "You want to be a sniper recon guy? That's not going to happen with the Jarheads. What you want to do is to become a Ranger." Then he pointed Scottie to the book *To Fight with Intrepidity*, which chronicles the complete history of the U.S. Army Rangers, beginning in 1622, when Rangers patrolled American settlements and offered early warnings on incoming raids, to World War II and the heroic exploits of Merrill's Marauders and Darby's Rangers, modeled after British commandos. Scottie was hooked.

He signed up for the Army on February 21, 2001. Seven months later, on September 11, he was at Ranger training when he and the rest of the world learned that planes had crashed into the World Trade Center and the Pentagon. In rapid succession, the United States launched not one but two wars, first in Afghanistan and sixteen months later in Iraq, and on both fronts it was the Rangers who led the way. The battlefield had dramatically changed since the first Gulf War a decade earlier, and the demands on special operations doubled, then tripled, and then continued to climb exponentially. Scottie headed to Afghanistan in 2002 and soon found himself living in a war cycle: several months in battle, a few months at home for more training, then back to war. He was indeed serving "at the tip of the spear," as he had always dreamed.

By 2006 General McChrystal's shift to time-sensitive targeting of high-value insurgents—what McChrystal called "F3EA," or "find, fix, finish, exploit, and analyze"—had changed everything for Ranger Regiment, which now focused almost exclusively on executing these raids. As a team leader Scottie Marks learned to move swiftly, without much advance preparation, in the fight to target and capture. During his early deployments his unit had had plenty of time to refine operations; they were able to devote a lot of men and a lot of planning to a single raid. All that changed when Iraq's insurgency exploded into a deadly efficient killing machine.

By the time McChrystal and his men redesigned the joint special operations team, team leaders like Marks no longer had the luxury of two or three days to assemble an operation and hit a target. Now they had fifteen minutes to create a plan. Each night the platoon sergeant asked Scottie's team to design that evening's operations— sometimes it was one mission, other times it was a whole series of them—and it was his job to deliver. As the years went on, Scottie Marks came to feel far more at home on his narrow cot at General McChrystal's special operations headquarters in Balad, Iraq, than he did in his king-size bed at his house near Fort Benning. He missed the war when he was away; it was his one and true home.

But one night in 2010, Marks and his team were engaged in a firefight with insurgents as they made their way to a building they needed to secure for another special operations team. As Scottie barreled out of the vehicle, ducking to avoid bullets that were hissing by him, he blew out his right knee and was forced to limp, with the help of a teammate, to the position at the rear of the building he had planned to guard. He made it through the night's mission, which was a success—his team located and captured the men who shot at them—but shortly thereafter Marks was evacuated to Kuwait, where he underwent surgery to realign his knee. The surgery too was a success, but Scottie's days of fast-roping out of helicopters, busting down doors, and jumping out of airplanes were officially over. His new assignment was to remain at Fort Benning and use the considerable knowledge and expertise he had learned on the ground to train the next generation of Rangers. While some of his fellow trainers complained about the assignment, Scottie found it hugely rewarding. His body may have had enough of combat after nearly forty-eight months in Iraq and Afghanistan combined, but his mind and his heart would never give up. Now he could be a gatekeeper for the Regiment, picking the new guys and training them to be superior soldiers. It was the next best thing to being a team leader in battle.

Scottie discovered that he had a knack for uncovering talent, and found that he loved wringing the best out of the hungry young men he taught. And he never lost his passion to be the best sharpshooter in the Army; when he wasn't teaching, he kept training himself to be as good a shot as Berenger in *Sniper*. He entered and won a slew of shooting competitions for active-duty special operations guys. Eventually Scottie got his dream teaching assignment: running the newly revamped marksmanship training program for Ranger Assessment and Selection. In preparation for his work, he and another Ranger traveled the country to find and learn from the best marksmanship teachers in America, and then they returned to Fort Benning to use that knowledge to develop new training tools and lessons that would meet the demands of the ever-changing battlefield. Scottie had thoroughly enjoyed the process of learning about the art of shooting and the pedagogy behind it. Soon he was nearly as proud that he could teach an eighteen-year-old Army private to be a highly skilled Ranger as he was of his own time at war.

And so, when it came time to train female soldiers to become Ranger enablers, it was no surprise that one of the first names to surface at Ranger Regiment's headquarters was Scottie Marks. What his bosses didn't know was that Marks had actually seen the need for a program like the CSTs when he was facing down al-Qaeda in Iraq. In his first few years as a Ranger, he and his fellow soldiers had little daily contact with women in the military. But once in Iraq, Marks often found himself thinking that his job would be a lot easier if he could call on female soldiers who could talk to and search women and gather actionable intelligence. In 2003 his unit lost three guys to a pregnant suicide bomber, and by 2006 as a weapons squad leader he had to do a lot of the questioning of Iraqi women whom his team encountered on raids. He knew the frightened Iraqi women were all the more terrified by his presence in their homes, and he kept thinking how much better for everyone it would be if women were doing the questioning instead.

Weeks before the first group of CSTs were ready for training, Marks was instructing Ranger trainees as head of marksmanship for RASP, the highly respected Ranger Assessment and Selection Program. And then one morning his commander informed him he would be spending the next couple of weeks organizing some new program for female soldiers who were headed to Afghanistan with a team of Rangers they would be enabling. When Scottie asked what he was supposed to prepare them for, the response was as broad as it was practical: "They need to be able to do what anybody else can."

He didn't, of course, get to Fort Bragg without some hazing from his buddies. "You're gonna have to train *girls*?" they asked him. "Seriously, dude? That sucks." But Marks wasn't thinking about the gender issue; he had worked with a whole slew of "enablers" in the course of his ten years and dozen-plus Ranger deployments—EOD guys, who hunted for and disabled explosives, and tactical psychological operations types—and he figured these girls couldn't be that much different. They had made it this far; how bad could they be?

Now, a couple of months later, Scottie was at Bragg preparing this first all-Army team of female enablers in a course that he and a few teammates had designed. It was to be a week of surprises for the veteran trainer and his colleagues. The first sign that things were different was the killer focus the women brought to the classroom for Scottie's opening "combat mindset" talk. These women didn't play around; they didn't fidget or elbow each other. They just looked damned happy to be there and 100 percent ready to go.

But then came the PT test. Scottie had seen their scores going in and knew they were strong; in fact, that was a huge factor influencing their selection to the Ranger side of the program. He set the distance for the first running test at two miles, and within moments of completing her run one of the CSTs was in his face. "Sergeant, this course isn't two miles," she threw at him. "I know what my two-mile run time is. It is not twelve twenty-five, it is twelve thirty."

"You want to put your kit back on and do it again?" he retorted. He sounded irritated, but in fact he was filled with respect for the soldier. These girls are *intense*, he thought. They reminded him of the men they were about to join. Scottie went and measured the distance of his course and in fact the soldier had been right: it was off by a whopping ten feet. She never put her kit back on, but she had proven her point just fine. The CSTs wanted no easy outs or cut corners—even if it was a matter of a few seconds.

By the end of the third day of training Scottie Marks was a CST believer. "These girls are the best I have ever seen in my life," he told one of his colleagues. "They are going to be our moneymakers—they'll prove this program. They're smart and fast and can do things that no other women can do." He thought about the outrageous myths troops routinely repeated about African-American soldiers before President Truman's 1948 executive order ending segregation in the armed services, including that they were cowards and lousy fighters. Fifty years of war had proven to the American public the heroic mettle of these soldiers, and Scottie Marks found himself guessing that someday, the same thing would be said about these pioneering women.

After the running test, the CSTs faced a brutal CrossFit workout in full gear—forty-plus pounds of weight—and Scottie watched as they attacked the chin-up bar. Then the trainers decided to test the women's limits a bit more, and moved the group to a twenty-five-foot rope that was dangling from a rafter in the gym. "Now," Scottie announced, "this is a warm-up for fast-roping that will come later. Saddle up and get in line."

"I don't think a lot of you will be able to do this," one of the trainers commented. "But let's give it a try." He demonstrated the technique, calling attention as he climbed to the coordinated movement of his arms and legs and the way they worked in concert. Then he nimbly descended the thick, braided rope, using the same technique but now in reverse. It looked simple enough.

Now it was the CSTs' turn.

The first girl, a fit soldier who had always prided herself on her strength, started up the rope but fell quickly back to the floor after making it less than a third of the way up. She shook her head as she landed. "Shit," she muttered, then stepped away as the next girl grabbed the rope and began climbing. She made it to the halfway point, but ran out of strength, too, and dropped to the ground. The third soldier, long and lean, but with less upper-body strength, started her climb strong but then stopped as her arms refused to carry her further and her inner thigh muscles buckled. Weighed down with so much gear, she dangled on the rope for a moment or two, then finally peeled off. And then it was Ashley White's turn.

Marks expected little from the one he dubbed the "megatron quiet blonde," or as one teacher whispered, "sweet enough to be a Disneyland greeter." The cherubic young Ohioan with the American-as-apple-pie cheeks stepped up to the rope without saying a word and slowly, and with great focus, began climbing. Up, up, up she went. She reached the top of the rope, touched the ceiling, then scampered back down. Most astounding: she did it all using only her arms. She reached the bottom and then repeated the climb up, touch, and descent. Then, for good measure, she did it a third time. Returning to the floor beneath the rope she wiped the sweat from her hands onto the pant legs of her uniform and nonchalantly returned to her place in line.

Holy fuck, Scottie thought to himself. His Ranger buddies were looking on with a mix of awe at Ashley's talents and amusement at Scottie's reaction.

Ashley saw the startled reactions from her instructors and teammates, and suddenly felt self-conscious. "I couldn't figure out how to use my legs," Ashley explained, referring to her improvisational style. "Easier just to use my arms." She shook her legs out as she spoke to relieve the muscle cramping, and looked down at her white ASICS tennis shoes.

"Well, well, well, White, shocking us all," Marks commented, then faced the CSTs who hadn't yet attempted the climb. "But listen up, everyone: you *should* use your legs, otherwise you're going to get tired out there when you're fast-roping. Don't try White's technique at home! Who's up next? Okay, let's go."

For a moment the others just stood there, speechless, then Tristan stepped toward the rope and the exercise continued. Amber, Ashley's PMT roommate, came up and patted her on the back. "Man, Ash, I didn't know you could do that," she said. "If I could climb like that I'd be telling *everybody*!"

The one person who wasn't surprised by Ashley's display of strength was Leda, who had been quietly monitoring Ashley's progress since March. All along she knew that this was a young soldier with special talent that had yet to be fully tapped. She was glad to see that the other CSTs were impressed by Ashley's prowess and observed that Ashley's confidence was surging. Finally, it seemed, Ashley was realizing that she did indeed deserve her spot in this nest of high achievers.

Leda herself fared less well in the fast-rope two days later, when the trainers led the women onto a testing ground that more closely resembled real-world conditions. Wearing body armor, she stepped onto the sixty-foot-high platform—roughly equivalent to the top floor of a several-story building—and prepared to descend. But for an instant adrenaline got the best of the veteran soldier and instead of grabbing the rope and sliding steadily downward as she had in previous trainings, she jumped off and barely caught the rope in her hands as she flew down its length, smacking hard onto the ground below. Marks raced over, saw bones in her leg jutting out at a decidedly unnatural angle, and thought to himself, Broken, for sure. But years of war had made the urgent situation his natural habitat, and he never shed his combat mindset.

"Looks like you're fine, Leda," he said reassuringly, as the medic who had been standing by ran toward them.

Leda, looking pale, tried to assess the situation.

"Don't look at your leg, Reston," Scottie commanded in a gentle but forceful tone. "Tell me what you had for lunch."

"Chicken," she immediately answered in a calm voice, but through clenched teeth. "I'm really sorry about this, Sergeant. I'll be fine." She, too, had been to war and knew how crucial it was to steady her nerves and keep her composure, no matter how dire the situation.

The medics carried Leda off and Scottie turned back to the rope. "Okay, next one up!" he shouted to Lane, who was standing on the platform awaiting her turn. Without hesitating she grabbed the rope and stepped off, but halfway down she peeled off the rope. This time Marks was ready; he saw her hands begin to slide, and swooped in to catch her just before she hit the ground. What the hell is going on here? he thought to himself. Next came Tristan, who made it almost the whole way, but ten feet from the bottom she too fell off the rope. She suffered a minor concussion but was back on her feet within a few minutes.

Finally they finished with the fast-roping, which had been as stressful for Scottie as it had been for the soldiers. Over dinner in the dining hall that night, he confessed his anxiety to a group of CSTs, including Tristan, Sarah, and Kate. "I've done over twelve combat deployments, and I have *never* been more scared than when I tried to teach you guys to fast-rope. My balls were in my throat the whole time!"

Sarah whispered to Kate, "Now they're going to say, 'See, girls can't do this.' I just hope they realize that all we need is more training, at least more than a day. This is just the first time some of us ever got to try it. So what if a few people got hurt? I *know* guys get hurt doing this all the time. No one ever says that means all men can't fast-rope."

In fact, it was only a few months earlier, on the bus to Fort Benning when they watched *Black Hawk Down*, that the CSTs had been reminded how deadly fast-roping can be. A Ranger goes to fast-rope out of a helicopter that is facing rocket-propelled grenade fire, slips, and falls to the ground below, leaving him bleeding in the middle of streets full of hostile fire. The accident was the first in a string of calamities that plagued American forces on a tragic day that ended with eighteen soldiers killed in action.

The next day began with a few hours of "dry fire"—shooting guns without ammunition—and learning the "three F's," for fit, form, and function, a sequence that ensured their weapons worked properly and as expected. The women would train on the M4 assault rifle and the M9 pistol, the guns that Rangers take on mission. The rifle was their primary weapon and the pistol the backup in case things went south while they were in a small or enclosed space such as a living room and they found themselves suddenly under attack.

Then they hit the firing range, a desolate spot in a broad field filled with patches of dirt. The women took their places underneath a bright blue North Carolina sky, stood before their targets of brown and tan paper silhouettes, took aim, and started firing.

Scottie began by demonstrating the correct stance and the proper foot placement for firing the M4. Then he went down the line correcting his students. He told Lane to place her feet wider apart and to keep her left hand wrapped tight around the hand guard just beneath the barrel while quickly reloading the magazine with her right. "Try it again," he said, then moved down the row of CSTs to check on the others and demonstrate proper technique. When he had worked with them all, he returned to the top of the line and was surprised by what he saw: Lane was going through the motions just as he had told her to. "Wait a minute, Mason," he blurted out, "what's going on here? You're doing it right! What's up with that?!"

"This is easier, Sergeant," she matter-of-factly replied, as taken aback by his question as he was by her adherence to his instruction.

Whoah, Marks thought to himself. This is a new one. They actually listen and then they do it right.

For years Scottie had taught would-be Rangers on the firing range and watched as they did exactly what he told them not to. He long ago had come to the conclusion that all these young soldiers learned to shoot watching Mel Gibson in *Lethal Weapon*, and therefore had no idea how to correctly fire a weapon. America's young men, he decided, were convinced they knew three things by heart and from birth: how to shoot their gun, drive their vehicle, and make sweet love to their woman. Scottie only needed to teach them one of those lifesaving skills, but it took him twice as much time as it should, and squandered much of his precious patience to boot. Now he found himself on the firing range with soldiers who required exactly one adjustment, followed by a lot of practice, before they started improving their skills and became decent marksmen. That was it. There was no ego to contend with, no pushback about how, "well, my dad taught me this so it must be right."

Unbelievable, he thought to himself.

The CSTs paired up and, crouched on the ground with their notebooks out as if they were interviewing the women they would meet, they prepared for a scenario in which the woman turns out to be a man in a burqa and they have to draw their weapon and shoot. Over and over he had them repeat their moves, starting from a seated position, moving to their haunches, and then drawing to defend themselves from the ground.

Fighting their instincts was Marks's first challenge.

"Drop the pen," he yelled at one CST as he pretended to overtake her. "You have a pistol, draw it, aim, and fire!"

Some, like Cassie, Kate, Kimberly, and Sarah, were comfortable with the Beretta M9 pistol because they had trained on it for years as MPs. But Marks quickly saw that he would need to spend more time with several others who had logged a lot fewer hours handling a gun.

Ashley, whom by now Marks thought "the sweetest girl in the world," was still struggling with the close-quarters technique. She may have been stone quiet and incredibly nice, but Scottie saw in her eyes the flint of a real soldier and he wanted to draw out that "killer" in her. Ashley was wrestling with the pistol, but he thought it was the newness of close-retention shooting that was throwing her off; she seemed plenty comfortable firing a weapon. He just needed to help her attack the source of her concern and do enough drills to make her feel confident in her own abilities. He worked to build the muscles in her hand, instructing her to hold the gun with just her thumb and middle finger, then keep pulling the trigger. After forty-five minutes of that, over and over, Ashley asked if she could please take a quick moment to stretch her cramping forearm. Marks gave her a moment to stretch, then had her back at it. "You gotta build your forearm muscles, White," he said. "All right; thank you, Sergeant," Ashley answered through clenched teeth.

But still there was something missing. Then, in a flash, Scottie remembered a special technique he learned from Mike Seeklander, a friend and expert shooter who had written a number of handgun training books and specialized in close-quarters shooting.

"Okay, gals," he said, "watch me closely." Using Ashley as a model, he looked her dead in the eyes. "First, you gotta draw your weapon fast. White, you gotta be ready to kill me. Get mad, goddammit. Mad enough to punch me in the face and want me dead. Because if you don't get me I am going to get you. Like this . . ." And with that he lunged toward Ashley.

"If someone is grabbing your gun you have to push their face away, wrap your arm around the back of your head, trace your body back down and around, and go underneath the gun to punch out and shoot in the pelvic area," he said, addressing the entire assembly of buns and ponytails. "That way you avoid putting your hand in front of the barrel so if you're pulling the trigger very quickly you don't end up shooting yourself in the palm."

Then he repeated the action, this time with real gusto. "All you need to do is sweep your gun underneath like this." He now arced his gun back to brush his imaginary long, lustrous hair, then pulled his hands down the sides of his body where they met at his waist before he rapidly lifted them back up and aimed at his assailant. "Now you say, 'I am beautiful and I love to shoot.' Think of *Charlie's Angels* and then pull the trigger!"

That did the trick. After they finished laughing, Ashley and the others repeated the sweep, professing their strength and taking down their assailant.

"Come on, White," Marks taunted. "Get *aggressive*, push back. I am right here in your face!" he yelled at her. "Get serious. Shove me away and draw your weapon."

"Roger that, Sergeant," she said, now bellowing back. "I am beautiful and I love to shoot."

"Angrier, White, can you handle it?"

Her cheeks and forehead began to redden and it was clear she had had enough of his goading. The next time he lunged at her the real anger showed. Her eyebrows narrowed and her mouth tightened as she shoved him back, hard enough to throw him off balance, and drew her pistol in four counts.

"*That's* it, White!" he yelled. "Excellent! That's what I am looking for. I knew you had it in you!"

One of Scottie's biggest concerns was how hard the CSTs were on themselves. Whether it was out on the range or in the role-playing scenarios doing searching and questioning, his trainees grew racked by frustration if they didn't improve quickly enough. It took him almost the full week to trace the source of the frustration, which at first he attributed to old-fashioned perfectionism. When he realized what was going on, toward the week's end, he assembled the entire group for a pep talk.

"All right, I am watching you all beat yourself up out there and I finally got it figured out," he said. "You guys have never been around a bunch of badass motherfuckers before who were as good as you are. Every single one of you is used to being the best female in the unit, hands down and no questions asked. And now all of a sudden you aren't."

A few of the CSTs nodded their heads without thinking.

"Listen," he said, "every soldier we pick is a diamond. She is an athlete. She is awesome. That's why you are here. This is just the first time any of you in all of your Army careers has ever found yourself in a pile of diamonds. You are pissed off, you feel lousy about the fact that the girl next to you is doing better at something than you are. But you're now a diamond among diamonds. And you've gotta stop being frustrated with yourselves. You *are* going to fail at things. That *is* going to happen when you are around people this good. Someone's better than you at something and you don't like it? Figure out why and do it better next time.

"Now get back to work."

Later on, walking back to his barracks and reflecting on his talk, Marks smiled to himself. Maybe, he thought, these girls aren't so different from the men I fought with after all.

At night, when they were done, the women replayed the events of the day and discussed the work that was still to come. Before passing out from exhaustion, some of them critiqued each other—not their actions, but their attitudes, and particularly their lack of faith in their own abilities. One evening Cassie told Tristan she had to be bolder at the firing range.

"Tristan, you have just *got* to own it when you are out there," she said in a tone bordering on disgust. "Man up. Stop acting like such a wuss."

Kate, who roomed just across the hall from Ashley and Amber, often overheard Amber joking with Ashley and encouraging her to be more aggressive, clearly trying to draw out her inner alpha. Kate wondered how it had come to be that all of them equated the idea of toughness with the male version of the trait when Ashley was clearly plenty decisive when it came time to act. Here was someone who was athletic to the extreme and good at what she did. But they were so used to seeing competence accompanied by shows of masculinity and aggression that they worried whether their teammate would succeed in the theater of war. We've all bought into it, Kate thought. Ashley seems so comfortable in her own skin. And we are all razzing her for it.

Most of the time, though, the women reminded each other of their achievements: the run times, speed at drawing a weapon, push-up count, rope-climbing skills. At the end of one particularly difficult day, Kate summed it up: "Everybody has something that the other girl doesn't. This is what makes us a team."

As the week wore on the women grew closer to each other and to their instructors. They marched in full kit at night, shot guns, and suffered through burning workouts every morning. Marks's other frustration, the one he never articulated publicly, was that he and his fellow instructors had so little time to prepare the women. So they stuffed a month's worth of learning into less than two weeks: the role-playing, shooting, searching, questioning, getting the mind ready for war. While they did get a few hours of night-vision device training, he had to squeeze most of it in during the day.

Marks and the other trainers recognized that these girls wanted to be part of special operations with every part of their brains and bodies. They were now his team, Marks thought, just as all those aspiring Rangers he graduated to the next phase of selection were his guys. He felt as surprised as anyone by the very real sadness he and the other Rangers started to feel when the week wound down to its final day.

And now it was time for his closing talk.

"All right, you guys, I want you to remember to go out there and be great. *Be amazing*, because you are. Don't forget any of the stuff we learned this week. Don't do stupid shit and always remember in the military perception is reality. So don't mess with your Ranger buddy. Hang out with your CST teammate at mealtimes and every other time of day. Stay away from trouble. And for godsakes, stay in the gym. That is going to be the *very* first way that the guys you serve with measure you. So work out *really* hard every single day and show those guys you mean some serious fucking business, just like you showed all of us. I'm proud of what you did here this week. Now go and do it even better out there with your Ranger battalion. Show them you belong there. Do the work, and they will respect you and make you part of the team. Pay your rent and they'll bring you out on mission every night. I know you'll make a difference out there."

Then he walked to the whiteboard and started writing.

"This is my phone number," he said. "If anything goes wrong in Afghanistan, if anyone is mean to you, I will skullfuck them. And I mean it. Just call me.

"Now go out there and get it done," he said. "Be *great*."

Now *this* is what I always dreamed of when I dreamed of joining the Army, Kate thought. She wasn't the only one who felt it had been the best week of her military career thus far.

A few days later, as the CSTs were enjoying two weeks of leave before their deployment, tragic news seized the headlines. On August 6, 2011, a rocket-propelled grenade blasted through an Army CH-47 Chinook helicopter in the eastern part of Afghanistan. Thirty-eight Americans and Afghans died, including twenty-two Navy SEALs from SEAL Team Six. The SEALs, according to Pentagon reports, had gone in as part of a team backing up Rangers on a mission to capture insurgents gathered at a compound in Wardak Province's Tangi valley. It was America's single worst day of casualties in ten years at war in Afghanistan, and the worst day in history for the Navy's special warfare unit.

Lane was home in Nevada visiting her brother and a group of his friends when she saw the television news headline. No one else seemed to notice. In the midst of preparing for war in Afghanistan herself, she couldn't believe how little attention any of them paid to all those war dead.

"You all need to tune in," she said to her brother and the others in the room, pointing to the TV, even though the newscast had moved on to another story. "These are the guys I'm going to be out there with. This country is still at war, despite the fact that no one even remembers it."

Back in North Carolina, Jason and Ashley were finishing up breakfast when the news broke. Jason's first instinct was to turn up the volume, but then he quickly switched the channel. His wife was home for just two more weeks and he wanted to focus on their time together. He had given up a spot at the five-month Maneuver Captains Career Course, once called the Infantry Officer Advanced Course, to be home with her until she left. Artillery, Jason's unit, had to fight hard to get those slots for its guys, and Jason had lobbied to secure a space in the July course. But when he found out Ashley would be leaving in August, he decided he had to turn it down. His wife was heading to Afghanistan with special operations and there was no way he would leave her during those last weeks before she deployed. The decision to stay was easy; harder was telling his executive officer and the other commanders who had backed him that his wife was the reason he wasn't taking the vaunted spot.

His superiors were unhappy and said so. "Don't burn a bridge," they said. "Don't you realize this decision isn't good for your career as an officer?"

Eventually he turned to his battalion commander, a man he knew from his time in Afghanistan and a leader who had a career—and a marriage—he respected.

"Hey, Stumpf, let me put it to you like this," his commander answered when Jason told him about the situation. "If anyone judges you for the decision you're about to make, fuck 'em."

Jason had never heard his commander utter a swear word in all the time he had served under him, even in the middle of the war in Afghanistan.

"Okay, sir, then I will go ahead and reverse my decision and take the September artillery course at Fort Sill," Jason said, referring to the course that would be useful but more traditional—and consequently less helpful to his career trajectory. "It will give me an extra month with my wife."

"I imagine I would do the same thing," his commander replied. "Your wife is going to Afghanistan. You two are newlyweds. Enjoy the last month before she goes over there."

Ashley was furious when Jason told her what he had done.

"I know why you did it, but you didn't have to," she insisted. "I would have come to see you on weekends."

"Ash, be real," he answered. "You would've been way too busy, and I would be full-on with a career course. It wouldn't have worked. You know that."

"And besides," he said, "I didn't make the decision for you. I made it for us."

Another difficult decision had to do with Ashley's parents, Bob and Debbie. She had told them little about the CST teams because she couldn't bear to have them worry. Jason initially tried to change her mind, urging her to at least tell them *something* about the program since she had always been so close to them, but he knew when it was time to back off, so he promised he wouldn't say anything to them.

She did take her beloved brother Josh into her confidence. When the White kids were small, Josh would take his little sisters down to the pond near their Ohio home. Now the trio headed to Florida for a nighttime fishing expedition on a giant party boat. Ashley and Brittany both caught their first saltwater fish during that excursion, and the siblings were reveling in the day's successful catch.

During the twenty-mile trip back to Pompano Beach, Josh and Ashley sat alone at the front of the boat, watching as the prow cut its pathway through the ocean.

"It's going to be a bit sketchy where I'm going to be," she began. "Jason just got back, you know, and he's telling me the Guard units are kind of ragtag over there, and I wouldn't be making much of a difference with them if I went to Kuwait. So I signed on for a special mission, a new one, which the Guard encouraged me to volunteer for. I'll be with the Rangers, not kicking down doors or anything, but as an enabler. I'll be going into more dangerous areas, getting much closer to real combat, but I'll be with the best of the best. And I'm going with an amazing group of girls who all made it through this pretty tough selection and training process. It's an incredible team."

He wasn't saying a word, so she paused, then asked: "What do you think?"

Josh knew she was telling him and only him because she knew he would understand and wouldn't try to stop her. Ever since he was a kid he had wanted to join the military, and as a high school senior had even been accepted to West Point. But when the acceptance letter arrived his then girlfriend, now wife, had been brutally honest with Josh: he could join the Army if he wanted, but she didn't want the life of a military wife with babies on her hips and a husband off at war. "I can't do it," Kate said. "I'm just not cut out for that kind of life." So Josh found another way to serve: as a state trooper, where he confronted the danger of the unknown every single night but at home in the U.S.A.

Josh knew how important his approval and blessing were to Ashley. He didn't have the heart to try to dissuade her, and he knew it was impossible anyway. He risked his life every night in his own job. Who was he to say she should stay home, safe and sound, when duty was calling her?

"Do it, Ash," he said. "You're so good at what you do. I can't tell you I won't worry about you every day, that I won't feel scared every second of your deployment. But I support you, and I understand why this is so important."

Now it was his turn to go silent. "Actually," he continued, "I'm envious of you. I wish I would have had the opportunity you have before you now. You're going to be great, and you're going to do such important things."

And yes, he promised not to share the details with their parents.

A few weeks later Josh, Kate, their little daughter Evelyn, Bob, Brittany, and Debbie White said goodbye to Ashley in Fayetteville just before her deployment.

Two days afterward, it was Jason's turn to see his wife off to war. They drove in his pickup to the Landmark, where the CSTs would meet to head to Pope Air Force Base, just outside Fayetteville. He tried to make small talk on the way and so did she. She reminded him she had left a list on the refrigerator of things around the house she wanted him to do while she was away.

Jason pulled up to the front door of the Landmark, the same place where Ashley's first adventures in Assessment and Selection had begun five months earlier. He pulled her rucksack and duffle out of the truck bed and set them down by the door.

"Okay, this is it," she said, as she stood before the motel's entrance.

"You sure you don't want me to help you carry your bags in?" he asked.

"No, no, no," she insisted. "You go ahead now." He watched her make the effort to stay strong and keep from crying in front of him and the other girls. This was not a group that welcomed tears. And he knew Ashley wanted to remain composed for him as much as for herself.

He hugged her and kissed her goodbye.

"I'll talk to you from Germany," she said. "I think it's okay to let you know when we're leaving for Afghanistan."

"Babe, I don't think you're going to jeopardize operational security by telling me when you're wheels-up—I don't think they're tracking that!" he said. "Pump your brakes and be calm; you are going to be fine."

"Okay, well, I'll text you and I'll start emailing you when we can," she said.

The silence was uncomfortable.

"What are you going to do the rest of the day?"

Jason smiled. Who cares? he thought. You are about to go to war.

"Oh, you know, usual stuff: put some gas in the truck, cut the grass, do the laundry . . ." His voice trailed off as he realized that he would now have to do all of those things without her.

"Maybe I'll get a pizza. I don't know."

The last time things were this awkward it was Jason who was about to get on a plane and go to war. I have no idea what people do when the shoe is on the other foot, he was thinking.

So he hugged and kissed her one more time.

"Don't be a hero," he said. "You have nothing to prove. You went and did something I have never done: be part of special operations and work with Ranger Regiment. You don't have to prove anything to me. Just promise me you are coming home."

"Okay," she replied. "I'll be okay." Jason got in the truck and slowly drove away.

In his rearview mirror he saw Ashley reach for her bags, then disappear through the sliding glass doors of the motel. He pulled into a nearby gas station and called his dad.

"Every time I see a C-17 for the next few hours I'm going to be looking up and wondering if it's Ashley. It's terrible being on this side of deploying—I never thought about what she was going through when she dropped me off," he said. "I feel like some stay-at-home dad. I'm the one who is supposed to be leaving."

As soon as he got home he sat down in the bright yellow kitchen where two nights before she had cooked salmon and potatoes for supper. He pulled out a calendar to start tracking the months until she returned home safely to him.

"It's the end of August by the time they finish getting fully in-processed," he calculated. "By the time they reach their base and really get into their jobs it will be September. The battalions will switch out in September–October so that will eat up a couple of weeks as the new guys settle in. Then we're looking at the winter months, when the operations tempo gets a lot slower."

He was making little scratch marks on the calendar as he thought out loud.

"If we can just make it to the winter and the first hard frost and snowfall when all the fighting quiets down, we will be fine.

"We just have to make it to November."

II

Deployment

8

Arrival, Afghanistan

★ ★ ★

Cassie sat bumping around in her seat as the lumbering C-17 flew east to Germany's Ramstein Air Base. Each of the CSTs had received a letter just before graduation, and Cassie now thought about its contents as she rode to war with her nearly twenty comrades-in-arms. It was a personal letter printed on gray and white stationery and was from Captain Tara Matthews, who had been program manager for the CSTs' classroom training that summer. For nearly three years Matthews had served in special operations as a team leader in civil affairs. Matthews had come home to Fort Bragg after deploying to Afghanistan and had run the summer training program.

Matthews had been effective and efficient, but the CSTs hadn't sensed that she possessed any deeply held views on their pathbreaking program or had considered its place in women's long march toward combat. Then, at the very end of the course, she surprised her students by sharing this letter, just as they were on the verge of starting their own tours in Afghanistan. Matthews was older than many of the CSTs, but only by a few years. But as they read her words, they heard the voice of someone who had seen a great deal and now wanted to share what she knew with a group of women with whom she obviously felt a strong connection.

Cassie had read and reread the letter she found inside the folder holding her graduation certificate, and although the note was addressed to the entire group, she felt that Matthews was speaking directly to her in the most personal way.

"The ultimate effects of this program on the coming generations are yet to be seen," she had written.

"Thank you for rising to the challenge of being female warriors in today's Army. I don't know if you recognize that your presence here has been foretold by the generations of women that preceded us in military service to the nation, and that you walk a path in advance of a more efficient and tested generation that will strive to follow you, and carry us into the future.

"The mission has not yet run its course. Don't limit your actions in pursuit of success. Take a measured course and a wide berth within your lines of operation. Show us all what you are capable of."

That's exactly what I intend to do, Cassie silently vowed.

"Know too that the eyes of the Army and, increasingly, the Nation, are on you. This is an opportunity for failure as much as it is one to succeed. Do not block out the voices of opposition, study them and defeat their words and prejudices through brilliant action."

Cassie had felt strongly from the beginning—perhaps more than most of the other women—that the CSTs were, whether they liked it or not, a group of trailblazers who had better not mess things up for those who would come after them. And she was awed by the women who had come before them, especially one female soldier who had gone out with the Rangers on missions long before the CST program was in place. The subtext of Captain Matthews's letter was clear: if one of them screwed up out there it wouldn't be just her mistake; it would belong to "all women." In her heart,

Cassie saw herself as just another soldier who was taking part in the ancient struggle to live up to her potential as a warrior. She didn't see herself as *a female soldier*, just a soldier. But Cassie's own path had shown her that there was still a long way to go before military women would have the same opportunities as men, from serving in infantry to attending Ranger School to trying out to become a full-fledged member of Special Operations Forces.

Like many of the women in Captain Matthews's course, Cassie had conditioned herself to swallow her disappointments and channel that energy into making herself better and stronger. But nothing had lessened the frustration she felt over her own suffocated potential. Until she joined the CSTs. The summer just past had been the best of her life: she, Tristan, Kate, Kristen, and Isabel—an intel officer stationed in Korea who was her roommate at selection and now her closest friend—and some of the other unmarried girls had spent nearly every night together, going to dinner and the occasional bar on weekends, then eating and working out together during the week. She was a long, long way from those lonely nights of doing crossword puzzles on the floor back in Iraq.

Cassie and her teammates had come to understand each other in ways no one else could, or probably ever would. They had forged a bond based on friendship and respect, cemented by the fact that they had never before known people like themselves. Women found them weird for wanting to go to war. Men found them threatening. For a long time Cassie thought this was a reality she alone had experienced, but then she got to know her new teammates.

And now this "band of sisters" she had come to love was about to split up and scatter to outposts across the country in teams of two and three. They wouldn't see each other for months, and perhaps not at all during the full, eight-month deployment. Cassie was eager to get to her base and start going out on missions, but she didn't want to think about saying goodbye to her teammates. Together they were making history, and while most of them remained focused on their personal goals rather than the larger backdrop against which their own trajectories would play out, Cassie found herself one of the few who were keenly aware of the moment. Perhaps it was the women's studies major in her, or possibly it was the ROTC Cadet. Or maybe it was the rucksack at her feet that was filled with books like Sebastian Junger's *War*, Marcus Luttrell's *Lone Survivor*, and Pete Blaber's *The Mission, the Men, and Me*, which follow platoons of soldiers or special operations units into some of the toughest battles America's troops have faced. Whatever it was, Cassie couldn't help but feel that this deployment was something that somebody, someday would want to know about.

Cassie had pulled the unfortunate duty of chalk commander, meaning she was basically the airplane's chaperone. It was her job to make sure all the names on the manifest were on the plane, and would be on tomorrow's flight to Bagram Airfield in Afghanistan. She led the gang of women in boarding the C-17, and was therefore among the first to feel the curious stares from the male soldiers who were hunting for space on the webbed seats along the plane's sides. A huge cargo pallet carrying supplies to the troops in Afghanistan filled the plane's midsection.

"What's going on?" one of them asked as Cassie settled into her own spot at the front, near the stairs that led to the cockpit. "You guys nurses? This *is* the flight to Ramstein, right?"

"Not exactly, and yes, it is," Cassie replied, offering up a half smile that indicated the conversation was over. The CSTs were by now used to being sized up as nurses or members of a softball team, and at the moment they were more concerned with getting some shut-eye than explaining themselves. As soon as the plane was airborne, most of them spread their sleeping mats and poncho liners on the freezing cold metal floor and were soon fast asleep.

Nine hours later, as the plane descended, they landed in Ramstein, not far from the Landstuhl Regional Medical Center, America's largest hospital outside the United States. Many of the most severely injured troops from Iraq and Afghanistan stopped here for emergency treatment and care before going home.

The CSTs slept that night at the Rhine Ordnance Barracks, a military way station not far from Ramstein. Or, rather, they tried to. After lights-out, a chorus of male voices shattered the evening quiet. Cassie, Sarah, Amber, and Kate, whose bunks were clustered together, rolled their eyes in the dark.

"My girl dances dirty, but she just fucking lays there in bed," one guy called to another in a voice that carried easily into the women's quarters.

"Oh, I'm a bad girl," came the reply, voiced in a high-pitched squeak designed to sound like one of these "girls."

"You're too hard," the second one continued, gleefully drawing out the last word.

"Just open your mouth already," the other one replied, dropping his voice a few octaves.

For Amber, this was the last straw after a long day. She needed rest and these clowns were standing between her and much-needed sleep.

"Hey, you, Casanovas, how about shutting the fuck up and going to bed!" she yelled in her loudest officer voice. "Some people are trying to sleep here."

Not another word was heard until the CSTs woke the following dawn.

They boarded a transport plane for the six-and-a-half-hour flight from Ramstein and the world they knew to Bagram Airfield, the largest U.S. military base in Afghanistan, and the war that waited just outside its heavily fortified gates. Ambien ruled the flight, along with headphones, as the women stretched out in the cargo area to grab the last bit of rest while they could. When the CSTs were awake they cracked jokes and swapped sarcasm about their fictional softball scores and the fact that their role was actually the "Coffee" Support Team for Ranger Regiment. Or that some would think the letters stood for the "Casual Sex Team." The laughter kept at bay the reality that it was combat to which they were headed, no more training or warm-up. As one of the CSTs later wrote to a friend, "I couldn't quite ever imagine what deploying would really feel like, but I thought I would be way more nervous than this. I guess I just feel ready to get started and trust my training and my own good judgment to do the right thing. It will be a steep learning curve, and I don't doubt that I will be yelled at a few times, but I know that's just part of the learning process."

At long last they made it to Afghanistan.

It's so strange, Sarah said to herself, once the plane was on the tarmac. She found the routineness of it all disconcerting. It doesn't feel like war at all—no one was shooting at our plane when we landed, no bullets ricocheted off the C-17 as we offloaded our stuff. It felt almost normal.

The Soviets built Bagram Airfield in the 1980s, during their war in Afghanistan. Located just sixty-five miles north of the capital city, Kabul, it was their main air base, but after the Russians retreated in defeat it fell into disrepair. The Americans began using the abandoned facility just after they entered the country in 2001, after the attacks of 9/11. At that time the facility was gutted, decimated by its problematic geography: stuck between Kabul, which the Taliban controlled, and the northern province of Panjshir, the last swathe of the country it didn't. Years of brutal fighting between the Russians and the Afghans—and later the Taliban and the Northern Alliance—had destroyed much of the lush vineyards that once surrounded the ancient city of Bagram.

Over the decade that followed 9/11, hundreds of millions of U.S. and allied dollars poured into the airfield, leading to a construction boom so intense that a Turkish firm built a cement factory on base to keep up with the rapid expansion of hangars, towers, runways, barracks, offices, and support buildings. By the time the CSTs arrived in late August 2011, Bagram had metamorphosed into a city unto itself, replete with a traffic-clogged, tree-lined main thorough-fare known as Disney Drive, named in honor of Army Spc. Jason Disney, who died in 2003 when a heavy piece of Russian equipment he was working to remove fell on him. The now-massive, nearly six-thousand-acre base had become a military and contractor city, home to a hive of different types of sleeping quarters, from huts and tents to formal dormitories and five large workout gyms, nine dining facilities, two Green Bean coffee shops, two Pizza Huts, two Subways, and a Popeye's Chicken. The base also offered a top-tier trauma center for treating the most injured troops, and a detention facility to house suspected Taliban and al-Qaeda fighters.

Bagram also attends to the emotional needs of the troops by providing two United Service Organizations centers. These were congressionally chartered and designed during World War II to lift the spirits of service members heading into battle and the families who awaited their return. President Franklin D. Roosevelt conceived of the USO in 1941 just as war began to look imminent; three months later Hollywood actor Bob Hope assembled a group of celebrities and together they put on an unforgettable show for airmen based at California's March Field. Then the war started and so did the massive mobilization of men from across the United States. In 1943, Hope and a few others entertained troops fighting in Europe and North Africa, and so began a tradition of USO tours that has never stopped. Over the years some of the biggest names of their era, from Lena Horne and John Wayne to Lou Rawls, Sheryl Crow, Toby Keith, Ben Stiller, and Stephen Colbert, have taken part in USO tours to support the troops. One of Bagram's USO centers is named for former Arizona Cardinals football star Pat Tillman, who gave up a promising NFL career to join the Rangers after the attacks of 9/11 and was tragically killed three years later by friendly fire in eastern Afghanistan.

Sarah looked with dismay at the wretched excess of a fortified city soaked in first-world conveniences, smack in the middle of one of the world's poorest and most conflict-ridden countries. She had been raised by her family to live simply, without unnecessary creature comforts, and what she saw was demoralizing. She felt disgusted by it.

People here on base are living like pigs, she thought. No wonder they say Afghans resent us. Who wouldn't?

For the CSTs, like thousands of other troops, Bagram was the final taste of America on the way to war. The soldiers heading to Ranger Regiment would stop there only a couple of days, just long enough to pick up gear, receive briefings, and process paperwork. They'd get their final assignments and—most important of all—learn which CST they would be paired with.

They would also be introduced to the Joint Operations Center, or JOC, a wartime nerve center where they received an overall intelligence brief on the kinds of missions that lay ahead and the various threats they would be facing. Most of the bases where they'd be serving would have them. At the start of America's decade of war, bureaucratic barriers prevented vital information from reaching troops serving in Iraq and Afghanistan. This information blockage was part of what McChrystal had tackled as JSOC commander. No central system existed to collect, collate, and coordinate the intel that was daily being uncovered in the increasing number of special operations raids on insurgent networks. This meant valuable information remained in offices, buried under stacks of reports, stuffed away in desk drawers, or, worse, consigned to the trash. Often it never reached the people on the ground who might best understand it and be in a position to use the many details it held—down to the smallest nuggets of data that could save lives. The JOCs were born to improve the flow of information by building local structures and systems in which intel could be gathered, shared, and acted upon in real time across special operations units and top-secret government agencies. These high-tech stations could be found in various regions of Afghanistan, sitting in the middle of towns and villages that regularly lost electricity—if they had it at all—and often had no running water. By the time the CSTs arrived, the JOCs played a central and vital role in the wartime landscape.

Sarah had never deployed to Iraq or Afghanistan before, and she marveled at the humming electronics hub that had eyes all over the country. She counted thirty TV monitors and well over one hundred computers. At each station sat delegates from a slew of government agencies, each with its own acronym. In shifts that ran all day and all night they pored over every iota of intelligence that came through, and interpreted and then distributed it. Sarah worked to learn the place's language: There was the TOC, or Tactical Operations Center; CFSOCC, Combined Forces Special Operations Component Command; BUBs and CUBs, Battle Update Brief and Commander Update Brief, respectively.

Kate, in the meantime, was astonished that senior commanders in charge of the special operations battlefield had taken precious time away from organizing and leading the fight to greet the CSTs when they reached Bagram. It appeared that the women's arrival in Afghanistan was new and unusual enough to justify this special, high-level welcome. She didn't imagine that many of the other enablers got the same kind of attention, and she took some comfort from the support the program received from these men, most of whom had spent the past decade in battle, either here or in Iraq. If it turns out that everyone else hates us, at least the guys at the top see the value of having us here, she thought.

Leda, still recovering from her pre-mission training injury and operating from her computer back in Virginia, had written up her suggestions for the CST pairings and submitted them to the sergeant major overseeing the program from JSOC's headquarters at Fort Bragg. She wanted to pair the least experienced soldiers with the most experienced ones, so the veterans could coach the newbies through the tactical and cultural challenges they would face. The role of officer in charge temporarily fell to Anne Jeremy, and now, with everyone gathered together in Bagram, she shared team assignments with the few who hadn't already received them.

"Ashley and Lane," Anne said, "you'll be going down south. I'll join in a few days, as soon as I finish the paperwork I have to do here."

She was headed to Kandahar. Ashley was dejected when she heard the news, and while she said very little, she was unable to hide from her colleagues the anxiety she felt. It was written all over her face.

Kandahar, in southern Afghanistan, was the Taliban's home turf, site of Mullah Mohammad Omar's 1996 political coming-out as the movement's leader. As the Taliban fought its way northward and took control of most of the country, including the capital city, Kabul, Mullah Omar remained in Kandahar and led his new government from his compound in the south.

It was from Kandahar Airfield (KAF), where Lane and Ashley would be stationed, that the Taliban staged their last stand against the Americans in November 2001, before they were routed and forced to retreat into the valleys and villages along the border with Pakistan. The insurgents spent several years regrouping after the first phase of the war ended and gradually reemerged to fight with formidable power once more. Now, ten years on, they had demonstrated to their enemies, the world's most sophisticated and powerful militaries, that they did not need to control the physical bases to control the actual narrative. The Taliban knew they simply had to outlast and outblast their opponents, and assassinate the civilians they suspected of working with the Afghan government and the foreigners who helped to support it. The Taliban's escalating ability to kill and injure Afghan civilians and launch spectacular attacks on U.S. and NATO troops was part of the reason that President Obama had announced the surge in December 2009. By the time the direct action CSTs arrived at Bagram in the summer of 2011, the battlefield they would join with the Rangers had become vastly more dangerous and unpredictable. Kandahar had become one of the most notorious hotbeds of the insurgency, home to a nearly endless number of IED attacks that claimed the lives and limbs of American service members.

But there was another, more personal reason for Ashley's anxiety.

She would be going to war with Lane, a fellow Guard member, not Amber, her summer training course and PMT partner with whom she had expected to work. CST assignments were, as it turned out, changing constantly based on the needs of the special operations teams, and Anne warned the girls they were likely to change again in the future. The one comfort Ashley had clung to—that she would serve with her close companion—was now gone. She told Lane as much as they waited at the airfield for the plane to take them down south.

Lane, for her part, felt guilty about disappointing Ashley, though of course she had had nothing to do with the decision. She had not gone out of her way to be warm and fuzzy to anyone that summer. No one would ever call her mean-spirited, but she shared Amber's no-bullshit demeanor; in fact, she was even more blunt and uncompromising when she encountered something she disagreed with. Part of it came from the way she was raised, with a lot of responsibility, little parental supervision, and only her brother and her track and field coach to lean on. But another part of Lane's toughness and uncompromising attitude stemmed from her rape experience. She had remained true to the vow she made after "coming out" to her fellow Guard members about the incident: she would never allow herself to be victimized or taken advantage of again. She didn't care who it was; she never was going to "tone it down" or stay "nice" and quiet in the face of something she believed was wrong no matter how insignificant. But Lane also felt protective of Ashley, not only because she was such a good person, but because she represented a kind of wholesomeness that Lane had never known. Ashley came from a supportive, loving family, and had a marriage that inspired every CST who met her and Jason. Lane wanted to see all of that goodness remain unsullied through the ugliness of war—as much, she admitted to herself, for her own sake as for Ashley's. So, however her new teammate might feel about working with her, Lane bucked herself up and embraced the role of the NCO determined to protect her officer, a second lieutenant with the angelic smile and kind heart. She knew Ashley felt unsettled about Kandahar *and* about her, and she promised to watch her partner's backside when things went haywire, as she was sure they would.

In fact, things were going haywire everywhere. That month, August 2011, when the CSTs were joining their new teams, was shaping up to be among the deadliest for U.S. forces since the war began. Along with the Americans who perished in the Chinook helicopter crash, more than fifteen soldiers had been killed in action in the southern provinces of Kandahar, where Ashley and Lane would be, and nearby Helmand. A number of other Americans had given their lives in eastern Afghanistan, where several CSTs would be posted. The women had arrived in Afghanistan at a particularly deadly period in the long war. The handover of security responsibilities from NATO to Afghan forces was just getting under way, and President Obama had announced plans to bring the war to its close, beginning with a major drawdown of troops by the end of that year. Bin Laden was dead, and most Americans rarely thought about the fact that their country was at war. "We take comfort in knowing that the tide of war is receding," the president had said a few months earlier. "Even as there will be dark days ahead in Afghanistan, the light of a secure peace can be seen in the distance. These long wars will come to a responsible end."

But for the newly minted CSTs the war was just about to begin. And if that month's casualty count was any indicator, a bloody fight awaited them.

Kate, who had been so offended by the critical response to her writing at the end of CST selection, wrote a poem to mark the beginning of her deployment.

We are living in a cloud of dust
Like a fog that settled in when we weren't looking and won't
move on

The further out the thicker it appears, and the only way you
  know you are in it is the grit in your eyes and the film
  coating your mouth.
I feel like I am on a moon or stuck in a book with lots
  of meaningful buildings and scenery, but all the people
  walking around are just characters that hold no sway in
  the plot,
Like a dreamscape that is a staging area between two worlds.
All of my history lies behind me, but perhaps my defining
  moments lay ahead.

Perhaps, indeed.

By the next evening the paperwork was finished and it was at last
time to go to war.

During the flight to Kandahar, the routineness of it all impressed
Lane, just as it had Sarah a few days earlier. After ten years in Afghanistan the air system ran smoothly; the CSTs hopped on the
hour-long flight between the two rapidly growing military outposts
just as easily as travelers on the other side of the world boarded a
Delta Shuttle to travel between Washington, D.C., and New York.
To make things even stranger, there were civilians on board their
flight from Bagram. When the plane touched down, Ashley and
Lane hugged the other CSTs on the flight headed to their own bases,
then stepped out onto the tarmac.

And the assault on their senses began.

"Wow," Ashley said, trying to keep her composure. "It really *does*
smell."

The first hot wave to hit them reeked of diesel fuel; it stormed
their nasal passages and stung their eyeballs, then insinuated itself in
their lungs. The second wave was purely human.

"Man, Jason told me about this but I didn't believe it could be
this bad," Ashley said, covering her mouth and hurrying to the

transport vehicle that was waiting on the airstrip. "Think of the smell of diesel, the smell of things burning, and the smell of shit, all swimming together," Jason had said, then he explained how decades of war had ravaged the country's infrastructure, including its sewage systems. The temporary facilities the military set up—basically collapsible port-a-potties—required a great deal of maintenance, which usually ended up half done at best. But even Jason couldn't have known just how prescient his words would turn out to be.

"Oh, I can't wait to tell him *this*," Ashley said, as she and Lane arrived at the camp where they would be living with the Rangers. It sat just downwind from the "poo pond," a place where multiple septic systems from across Kandahar Airfield dumped the product of 1,800 portable toilets—enough to serve thirty thousand military personnel and civilians—into a huge, mud-colored, semi-treated sewage stew of feces that was roughly the size of Lake Michigan. The stench of the poo pond was aggravated by the dry, summertime Kandahari heat.

A rugged-looking young Ranger wearing the Regiment's workout uniform of black shorts and a tan T-shirt had picked them up in his truck at the airstrip and now deposited them at their barracks.

"Hey, welcome," he said, with a casual air. "Glad you're here!"

Oh, God, this actually is happening, Lane thought to herself, amazed by how informal and welcoming he was. She felt like she was in a movie, one she hoped she would enjoy remembering one day when she was a lot older. Right now she just had to survive—and make sure she and Ashley proved themselves quickly.

A sergeant major was there to greet them as they hopped out of the jeep, and he was all business. "Welcome," he said, and pointed to their barracks. "Here's where you'll settle in. You guys need to get your kit ready and be all set to go tomorrow. I want you on the bird out on mission tomorrow night. Let me know if that is a problem." The way he said it, he made clear he would hold the women to the same standards as everyone else; no special treatment. He was deadly serious about the business his Rangers did every night, and he wanted to make sure they were, too.

Both women knew that Rangers typically get thirty-six hours from their arrival in-country to their first mission, and since the first sessions back at the Landmark Inn every CST had lobbied for the same high standards to be applied to them. Ashley and Lane had discussed this on the plane from Bagram. They didn't want to be eased in; better to get the first mission behind them as soon as possible. "We'll be ready to go, Sergeant Major," Lane answered without hesitating.

They made their way inside the reinforced building—at least they didn't have to sleep in tents, Lane thought—that would be their home for the next eight months, and to their new quarters: each had a twelve-by-twelve room she would share with a roommate or two. Subtracting the space occupied by bunk beds, dressers, and a wall locker, there was little room left for moving around. Down the hall was the bathroom: four toilets, four sinks, and three showers. Only a narrow hallway separated Ashley's room from Lane's. If they yelled loudly enough they could speak to one another without leaving their beds.

The first female soldier they met was Meredith Rose, a medic and Iraq veteran who, it turned out, had learned the CST mission on the job. She had simply been asked by a commander one day if she thought she could "run around and catch terrorists" with the special operations guys. Meredith knew the only answer to give was "yes" and a few days later she moved to Kandahar and began going out with the Rangers to search and question women. She had been there ever since.

Meredith lost no time in organizing a tour of the barracks for the new arrivals. "We get to clean those ourselves, so keep your flip-flops handy," Meredith said, pointing to the showers. "There are a couple of other girls living here—you'll meet them. We all live on this hall."

As she stepped into her room once more Ashley saw another young woman—a brunette, petite, like she was, sitting on one of the beds. Ashley put her hand out and introduced herself.

"Great to meet you," the young woman answered. "Tracey Mack. I'm in field artillery."

She pointed Ashley toward the other bunk across from her.

"It's not much, but it works," she said of their little room.

"You guys hungry?" she asked. "You haven't eaten yet, have you? Let me take you down to the Boardwalk."

"The what?" Ashley asked.

"You'll see," Tracey answered.

The field artillery officer had faced her own challenge of fitting in six months earlier when she arrived in Kandahar as an untested, twenty-four-year-old second lieutenant serving as the resident expert on the High Mobility Artillery Rocket System, known as HIMARS.

The daughter of an Army veteran father who had worked as an MP, a dog handler, and an investigator during his thirteen-year military career, Tracey had entered ROTC during her freshman year of college. After graduation she was devastated to receive her assignment to the Army's field artillery branch. Like Tristan, she loved the idea of being out in the fight, but all those jobs closest to the front were still closed to women. Instead of leading people in battle, she'd be managing paper clips, Excel spreadsheets, and Xerox machines back at headquarters. Fate turned, however, to offer her an opportunity: an assignment at Fort Bragg under a particularly open-minded colonel.

"Hey, we're excited to see you on our books," he emailed. "Our unit needs a leader and your battery is going to deploy next year." Tracey leapt at the chance to be a platoon leader. Even six months earlier only a handful of women in the *entire* military would have had that chance. And now she was one of them, here in Afghanistan.

When she first arrived at Kandahar in the spring of 2011, the petite and perky Lieutenant Mack knew she made an easy target for the rough-and-tumble Rangers who had lived according to combat's clock for an entire decade. She imagined they saw her as some smiling little girl who was hard to take seriously. She, in turn, felt intimidated by their years of battlefield experience and the intense camaraderie that was born of all that time in the fight together. Any one of these men would have died for another, she thought, whether they liked him personally or not. They had seen the entrails of friends and the brains of enemies and survived fighting that had changed them as people. She considered trying to make herself more "masculine" and harder-edged for the sake of fitting in by being less upbeat, less friendly, and a lot less jocular than she truly was, but in the end she figured that being fake would be even worse than being ostracized.

So Tracey launched a mission to prove herself. She would stand alone to the side each night in the JOC and learn the rhythms of the missions as she watched them play out, in real time, on the screens before her. She saw that the Rangers were straight-shooting: their guys' lives were on the line out there and all they cared about was what each soldier brought to the table and how well he—or she, in the case of their enablers—could do their job. One night the planes that usually provided air support to the Rangers were prevented from flying because of lousy weather and she offered up her artillery system. After three months of pitching her capability Tracey finally got to demonstrate it, as the GPS-guided artillery struck the target dead-on. Once the men who had seen her around the JOC for all those months saw that she could deliver under the extreme pressure of combat—and could take being ribbed from time to time—they accepted her.

Now here she was, introducing the new gals to KAF. She felt hardened by her last six months at war—she had seen too many flags flying at half-staff as special operations guys got killed by IEDs or enemy gunfire. She marveled at how fresh-faced Lane and Ashley looked to her now.

"The Boardwalk is where we eat when we need a break from the DFAC," Tracey told Ashley, using military shorthand for the on-base dining facilities. The Boardwalk was KAF's global shopping and eating promenade. Want a hot dog? Try Nathan's Famous. Latte? Grab one at the Canadian coffee shop Tim Hortons. Burgers and much more could be found at the Kandahar branch of T.G.I. Fridays, complete with its cheery red and white awning.

But no amount of American consumer merriment or salmon baguettes or chocolate croissants or waves of barbed wire and Hesco bastions could keep out the threats that lay in wait just beyond the fortified base. They lived in the heart of Taliban territory surrounded by an increasingly bold insurgency committed to its fight.

"Pizza or gyros?" Tracey asked Lane and her new roommate Ashley. Nothing else was open at the moment—it was 10 p.m. Nearby hung a banner featuring an attractive blond woman with glossy red lips holding her sandwich and looking enticingly into the camera with the words "GYROS (YEEROS) for HEROES" in big, dark letters above the locator, "KANDAHAR RESORT."

"The gyros are pretty good, actually," Tracey said.

"What's a gyro exactly?" Ashley asked sheepishly. Tracey showed her the brown beef wrapped around the silver spit on which the lamb circled around and around. The long line of service members queuing for the seven-dollar pita sandwich spoke to its popularity. "All right, let's try it."

First meal in Kandahar and already it's an adventure, Lane thought to herself as they walked back to their new rooms to finish unpacking their gear and head to bed.

She looked down at her black Timex.

Tomorrow at this time we'll just be getting ready to go out on mission . . . Lane thought. And she remembered the words Captain Matthews had left for them.

> *Take a measured course and a wide berth within your lines of operation. Show us all what you are capable of.*

Lane promised herself she would do no less.

9

Operation "Fit In"

★ ★ ★

Hey, Ash, check it out!" Lane yelled. She was pushing a large box toward Ashley's room with her boot. The girls had been eagerly awaiting this package from Fort Bragg. The carton displayed a large letter *P* encircled by a *C*, the logo of Crye Precision, a New York City–based company founded by two Cooper Union graduates in 2000 to "revolutionize the soldier" by creating a new line of camouflage uniforms and body armor for the U.S. Army's Special Operations Forces. The Cryes were designed to work in every environment where America's soldiers deployed, from desert to forest to swamp to city, and in every type of climate, elevation, and light condition. Members of Ranger Regiment wear the Cryes every night on mission, and the CSTs had lobbied Leda relentlessly for the same uniforms. She, in turn, had pushed relentlessly on her team's behalf. The CSTs thought they looked ridiculous out there wearing their regular Army "MultiCams." As if they didn't stand out enough.

"It's like Christmas," Lane joked as she pulled the green and brown uniforms from the box and started handing them out to her teammates.

The soldiers laughed, but their reverence for the Cryes was real. They were undeniably proud to have the chance to wear the uniform worn by the Army's hardest fighters. And with their built-in kneepads, the Cryes would be a big help when the CSTs took a knee after running out of the helicopter. The Crye top was another prized item with its elbow pads and lightweight, breathable material that minimizes sweat under body armor. It also has a high, zip collar that keeps gear like rifle straps from brushing and irritating a soldier's neck. The Rangers who popped their collars reminded Lane of John Travolta in *Saturday Night Fever*, and for weeks she would think about Tony Manero on the dance floor every time she boarded the bird alongside her platoon.

"Uh, Lane, look at this," Ashley said, parading up and down the tiny space between their bunk beds. She was drowning in camouflage that was at least two sizes too big: the waist was a solid eight inches wider than her hips and the waistband nearly reached her armpits when she pulled the pants up. The shirt was so tight it felt like the top of a wetsuit. Thank goodness no one will ever see it, she thought, since she would always be wearing another top and full body armor over it.

She looked like a little kid borrowing her parents' camouflage, and Lane was nearly doubled over with laughter.

Lane had the opposite issue as Ashley: her pants were tight in spots where they should have been loose and loose where they needed to be tight. The area around the groin, which featured a nylon-cotton blend zip fly with a handy Velcro closure for quick action, was somewhat puffed out because something the manufacturers had intended to cover was missing.

"I don't think they planned on girls wearing these," Lane deadpanned.

Ashley asked around to see if any of the Rangers had suggestions for remedying her wardrobe challenge. She got lucky and scored a handsome pair of green suspenders that did the trick; from that moment on they became her signature.

Of course, their sartorial problem was hardly a first for women in the military. In World War II, the Women's Army Auxiliary Corps had been supplied with uniforms made by manufacturers that only produced clothes for men. Women's garment makers charged higher prices for every item and the Army wasn't about to pay more to outfit the ladies. One woman in the 1950s noted that the women's uniforms looked like they "were intended for a race of giants." Mildred McAfee, the first director of the WAVES (Women Accepted for Volunteer Emergency Service) in the U.S. Navy, complained they "looked like a comic opera costume." Nothing, it seemed, would fit a woman's form: jackets had heavy shoulder pads and were tightly fit in the chest area; skirts were too narrow for a woman's wider hips. Shoes and neckties were deemed unfeminine. The basic design may not have been "all that bad," one servicewoman said, but "the end product could not have been worse from any standpoint."

Things didn't improve much come Vietnam, where women's uniforms crumpled in the heat and disintegrated after the repeated washings required by the tropical humidity. Most women ended up wearing men's fatigues and boots, even though their official uniform in theater was a two-piece outfit complete with skirt and pumps. When the Women's Army Corps director demanded that women wear the traditional outfits, a Corps major protested that "WACs are in Vietnam to do a job and not to improve the morale of male troops." Finally a commander stepped in to de-escalate the fashion war and allowed that the WACs could keep on wearing the tropical fatigues "if desired." Most did.

Things in the twenty-first century had most definitely improved since the days of mandatory pumps and skirts, though strange-fitting uniforms abounded. Now, in 2011, at least the CSTs could wear the same clothing as the men they went into combat with, even if they required some adjustment to make them work.

The next hurdle for the CSTs concerned office space. The women had been given a room on the second floor of the Tactical Operations Center, or TOC, far from the Rangers' team rooms on the bottom level, which meant they had to run up and down the stairs all day to learn about missions, intel, and anything else that was happening. Anne told one of the Ranger platoon sergeants that she wanted to move her teammates downstairs.

"Honestly, I don't know if you guys can handle us—we're kind of a crazy bunch down here," the Ranger said, half joking. In any case, he added, there was no free office space near the team rooms.

"Oh, that's okay," Anne replied, undeterred. "We'll just take over the broom closet."

And so the CSTs spent an entire day cleaning out an old house-keeping closet that happened to be next door to the briefing room, and transformed it into the semi-official headquarters of the Cultural Support Team. It was big enough to hold a few desks and computer stations, and they settled right in. Ashley surrounded her computer with photos featuring her baby niece, Evelyn, her beautiful twin sister, Brittany, and snapshots of her and Jason. She also made it her business to keep everyone well fed, just as she had back at Bank Hall. Jason was sending regular care packages stuffed with all the sweets she loved, especially gummy bears and M&Ms, which Ashley stored in big jars positioned around the office/closet for visitors to enjoy. Ashley's mom also sent goodies, including her rich, homemade chocolate chip cookies, which somehow managed to arrive in Afghanistan still gooey.

One day Anne was telling Ashley about how great the food was on the base where she served during her first Afghanistan tour, and Ashley had an idea. "If you get us a breadmaker . . ." she said. In no time the machine had arrived and Ashley's mother was sending special bread mixes and all kinds of ingredients from Ohio. Ashley broke the machine in with a batch of raisin bread, and the entire hallway soon smelled of freshly baked bread. Rangers stopped in to try the treats and joked that the CSTs were just trying to torture them with the smell of home. Back in Ohio, Mrs. White would laugh over the phone with Ashley during their weekly Sunday phone calls at the fact that her daughter was baking even while she was at war. Some things never changed.

In reality everything had changed as day became night and night became day. Each "morning" the CSTs woke up at 1 or 2 p.m. Usually they headed right to the gym for a CrossFit workout, rope climbs, and toe-to-bar leg lifts. They completed dozens of lunges, then a series of Olympic lifts and pull-ups. Then they practiced rope climbing. Ashley had raised her own thirty pull-up standard and found herself getting stronger each week. Then, when time and briefings allowed, came a long run around the base, sometimes in full kit and sometimes wearing just the Ranger workout gear of black T-shirt and shorts. After that it was time for "breakfast," which came when most of their friends and family back home would be eating dinner. Before they commandeered a pickup truck they could use for the quick ride to one of the dining halls, the CSTs requisitioned boxes of Special K with Strawberries and packets of oatmeal they could eat in their rooms or at their desks while working on the computer. They would spend the "day" figuring out what the actual night would hold, attending intel briefings and pre-mission briefs, and getting their minds and notecards ready for the evening's mission. By 10 p.m. they were prepping. If all went well and even close to what they had expected, they would be back on base in the early predawn hours. Then they had "dinner," usually known as breakfast, and headed off to their post-mission brief. By the time that finished it was time to wind down, usually with an episode of *Glee* or *How I Met Your Mother* on someone's computer in the office. Ashley often turned to the movie *Bridesmaids* for her post-mission mental recess. Then the CSTs would make the short walk back to their rooms, change for the gym, do their workouts, and finally grab a few hours of rest. The next day they'd start the whole routine all over again.

The soldiers quickly learned that no night was the same as the one that came before. This was the reality of life in special operations. That was the reason the men trained all year, and it was one of the reasons the Rangers had been so apprehensive about having the CST women attached to them. Beyond the issue of gender, their far shorter and entirely different training cycle made them seem a dangerous liability. "You don't rise to the occasion when things go wrong," Sergeant

Marks had told the women in pre-mission training. "You fall to your lowest level of training." The urgency, the fear, and the sensory assault of war destroy the response instincts of most people in the heat of the moment. This truth made constant training not just important, but essential to survival and success in combat.

And yet, the handful of weeks of training in search and tactical questioning were now paying off for the CSTs at war. Each week the women shared stories on their internal email of what they found in Afghan households, the different scenarios they had faced on mission and how they had handled them. In the eastern part of Afghanistan, a week or so in, one CST discovered an AK-47 buried in the ground just beneath a woman she was searching. Kimberly and her partner, on their first night out with a decidedly skeptical team of SEALs, had found the intel items the team sought wrapped up snugly in a baby's wet diaper. Out one night with her Ranger platoon, Cassie was called up to the front of formation to help calm a young girl whose father was known to be part of a group planning attacks on Afghans and Americans. The U.S. and Afghan forces hadn't yet cleared the house, but the Rangers didn't want to enter the compound while this girl was screaming at ear-piercing levels certain to wake the entire village. Cassie knelt with the girl and explained that she too was very close to her father, and she understood the girl's desire to protect her dad. But, Cassie told the girl, her father was doing some things that were killing her countrymen and U.S. soldiers. The girl told Cassie to go to hell and spat obscenities at her in a fury of angry Pashto, but while the two women interacted, the Rangers were able to clear the house without incident.

Slowly the CSTs were waging and often winning the battle to belong: letting their work speak for itself, acknowledging that they weren't Rangers but wanted to make a difference out there, going to the shooting range, hitting the gym, and marching their asses off each night without falling out. It was a fight every CST knew would be won slowly—and could be lost in an instant.

10

The "Terp"

September arrived and with fall's advance came a slight respite from the Kandahari heat.

Like the war in Afghanistan, the CST role itself was constantly evolving, most significantly in the makeup of its teams. Lane had just left Ashley and Anne in Kandahar for a base in another region. Sarah had moved as well. Instead of the pairings of two that had originally been envisioned, most of the women were now going out on their own with just an interpreter. The demand for CSTs from special operations was high enough that the women were spread out as widely as possible. And so as they were getting to know their fellow CST teammates better, they were also getting closer to their interpreters, the civilian women and men without whom they had no shot of doing their jobs each evening. As the CSTs came to learn, the interpreters were some of the bravest and most effective members of the special operations teams, even if their work was among the least known—and least appreciated. Demand from the entire U.S. military for Pashto-fluent and physically fit interpreters far exceeded the supply. The civilian contracting firms that specialized in recruiting the interpreters could not come near matching the surging demand from American forces.

This was hardly a new challenge for America's military. The Civil War had been the last battle in which all sides spoke the same language. In the months before Pearl Harbor the United States began recruiting second-generation Japanese-Americans and trained them in working with Army soldiers at the Fourth Army Intelligence School in San Francisco. After the 1941 attack the school was moved to Minnesota, since by that time anyone who asserted Japanese heritage was officially banned from America's West Coast. Historians would later attest to the extraordinary contribution of the Japanese-Americans during World War II. James McNaughton wrote: "Their courage, skill, and loyalty helped win the war sooner and at lower cost to the United States than would otherwise have been possible." During the American occupation of Japan "they helped turn bitter enemies into friends, thus securing the victory and serving as a bridge between the two cultures." Women played an important role in this effort; the WACs recruited American women from Japanese and Chinese families, some of whom spent the war years in Camp Ritchie, Maryland, analyzing seized Japanese documents.

But the Pentagon found itself utterly unprepared for the language demands that the twenty-first-century, post-9/11 wars placed on its troops. Finding language-skilled, battle-ready translators proved a major challenge, and Afghanistan was a lot harder to staff than Iraq because the Afghan and Persian communities in the United States were only a third the size of the country's Arabic-speaking population. Pashto, one of the two official languages of Afghanistan, is not spoken in huge swathes of the world, which complicates the task of finding translators in neighboring countries. The lost-in-translation dilemma highlighted a far broader problem: America lacked language skills in the places where it was fighting, and it was up to the military to find a solution. One of Admiral Olson's priorities was an initiative called Military Accessions Vital to the National Interest, or MAVNI, whose goal was to increase "our level of regional expertise through the recruitment of native heritage speakers." The translators had to be resident, legal noncitizens already based in the United States, and in exchange for their services they were promised an accelerated push through the opaque process of naturalization.

Speakers of Pashto and Dari, Afghanistan's other national language, were eligible for the program, but there were precious few native speakers who could provide the linguistic firepower the war required. So the U.S. military and its civilian contractors went hunting for candidates in the nation's largest Afghan-American communities, from Northern Virginia to Southern California. Private contractors paid several times what the military could, with salaries hovering around the $200,000 range, but even so it was a challenge to find people who met all the qualifications—especially women.

For the CSTs, who were busy getting used to their unusual new assignment, the ideal "terp" was a female who understood Pashtun culture; spoke American English as well as they did; grasped how special operations functioned; could relate to and connect with Afghan women and children in a hot moment; embraced the women's mission; was athletic enough to keep up with the Ranger men while wearing body armor; and could speak most dialects of Pashto.

Ashley had the good fortune to actually get to work with the ideal terp, a young Afghan-American named Nadia Sultan.

Nadia had come to the United States in the late 1980s when she was only one month old. Her parents were Afghan refugees from Kandahar, fleeing their country's nine-year war with the Russians, which was then taking especially bloody turns through the surrounding cities and their own neighborhood. They first stopped in Pakistan, where Nadia's mother gave birth to her baby girl, out of concern that the United States wouldn't let them in without health insurance. Once in America, her family spent its first few years in New York City, among a tight-knit neighborhood of Afghans; then they moved to Orange County, California, where a larger and more established community of Afghans was forging a new life. Nadia grew up a real Orange County girl; the raven-haired stunner never left the house without flawless makeup and a fresh manicure.

Nadia's family may have left Afghanistan, but they did not shed all the traditions of their native home. Nadia and her sister were raised in an insular Afghan-American community to study, find a job, and marry a successful fellow Afghan-American approved by their parents. After that they were to begin having babies—as soon as possible.

But once she was in college, Nadia swerved from the preordained path her parents had tried to forge for their girls. She worked at a bank while studying at the University of California and graduated at the height of the financial crisis, a time of few jobs and stiff competition. Initially she had wanted to work with the police or FBI helping to rescue abused kids. Then she had heard about the interpreting gig from an uncle in New York; several of her cousins had already accepted positions and departed for Afghanistan. Nadia decided that if she could interpret for Americans doing humanitarian work in her parents' homeland, she would go, too, and get experience that would help her when she returned. She was energized by the idea that she could make good money doing a job she believed in while also serving the nation that had given refuge to her own family when it was too dangerous to stay in Kandahar.

But Nadia's parents knew enough of war to question her idealism. They were furious when she shared her news, and exploded in anger. Neither could believe that after all they had lost and all they had risked—their own lives included—to get to America, their daughter now wanted to go back there. "The Taliban are going to kill you!" her mother cried in Pashto. "They will murder you as soon as they lay eyes on you. And you cannot escape them, because every day there are rockets landing at the bases. If you go there, you are going to die."

Nadia heard the same thing from nearly everyone in her family, but she ignored their entreaties and pushed ahead with her plans. She landed at Bagram Airfield in the summer of 2009, and three days later started her new job. Colleagues "welcomed" her the same way the commanders had received the CSTs: as if she had been there for years and was ready to hit the ground running without any breaking-in period or on-site training. Only she had had no training. She began working twelve-hour shifts interpreting at the base at Bagram, translating for the Americans when they brought in high-value detainees who supported the insurgency, and trying to help gain intelligence that would foil future attacks. She told her company she wanted to do more humanitarian work, like distributing food or opening schools, but they told her that unfortunately, this was the only work they had just then. Orange County and the days of mani-pedis couldn't have felt farther away.

As she encountered Afghans from around the country, Nadia couldn't believe how her parents' countrymen were living. She had never seen so much suffering, had never interacted with people for whom food, shoes, and water were luxuries. Her parents had described Afghanistan as a land of plenty, of monster-size watermelons, juicy pomegranates, and newfangled electronic gadgets that people from India and Pakistan flocked across the borders to purchase. But all Nadia saw was insurmountable poverty and the fragility of human life. The only thing she had in common with the Afghans she met was their language.

She vowed she would never tell her parents how bad it really was. Their Afghanistan now existed only in their imaginations, and she wasn't about to destroy it.

During her first two weeks at Bagram, Nadia struggled to endure each day. She hadn't adopted her own "combat mindset" yet, and she had been ill-prepared for what she would witness and hear. She remained stoic on the job, but returned to her room after each shift to cry for hours, only to turn around and head back to work. She wondered whether she could keep doing the job, regardless of how much money she was earning. We need to get our troops out of here; these people are from a different century, she thought. We need to leave this place and never look back.

Nadia was equally disgusted by the partying all around her. Civilian contractors and NATO troops on base stayed up all night, drinking and reveling until dawn. She couldn't think of anything more inappropriate than dancing in a war zone. How on earth can these people be out all night partying when men and women are dying right outside these gates? she wondered.

Time and war, however, changed Nadia, too, and gradually she became desensitized to the incongruous excesses of her new environment. After three months she stopped crying about her work. She even stopped taking it back to her room with her. And she stopped judging the partyers, though she never joined them. They weren't bad people, she decided, they were just trying to survive. They are living day by day in their minds, as we all are, because no one knows what the next day will bring, she thought.

By the end of 2009, just before the U.S. troop surge began, the social scene got even more extreme. Many more interpreters came to Afghanistan, including some women Nadia knew from New York and California, and in dismay she watched these new "desert princesses" grab their seats at the "man buffet" they found on the bases. The old joke was a true reflection of life in a war zone: "twos became tens and tens became twenties." Nadia herself—young, beautiful, and on her own—had an abundance of offers and suitors. "I would work three jobs to support a wife like you," one told her, but she paid meager attention. This is not the real world, she reminded herself, and in time she and the other young, Afghan-American female terps forged a unique bond given their outsider status. They were civilians on a military base, Afghan-Americans whose loyalties were questioned by both the Afghans and their fellow Americans, and outsiders even to their own families; the elders thought it outrageous that these young women would choose to live there, in the middle of a war fought by men, instead of "having babies at home, where they should be."

Six months into the job, Nadia realized that the shallow, label-conscious Afghan-American girl she once was had disappeared, and in her place was a steely professional with a front-row seat to the war in Afghanistan. Her work put her in direct contact with combatants and she—the spoiled girl from Orange County—was now part of the effort to stop attacks and learn where the insurgency's leaders and their supporters were hiding. Nadia had by now met countless individuals who wanted nothing other than to kill her, and she had communicated with dozens of regular Afghan citizens who were destitute, uneducated, and now fully ensnared in a war much larger than they could comprehend. She could no longer bear to hear from friends back home about boyfriend issues or Botox woes. People are dying every day, all that is just so meaningless, she thought. But she never expressed any of this out loud; she just kept herself focused on her work. Gradually she became more confident in her own abilities, and developed a fine-tuned instinct for when someone was lying. She also found her own voice and stopped hesitating when she had an insight to offer military personnel for whom she translated. If she believed they were following a dead end, she would say so, even though some of the American leaders didn't want to hear her views. She was only an interpreter; "just tell them exactly what I am saying," they would tell her, oblivious to the fact that some of the words they used didn't even exist in Pashto. But with time, many came to trust Nadia, and regard her as a partner who could offer insights into dangerous situations at high-stakes moments.

In spring of 2011, her bosses recruited her for a special assignment: a new mission that would take place out in the villages, not in the relative safety of Bagram. It was a new type of job for female terps: they would be assigned to American female soldiers who were out on raids searching and questioning Afghan women and children in insurgency strongholds. There was a color-coded shorthand for the special operations task forces. Nadia's male colleagues now ribbed her for joining this new one they jokingly called "Pink Team."

She didn't want to take the assignment at first. She had planned to return home to California by 2012 and move on with her life: she wanted to do that long-postponed humanitarian work and maybe go back to school. But her bosses were even more desperate than usual for her to take the job; there were precious few Afghan-American females willing, daring, and fit enough to do the assignment. And she knew that if she didn't go, the responsibility would fall to her teammates, some of whom were older women hardly athletic enough to go out on missions and others who were younger and had small children back home in the States. She felt it was her duty both to her country and to her colleagues to do what she knew she could. She would sign up for "Pink."

Overnight, she went from the relative luxury of life at Bagram to a tent on an Army base in a province where cell phone networks stop functioning after 6 p.m. because insurgents use them to blow things up. On her first night out with the Rangers she feared her mother had been right all along: she might not make it home. Her stomach tossed in terror as she realized she had had no training for helicopter rides through pitch-black skies, or rough landings on fields of sand that kicked up a storm of dust and made breathing impossible. Nor had she trained for the miles-long treks through unknown territory. She wore a baggy Army uniform and carried a night-vision monocular, a device that has just one eyepiece and therefore a drastically reduced view of the objective. She had been trained for just a few hours to use it by a CST. It put an eerie green haze over half the landscape, making things even more terrifying. Running for her life alongside the Rangers, Nadia wondered what the hell she had agreed to. On her first night she choked on sand and threw up as soon as they neared the intended compound. "We have to keep going!" a Ranger yelled back at her as they ran. "No stopping, pick up the pace!" Eventually she did.

Nadia felt like an outsider once again. Even some of the CSTs were impatient with her, insisting that she work faster in the field. She wanted to answer, "Girl, do you understand I am from Orange County and have never done this kind of job before and have zero training for it?" But she said nothing, and just worked harder.

Mistrust between the U.S. soldiers and the Afghan forces they were there to train abounded. The grim threat of insider attacks frightened the Americans; an Afghan border guard had recently killed two NATO service members in the northern province of Faryab, and no one was sure who, exactly, was collaborating with the Taliban to pull off such acts. In the dining facility one day Nadia overheard a fellow American, a soldier, say he didn't want to eat with the Afghan forces because he could be seen as a disloyal "defector" who might be working with the Taliban. She added this to her list of worries: that she, too, would be seen as someone with ambivalent loyalties simply because she dined or spoke with the Afghan forces to whom they would soon hand over security responsibilities. Men in the Afghan army shared with her their dreams of moving to America, and how those dreams collided with their genuine mistrust of American motives. Nadia tried to convince them that the Americans really did want to help the Afghans, and how hard the immigrant life in California had been for her family and so many others. She tried to build bridges between the Afghan men and the American soldiers who led the missions, but she found few takers. It was a cultural gap that felt nearly impossible to overcome.

In the summer of 2011, after her first round of CST missions, she agreed to be transferred to Kandahar. She knew it was full of IEDs and the site of constant firefights, but she now trusted the special ops guys with her life. Besides, their first interpreter there had broken her wrist; she hadn't lasted more than a few weeks in the job. And there was no one else to do it. But first, Nadia would return to California for a family wedding.

The trip home turned out to be a disaster: Nadia found herself feeling as isolated as she had during those early days at Bagram. No one in Southern California acted like there was a war going on; it simply never came up in conversation. "Why are you so down?" her family and friends kept asking. "You seem so bitter." But Nadia simply felt disconnected—from her family and her "real" life. I've just been bitch-slapped by reality, she thought as she watched the bride and her friends dancing carefree and full of joy in the wedding hall. They haven't got a clue.

She may have been a civilian in the conflict, but war had changed Nadia, and when she left California for Afghanistan she wondered if she would ever again feel connected to people who hadn't seen combat.

By midsummer she was settling in in Kandahar, and the new crew had arrived: Ashley, Lane, and Anne. Nadia was nervous; building rapport was important in a job that demanded they spend so many hours together preparing for, flying to, and, most important, placing their lives on the line during the mission. She found herself anxiously wondering what sort of women these soldiers would be. Nadia found her answer in the ladies' room, of all places.

The four women—Ashley, Anne, Lane, and Nadia—were in the washroom getting ready for the first meeting of the day when Anne and Lane broke out their traveling cosmetic kits. It was a small gesture, but for Nadia, it spoke volumes.

During her years overseas she had been around a lot of military females who frankly frightened her. They conveyed the impression that any sign of femininity would be perceived as weakness. But here, in this tiny bathroom, were three incredibly fit, Army-uniformed, down-to-earth gals who could embrace being female and being a soldier in a war zone. She found it refreshing—and inspiring.

"Oh my God, you wear makeup!" she burst out.

Anne laughed as she put the final touches on an abbreviated makeup regimen.

"Oh, yes, always have to have mascara on," she replied. "I am blond and look like I have no eyelashes. I don't want to scare people!"

"Me, too," Nadia answered, relieved in a way she hadn't felt in months. "I mean, I obviously have brown hair, but I always have to do my eyeliner and fill in my eyebrows. Anything else, I don't care, but those two things absolutely have to happen for me to be ready to face the day."

Then the soldiers and their terp headed to the briefing room. This is the dream team, Nadia thought. They are confident, they love the work, they are tough, and they know how to put on eyeliner. They love the guys they work with and want to help; they aren't scared or intimidated, just ready to go out. Meeting them helped convince Nadia to stick with the job. I can totally do this, she thought. I want to see these girls succeed, and I am going to stick it out and do it for them. Already she had sprained her ankle while out on mission and gotten more than a few scrapes and bruises. She worried she would get her face banged up or much worse one of these times, but she was going to stay at least until the following March, when her contract ended once more.

Over the next few weeks Nadia regularly went out on mission with Ashley and became one of her regular interpreters. She admired Ashley's resilience in the face of difficulty, as when she struggled one evening with the faulty batteries in her night-vision goggles, and took in stride the fact that her warning light had been on toward the end of the mission despite fresh batteries. She saw Ashley was determined to improve her work, and had no ego barriers to overcome. The feeling was mutual, and it wasn't long before Ashley trusted and felt comfortable asking her more experienced interpreter for advice about effectively talking with the Afghan women and children.

If Nadia had been "the ideal terp" when she got the CST assignment, she was now, six months later, even more skilled in her work. An interpreter's job is to hear all the nuances in the language that both sides use to communicate, but also to read their body language and facial expressions for further clues. In reply to Ashley, Nadia described what it was like from the perspective of an Afghan woman to be questioned in the middle of the night by fully armed soldiers. The last few months had showed her how much of a need there was for this job; she had seen how the Afghan women clung to the female soldiers once they realized they were women. But she also wanted to share words of caution.

"Listen, some of those people out there could get an Oscar, they lie so well. And straight to your face, without even thinking about it," she warned Ashley. "They'll tell you they don't know anything about what is happening in their homes, and sometimes they don't, but oftentimes it turns out to be a lie. So listen to their answers. Don't go in like a bat out of hell, all aggressive, because they will simply shut down. Sometimes these women really want to talk to you, but they are so terrified of the guys we work with and afraid of the Taliban propaganda that says American soldiers enter their homes only to attack them. You are there to keep them safe, and if you stay confident and composed you'll be fine. They pick up on your disposition. They may be illiterate and they may never have been to school. But even if they can't read or write they are smart when it comes to nonverbal communication, and they will be looking to read you from front to back. Never let anyone know the violence that you are capable of. Keep steady, and keep confident."

Just a few nights later, when the two went out on a mission together, Ashley had the chance to put all that advice—and then some—to work.

The evening began like any other, with Ashley doing her part at the pre-mission briefing. "I am CST, I will be standing at X point at X time on this mission; my objective is to secure the women and children . . ." It had all become fairly routine for her now. She had recently written to Jason that it was surprising what one could get used to at war.

She and Nadia boarded the bird together for a short flight. The mission was to find a man suspected of having strong connections to insurgent networks and who was helping to fund Taliban attacks. Nadia confided to Ashley that ever since so many SEALs had died in the August crash, she was terrified of flying on helicopters. A friend and fellow interpreter who frequently worked with that SEAL team had been involved with securing the crash site. Thirty people she saw every day simply never came back to base and she hadn't been the same since.

Nadia was now seized by the fear that she would be next, and every time she boarded a helicopter she instinctively did the most American thing in the world to calm her fears: she prayed. But the moment she began to whisper the familiar words, she realized she had to stop.

What is racing through their minds when they hear a Muslim say "God is Great"? she asked herself, looking around at the Rangers and their military enablers who were seated all around her on the metal benches. These guys are going to think I'm a suicide bomber here to detonate myself, she thought. Her eyes filled as the reality settled in: here she was about to run off a helicopter into the black of night to fight her country's war and she couldn't even ask God to keep her safe because she would be seen as a "defector" by her fellow Americans. But that was the way things were. She whispered "Allahu Akhbar" to herself instead.

Nadia had confided much of this to Ashley, who usually carried her St. Joseph's medal and her prayer card with her on missions, and the young lieutenant had figured out the rest. She did what she could to ease the anxieties of her friend and mission partner; she would give Nadia the thumbs-up as they boarded the bird, and offer her a reassuring smile that promised it was all going to be fine, just another night's work. It was easy to get separated out there in the dark night, among fifty people on rugged and unknown terrain, so the two stuck together when they reached the objective. When they reached the compound another translator called out to the insurgent on the loudspeaker in Pashto. All the while, Ashley never moved more than ten or twelve feet from her terp.

Once inside, Ashley gathered the women and began by explaining, with Nadia as her voice, that she was an American soldier and she was there to keep them safe. No men would come near. She put on her blue nitrile rubber gloves and began searching the women and kids, keeping up a constant patter of questions in a gentle but confident tone. With her terp beside her, perfectly mirroring Ashley's inflections, the team got to work.

The women answered Ashley's questions and she scrawled down in her notebook the information they shared. Confirming identity is notoriously hard in the villages of Afghanistan, particularly those where the insurgency is strongest, because so many people use similar nicknames, and most of the men have invented elaborate stories and created false identities to evade foreign and Afghan soldiers. That night it was Nadia's questioning, and Ashley's subtle recognition of what she had done, that allowed the two to swiftly confirm the insurgent's identity without giving anything away on their faces to show the importance of what they had just learned. That confirmation allowed the Rangers to use evidence they had found in the main compound plus other items on the ground to connect this man with the attacks. And it allowed all of them to get back to base faster than they would have otherwise.

She may have been skilled in her job that night, but it wasn't long before nature got the better of Ashley. The importance of drinking water while on mission had been pounded into the women during their summer of training. "Dehydration is a potent enemy," Scottie Marks had bellowed over and over again. But no one had prepared them for the reality of being out there all night for hours on end, trekking, talking, and flying, while taking in all those liquids. The body at a certain point cannot be ignored, and Ashley's bladder had been demanding attention for hours. The Rangers, of course, had no issue; the moment a bird landed, a whole slew of soldiers would file out and relieve themselves right there, under the stars. But for women, it was a lot more complicated. Some, like Ashley's partner Lane, trained their bladders by religiously pacing their water intake and sprinting straight to the restroom the instant they returned to base. Others used the "Shewee"—a plastic funnel that comes in "NATO green" and allows women to pee standing up. So far Ashley had held her body in check, like Lane. But this night, the metal plate of her body armor had begun pressing on her bladder and she was in agony. At last she asked a nearby Ranger if he would stand lookout while she scampered just a few feet away to answer nature's call. All was well for a moment. And then:

"Who the hell is taking a piss out here?" a Ranger providing overwatch—additional cover for the unit in case an enemy suddenly materialized—asked over the radio once his ears caught the sound of a bladder emptying.

Silence.

"Hey, what's going on out there? Who is peeing? I can hear you . . ."

Ashley was busted, and knew she had to answer because any uncertainty while the platoon was out on the objective was unwelcome, to say the least.

"Uh, it's me," she said for all to hear. "White."

"Oh, *wow*," the Ranger answered, in a surprised tone. The last thing in the world he had expected to hear was a woman's voice.

"Uh, hello, White!"

The story of the exchange spread quickly among the CSTs, particularly since it came from "the quiet one" who, now that she had done the deed publicly once, decided it really wasn't a big deal and would do so again. For weeks it was a joke among the female soldiers: "Uh, hello, White!"

Ashley never shared these stories with Jason—in fact she rarely spoke to him about what she was doing, given the sensitive nature of the work. To her mind, even uneventful trips to the latrine fell under the generic cone of silence. Jason always joked that Ashley had exceeded the speed limit maybe twice in her life; he could say with confidence that she would never be the loose-lipped soldier who would breach operational security.

But she did begin to pen a letter to tell him about one mission she would never forget, which had taken place a few days earlier.

It was her third time out with Ranger Regiment, she wrote. She and a translator—she didn't name her—had flown by helicopter to a compound that was thought to be surrounded by IEDs, and landed just a half mile away from the objective. In districts where the risk of such explosives was high—including many around Afghanistan's south—the special ops teams often flew in as close as they could to minimize the risk to their soldiers' lives, by crossing as little risky terrain as possible. The men they wanted heard the helicopters landing, and the Rangers watched as thirteen fighters bolted out of the compound. The soldiers started throwing "flash bang" stun grenades to stop or at least slow them down and give the assault force a chance to catch them. But the nonlethal "bangers" didn't do a thing except make some noise; the insurgents had a head start and were now running with their weapons. Immediately air-to-ground containment fire started to rain down to keep the men from getting away, and all hell broke loose.

At that point, her letter continued, Ashley was standing in the open air of the main compound's courtyard, questioning the women and children. She and her terp had finished searching everyone and now were speaking with the children and their mothers. Ashley had just begun to ask a question of one of the young wives when she heard the sound of gunfire popping all around her.

She leapt toward the women and scooped up the kids in front of her. "Let's go!" she yelled, as insurgents opened fire on the Rangers from the other side of the courtyard. One of the wives grabbed her arm and followed her to a corner of the courtyard.

"By this time I was already in the main compound doing my job and all of this was happening," Ashley wrote to Jason. Then the Americans answered from the air. "I remember when they were firing at these guys, the brass from the machine gun falling right over top of us."

Instinct and training took over, and Ashley threw her body on top of several children as the rat-a-tat of gunfire boomed over their heads. The women and their little ones shrieked and cried amid the chaos of rounds of machine-gun fire flying just above them.

No one on the American side got hurt, and the women and kids were unharmed. When it was all over, Ashley wondered at the relative composure of the women, who returned to their compound and gathered in a circle on the ground.

When she got back to their camp that night, Anne and Lane were waiting up for her. They had watched the entire mission, second by second, on a live feed in their office. The soldiers were just a bunch of blurry dots, and at the start of the action Lane had joked, "Maybe we should have her jump up and down for a second when she's out there so we know which blip she is." Then the firefight began.

"Jesus, they made contact," Lane said. For the next few minutes they held their breath as small dots and bursts of firepower that looked like comets crossed the grainy, black-and-white feed. Lane and Anne stayed glued to their monitors until the mission ended. The war they had joined for the next eight months suddenly looked a whole lot more real.

"Holy shit, what happened tonight, Ash?" Lane blurted out as soon as her teammate walked through their office door to prepare her post-mission brief. She wanted to hear all about it; truth was, she was a little jealous. She pulled Ashley in close in a bear hug. She could see the exhaustion in her friend's face.

"I dunno, I was with the women and kids . . ." Ashley's voice trailed off; she felt no urge to share the details of what it felt like to worry about getting shot at or have hot shells ricochet off your back or hold tight a frightened child who's staring at you wide-eyed while gunfire erupts all around. "I had no idea what was happening outside." Then she sat at her desk and began preparing notes for her brief.

A few days later, during a call to Jason, she mentioned—in that offhanded, selfless way that her father often called "classic Ashley"— that she had gotten her Combat Action Badge as a result of the night's action. She was among the first CSTs on her team to get the award, a two-inch silver emblem depicting an M9 bayonet and M67 grenade surrounded by an oak leaf, but all she could say was that she didn't think she deserved it. "I didn't do anything," she insisted. "Seriously, all I did was do my job, even when things were going crazy. The training just kicked in. It's really not a big deal."

His response was full of pride. "Everyone at war faces their fight-or-flight moment, and you not only passed your test, you made sure the others were safe, too. I can't wait to hear all about it, all the details of the mission you're allowed to share and what it was like for you.

That conversation was what had led her to write the letter, so she could share a few of the details he craved.

Ashley knew the badge was, in fact, a big deal: a rite of passage that Jason had earned during his deployment. All the CSTs wanted one, and were keeping close track to see who would earn it first. The award was conceived in 2004 by an Army major who argued that the changing nature of twenty-first-century wars created a need to honor every soldier—regardless of military occupational specialty—who personally engaged with the enemy during combat operations. Only infantry soldiers had been eligible for previous combat awards, but the insurgent warfare of the new battlefield had no front lines, and it was no longer just the infantry guys who faced enemy threats. Truck drivers like Lane, medics like their bunkmate Meredith, and military police like Kate regularly took fire and confronted IED threats. Among the first recipients of the Combat Action Badge in June 2005 was a female Army sergeant, April Pashley, who had served in Iraq with the 404th Civil Affairs Battalion.

But Ashley didn't say a word to anyone about the award—including Tracey and Lane—until days later when it echoed across the barrack's grapevine that "White got her CAB."

"How could you not tell us?" Lane asked, incredulous, when she heard the news.

Ashley just shrugged and looked down at her Gore-Tex boots.

"It's not that big of a deal," she said, and that was it, subject closed.

On the phone Ashley had promised to tell Jason the whole story just as soon as she could, which is why she was composing a letter that night. But a Ranger leader entered the broom closet, saying, "White, we're going out tonight." Special operations commanders wanted to keep the pressure on the Taliban, al-Qaeda, and all their networks and associates, and the op tempo was high. Finding time to write a thoughtful letter was proving harder than she thought.

Ashley would finish the story later.

11

Climbing Mountains
in the Night

★ ★ ★

I am going to die, Amber thought.

She was clambering up a mountain in eastern Afghanistan on this fall night, through a dense grove of trees that blocked nearly all the moonlight she knew was there. I think we are now walking around the only wooded part of Afghanistan, Amber thought to herself. It was pitch dark, and she was accompanying a team of elite soldiers she had never worked with before. She had never seen vegetation like this before in Afghanistan; it was bizarre. Every other mission had taken her through a rocky, bare moonscape that was good for line-of-sight visibility because it minimized the possibility of surprise. At first it had felt like any other "infil" as craggy mountain peaks loomed over bare earth. Then, suddenly, the landscape gave way to forest. Now she was navigating a mountain whose dense, tricky terrain seemed to be part of the enemy's plan.

She chastised herself for sweating like a three-hundred-pound fat kid.

Check yourself, Amber. Check your breathing, she commanded. Dodging a tree, she kept up the internal conversation that forced her to focus: Step by step. Don't slip into a crevice or fall off the face of the mountain and die. Don't do anything stupid. Pay attention.

Her quads burned as she scaled an incline so steep that the muzzle of her M4 nearly touched the earth. Amber's ankles felt as if they would break into little pieces of crushed bone. Her interpreter, Jimmie, a young Afghan male whose name wasn't really Jimmie, held on to her shirtsleeves as they jumped over crevasses, working to avoid getting smacked in the face by tree branches or tripping over roots and vegetation, all the while trying to keep up with the far more experienced Rangers. The sheer expanse of the mountains all around her served to focus her attention. Until now she had never truly appreciated how barren most of Afghanistan is, and how much easier that made most special operations missions. She pledged if she got off this mountain alive she would never take that spare landscape for granted again. As she lumbered through the darkness, carrying her fifty-plus pounds of gear and body armor, her mind wandered to the war in Vietnam. She wondered what went through those soldiers' minds as they trudged through the endless jungles trying to clear the trees, insects, and critters out of their way while keeping themselves and their buddies from getting killed. She always felt the deepest respect for what those guys went through, but it wasn't until now that she fully appreciated the hell it must have been. She did appreciate, however, the fact that her female legs were among the shortest of anyone's out there, making the trek longer and harder. But Amber would collapse in a dead heap before admitting that leaping over four-foot-wide gaps in the earth on a steep mountain in the middle of the night was a challenge for her. Part of her was secretly glad to observe she wasn't the only one struggling; a big guy next to her, another enabler, spat out colorful obscenities describing the terrain as he marched.

"Aren't you glad I had you do kit runs?" she called back to her translator, referring to the drills she had made him do to make sure he could keep up on mission. Jimmie grunted his grudging assent.

At long last they clambered down the mountain for the final time and reached a tiny village nestled in the valley and circled by mountains on three sides. The intel teams said the insurgent they sought played a central role in organizing Taliban IED attacks and moving foreign fighters around the area. The threat level was high—even higher than usual—and everyone was on alert as the line of soldiers cut across the night.

The Rangers' translator called out for the men of the house to come out. Soon the assault team entered the compound.

In another part of the compound, separate from the women and children, the Rangers began working to ascertain the identities of the men of the house, as well as to locate any weapons or explosives.

"CST, get over here," a voice called out on the radio. Amber hurried to the spot where six women and nearly a dozen children stood together, about a hundred yards away from the compound. Inside the house the Rangers were doing their work.

"I am Amber," she told the frightened group, looking the women directly in the eyes as Jimmie translated. "I'm an American soldier and we are here to help keep you and your children safe. We will make sure that none of the soldiers come near here."

Slowly she put on her blue nitrile gloves, and softened her tone. "I am going to start by searching you—this just helps us all to stay safe." Then she removed her helmet to make herself look less scary, and make it clear she was a woman, too. One of the children immediately stopped crying, and Amber draped a teal-colored cotton scarf over what she now called her "combat braids": two long, blond plaits of hair that extended from just above her ears to her mid-shoulders. The higher-ups had told the CSTs they should be able to prove quickly and uncontrovertibly that they were female while out on the objective; this would put the Afghan women at ease, which in turn might encourage them to speak more freely and share valuable information. The CSTs had joked about being asked to shed their helmets on target and how insane that would sound to most of the guys they worked with. "Hell, no," one of the Rangers told Amber, "You'd never catch me doing that." But they all agreed that making sure the women saw and understood who they were dealing with mattered most. Amber had turned to the braids as a solution; they allowed her to look feminine without her hair getting caught in her helmet.

Amber pulled Jolly Ranchers, Tootsie Rolls, and Dum Dum lollipops from the pockets of her cargo pants as she searched the children. "Hands out," she said, and a half dozen little hands tentatively reached out to accept the multicolored treats in clear, cellophane wrappers. The little boys were all curious about which candy the other was receiving; the tallest—she guessed he was the oldest—began divvying them up among the other kids. As they stared at the exotic treats, Amber gently patted each one on the shoulder. Once she was done she gave the kids the internationally recognized gesture of success: a hearty high-five. No one expected the kids to be carrying weapons, but they certainly could be given things to hold by men in their family who might think they were an ideal place to store whatever they didn't want found.

The women were watching Amber carefully, and soon realized she was not there to harm them or their children. So far she had stayed true to her word and kept the men at bay. One began speaking quietly.

"The Taliban are all over the village," she said. "They hide up in the mountain and they are always coming down here to make us give them food and a place to stay. They know you guys come in here, but they also know you leave. And so do we."

Amber was taking notes as the kids tugged at her Crye top, peppering her with questions in Pashto. Jimmie kept up a constant patter of translation, and Amber got to the point, asking about the men in the village and what they were up to.

Soon she was interrupted by a Ranger on the radio: "CST, what is the count?"

"Five men, six women, twelve kids," she replied. The women had explained to Amber who was there at their home that night, and now Amber shared her tally of the total number of adults and kids gathered at the compound. The women and kids stood there with her. The Rangers should have found five men inside.

"Are you sure?" he asked. "Check your count again."

Amber turned back to the women, and through Jimmie confirmed the number.

"Yes," she said, "I'm sure."

"CST, check again," she heard the Ranger leader say. There was a tone of urgency in his voice.

Amber was frustrated, but figured there had to be a reason. She and Jimmie went back over what the women had told them. The number of men was definitely five.

"Confirmed. Five, it is five men, six women, twelve kids."

On the other side of the compound, the Rangers now realized they had a serious problem: they saw only four men in front of them, all of whom had now been removed from the house and brought to an area outside for questioning. The CST had given them a different number. Where the hell was the fifth? In recent months this Ranger unit had faced a series of barricaded shooters, gunmen who were hidden inside a house and would start mowing down American and Afghan troops the moment they entered. Everyone was quietly tense, wondering if a fifth man was about to let loose on them.

Finally one of the four men confessed that there was indeed another man inside. A Ranger stealthily approached the front entrance and rolled a flash bang through the door, in hopes of drawing the insurgent out of his hiding spot without having to open fire. All the rules said they had to try this first, before resorting to firepower. A bolt of light flashed after the explosion, and smoke filled the room.

Nothing.

"Okay," Amber heard through the voice in her headset. "Send in the canine."

Another enabler, this one a professional dog handler, led a large dog wearing a harness to the entrance of the compound and gave a command that sent the dog lurching into the house. This much-loved animal had years of special training and service under his collar. His specialty was sniffing out explosives and finding hidden enemy combatants, and he was one of a long line of dogs that have worked overseas with America's armed forces.

The United States military officially began using canines in World War I and by World War II more than four hundred scout dogs were taking part in combat patrols, finding and hunting the enemy. After Pearl Harbor, a group of dog breeders formed "Dogs for Defense," with the goal of building a well-trained canine force in the event America went to war. Come Korea, roughly 1,500 canines performed guard duty with the Army while others joined patrols. During Vietnam, with its close-quarters combat in treacherous terrain and tropical climes, dogs were once again called into action: around four thousand joined patrols to hunt for weapons and enemies, and served duty on army bases, especially at night when soldiers were most vulnerable to attack. But many of the dogs that served alongside U.S. soldiers never made it home; some were euthanized and others abandoned in Vietnam once troops pulled out. After 9/11, however, the need for dogs on the battlefield became acute once more and thousands deployed. This time Robby's Law, named for a military dog that was euthanized when he no longer had the strength to serve, ensured that American soldiers who wanted to adopt the loyal dogs they handled could do so, as could other American families stateside. By the end of the first decade of the Iraq and Afghanistan wars, military working dogs had served in Afghanistan as bomb detectors, de-miners, people finders, scouts, sentries, and therapy providers at bases all across the country. In 2010 alone, military dog teams found more than twelve thousand pounds of explosives in Afghanistan, according to the military. Along with their handlers, some of the dogs were trained to slide down a rope or jump out of a helicopter. Like their fellow servicemen they had been killed, blown up, and injured by gunfire. For special operations, the dogs' abilities and instincts had become critical assets: a

Belgian Malinois named Cairo had even joined the Navy SEAL raid to capture Osama bin Laden.

Now, with the pressure mounting at the compound in eastern Afghanistan, the agile dog bounded inside. Suddenly Amber heard through her headphones the sound of gunfire. She tried to focus on the conversation she was having with the women, but it was hard to ignore the rapid tat-tat-tat of shots being fired. Jimmie was in the middle of an extended translation when Amber realized the men on the radio were talking about a soldier who was hit. The barricaded shooter opened fire the moment the dog cleared the doorway, and one of the Rangers standing close to the breach had caught a bullet just under the ribs.

Amber heard a call for the medevac. She was still outside the compound, and could see nothing inside its walls, but she knew the situation had turned lethal. Still, she was determined to keep the promise she had made to the women and children to protect them from whatever happened. One of the women was struggling to nestle her baby in her gown, and without thinking about it Amber removed her teal headscarf and handed it over. Despite the gunfire all around them, the mother actually had the presence of mind to thank her. Amber studied the woman's face, now illuminated only by the circle of light from her headlamp. She looked thin, maybe even undernourished, beneath the many layers of dresses and shawls. Amber thought this woman could be around the same age as she—close to thirty—or she could be fifty. There was no way to tell. These women's lives are so hard, she thought.

With her questioning done, Amber tried to pass the difficult minutes that followed in conversation. One of the women talked about the family of the insurgent who lived at the compound and the very regular presence of the Taliban in their neighborhood. "The mountains are full of their men," she said. She described the violence the Taliban soldiers regularly meted out to anyone who cooperated with foreigners. Amber tried to reassure her that the Americans were here to help and only wanted to make the area safe for the local population—families like hers, as well as the Afghan soldiers and U.S. troops who were operating in the area.

The boom of an incoming medevac helicopter interrupted the conversation. It landed around fifty feet from where she and the women and children were huddled, and Amber watched in awe as the pilot glided the enormous machine onto the only patch of even ground that could safely accommodate it. The high mountain faces that surrounded them made flying in the pitch dark treacherous; she couldn't imagine how he managed to find the one tiny rectangle of airspace in which he could safely maneuver to a landing. Technology would help, but years of training, experience, and exceptional skill were what made feats like this possible.

Just then Amber heard the Rangers yelling over the radio to pull the women and children farther back. The shooter was still inside, and they were not about to see any more Americans shot or killed that night.

By now hours had passed since they first landed near the village. Between trekking up and down the insanely steep mountain, reaching the objective, flushing out the shooter, and getting their injured Ranger to safety, they had used up nearly all their limited hours of darkness. Shards of daylight began to lighten the sky. Amber wondered whether they were facing the dreaded "ROD"—remain over day—and hoped they weren't. No one wanted to be there come dawn; the Americans and the Afghans would be juicy prizes in this Taliban stronghold if they were still on that hill when the sun rose. She eyed warily the hills that surrounded them and held her M4 assault rifle even closer.

We'll be Taliban breakfast, Amber thought to herself.

"CST, let's go. *Now!*" the Ranger first sergeant ordered.

Amber looked around at the women and children she had just spent the entire night alongside. They may not have spoken English, but they understood the voice command Amber had just received.

Their safety blanket was about to be taken away. The children began to scream and cry in Pashto. She could feel how scared they were now that the Americans had come and gone and found out about their relative, who happened to be an insurgent dedicated to fighting the foreign forces.

She hoped that her being there had made things less terrible for them, but right now she had to get the hell out of there. She offered her goodbyes, grabbed Jimmie by the sleeve once more, and began running out of the village behind the other soldiers.

As they bounded out of the village, Amber glanced back at the crying family. She wondered what would happen to the young woman who had wrapped her baby in Amber's scarf. Or the small girl with the wide, brown eyes who so loved the Jolly Ranchers? She didn't know and never would. She had done as much as she could. And now it was time to go.

Time had proven to be a formidable enemy. They missed the nighttime window in which a hulking Chinook could safely land and whisk them back to base. It was too risky, so now their only option was to run to the closest forward operating base and catch a ride back.

It was five miles away and a glint of light could be seen in the sky overhead. The platoon was running through the last moments of darkness, praying they could last just a bit longer under the disappearing cover of night, when Amber heard the sound of small arms fire. Bullets started spraying all around them as villagers greeted them with round after round.

Amber kept moving and studied the men in front of her, watching as they switched from a fast sprint to an unpredictable pattern of running and ducking, using buildings for cover. She had never had proper infantry training, only a half-day tutorial in the CST summer course. The Rangers, on the other hand, specialized in this kind of combat evasion and had prepared extensively for precisely this kind of situation. *Guess I am in for some on-the-job training,*

Amber said to herself with a dose of gallows humor. Imitation is the best form of avoiding a fatality, or something like that, she thought.

And so, when the Rangers zigged, Amber zigged; when they zagged, she did the same. She mimicked every movement they made: they looked up and down the street, she looked up and down the street. They "pied" corners—a technique for rounding a corner in a dangerous situation that minimizes exposure to the body—and Amber pied corners, ducking, crouching, using the compound walls for cover without actually touching them. Her mind flashed back to action films where the hero dodges gunfire while running at top speed. She always wondered how they managed to stay alive, and now here she was doing it herself, in daylight no less. It all felt surreal, as if she were trapped on a film set. Only the sounds and the sights were undeniably real. She was glad to see she was keeping up with the Rangers, and surprised by just how fast adrenaline and the desire to avoid getting shot propelled them all forward in all that gear. Even Jimmie was close behind; all the sprints had served him well.

Holy fuck, Amber, she coached herself as they tore through the village. Just do what these guys are doing and *do not* screw up.

She kept running. Do not let it be the girl who gets the bullet.

It wasn't just that Amber didn't want to get shot for her own sake. She knew that if *anyone* got hit right now the entire platoon would have to slow down to carry that soldier out. She didn't want to put anyone at even greater risk than they already were.

Then over the radio she heard one of the leaders congratulate the unit for their part in making the "Mogadishu Mile." It was a tribute to the Rangers who got pinned down on the streets of the Somali capital city in the Black Hawk Down incident. I gotta hand it to 'em, Amber thought. These guys don't lose their sense of humor even under fire.

At long last they reached their destination: an American FOB, or forward operating base, where a helicopter could safely land and carry them home. Amber thought the noise of the gate creaking open might just be the happiest sound she had ever heard.

It wasn't long before she was strapped into a noisy helicopter, the air filled with the smell of sweat mixed with gasoline, dust, and the gun oil CLP. Basking in a moment of pure relief, Amber realized she was ravenous. She promised herself she would always remember to bring a snack on future missions. Then she looked around at all those fighters, the guys she had dreamed of joining, and felt pure joy.

I have gone cliff diving, executed FBI search warrants to drug-dealing gang members, jumped out of planes, she told herself. But nothing matches this high. She imagined she could stay up for two more days if she had to. Going out to get bad men who were killing innocents and fellow soldiers and then living to tell the tale—well, making it to the other side of all that was a drug in itself, and Amber was sure that nothing else, ever, could match it.

Man, these mountains are majestic, Amber thought as the helicopter lifted them off the ground and over the trees that had, hours earlier, held so much gloom and terror. The sun rose in streaks of brilliant orange and red to greet them.

An hour later, back on base, she sat eating a microwaved s'more and listening to the team debrief the mission: what they had done right, what they had done wrong, the information they had gathered. What they needed to do better next time.

"Oh, yeah, hey, CST, good job out there," the Ranger who led the brief remarked. "You corroborated the fact that we were missing somebody."

In that moment she felt part of the team. Even if she still had a lot to learn on the job, which she did, she had contributed to the mission. And she had taken fire without crapping herself.

I love this job, she thought as she collapsed into bed that morning.

12

Making a Difference

★ ★ ★

There," the CST pointed. "There he is."

Sarah Waldman, MP and former Girl Scout who loved sewing as much as survival training, stood before a cluster of surveillance monitors at the operations center. She was pointing to a blurry dot on the screen, an insurgent called "Hamidullah" whom the Rangers had been watching on-screen for more than a dozen hours. Her job was to serve as a second pair of eyes during the daylong surveillance, a backup to the officers and team members whose duty it was to watch every bit of footage coming in. The fact that a Ranger leader had given her this assignment was a backhanded compliment: the monitoring work was tedious and hard on the eyes, but it was undoubtedly important. Sarah was proud to have been asked, and for hours had been focusing intently on the monitor.

In the last few weeks Sarah had swung between epic frustration and sublime fulfillment with her new role. Some nights the Ranger forces brought her out on mission and put her to work; those nights she loved. Other nights they would tell her there was no room on the helicopter or they didn't need her; those nights she loathed. She spent the down nights strategizing with Leda about how best to argue her case to the platoon's commanders.

"Give it time," Leda advised. "CST is entirely new for these guys; let them see what you can do and let your work speak for itself."

Sitting and doing *nothing* while her team went on mission was frustrating, but Sarah knew Leda was right.

All over Afghanistan the U.S. military's counterterrorism teams rely on technology to verify and amplify the intelligence gathered and help them "see" what is happening on the ground. Via satellites, balloons, manned and unmanned aircraft, the last decade of warfare has witnessed an explosive growth of visual sensors, "eyes in the skies" that offer a window on sites the American military could not otherwise observe. *Air Force* magazine called the new intelligence-surveillance-reconnaissance—ISR—"a revolution" that's changing the way war works by bringing superior technology to the battlefield in ever-more-real time. Or, as General McChrystal's intelligence chief wrote in 2008, "airborne ISR has become critical to this war because it offers persistent and low-visibility observation of the enemy as well as an ability to detect, identify, and track him" in places where foes can easily "camouflage" themselves among civilians. This revolution began in Bosnia, but came into its own in the years following the initial invasions into Afghanistan and Iraq; by the time CST boots hit the ground in Afghanistan, its impact was visible all across the country. The presence of the sensors lowered the number of casualties by allowing the military to stop attacks before they could occur. They also allowed commanders to get a better sense of where and how the insurgents were operating so when they did pursue them, they could minimize the risks to innocents.

In the JOC, teams of specialists working with the Rangers had been watching Hamidullah most of the day as he got on and off his motorcycle, making his rounds throughout the village, traveling from stop to stop to meet with his contacts. Intel folks understood he was a central figure in a plot to bomb a target in a nearby town center—a high-visibility attack designed to strike a crowded location at a busy time of day and terrify as many as possible. The goal of Sarah's commanders was to stop him before he struck.

Sarah carefully kept her eye on the blurry figure as it moved through the crowded streets. Finally, she saw Hamidullah stop before one of the biggest and most impressive compounds in the area. The building was built in Alexandrian style and boasted fourteen-foot walls with high towers rising from every corner. The house looked sturdier and more expensive than most in the area, as though it had been constructed from cement, usually imported from Pakistan, rather than the dirt or thatch that covered most houses in the insurgency-controlled rural areas. Most of those homes proved vulnerable to the harsh extremes of the Afghanistan climate, and looked like they might easily give way during even a modest storm. Like many of the compounds in the area, this one housed several extended families behind thick walls that offered privacy by making the house impossible to see from the outside. Inside, a network of narrow lanes connected one home to another, and a series of spacious courtyards provided areas for children to play and women to socialize. The families frequently consisted of one man with multiple wives and many more children, plus assorted visitors. This meant there might be three, four, or five men at home at once, along with at least three times as many women and children.

Minutes ticked by and Hamidullah stood by the door. On the other side of the wall, Sarah could see what appeared to be children playing. Then another figure came out and quickly returned inside, bringing the little ones with him. The children came back out and an adult brought them back inside again. She watched as Hamidullah rolled his motorcycle down the road by the handlebars to the entrance of what looked like a guesthouse and covered it with a sheet. A door opened and he quickly disappeared from sight.

Having confirmed the insurgent's presence in the compound, a team of Rangers filed onto their helicopters that night. Sarah initially worried she would be held back, since he was thought to be armed and official guidance from the higher-ups required that a CST remain on base if there was arduous terrain or an imminent threat of "contact"—meaning getting fired at or shot. But she had seen the compound Hamidullah entered and so had the Rangers. Kids lived there, which meant women nearly certainly did as well. Her services would be useful. Sarah, like all the CSTs, understood that contact could come at any time on any night, on any mission—they were *never* safe, and they accepted that. They had come to Afghanistan to do a job, not to be protected from the hazards of the work. This time, she was asked to join the operation.

She now found herself running off the bird with members of the Ranger platoon and walking toward the very same walls the insurgent had recently passed through. Once they reached their destination she waited for the assault team to do its work.

From a hundred feet back she watched as the Rangers cleared the compound and entered the guesthouse. The U.S. soldiers and their Afghan counterparts moved from room to room, silently hunting for explosives, weapons, and intelligence items.

"CST," she finally heard over the radio. "We need you here." Sarah and her interpreter, Wazhma, moved inside the compound to the living area and found a woman and children huddled together, nervously watching every move of the men who had summoned her in. Sarah could feel their terror.

She began by addressing the only adult in the room, who turned out to be the woman of the house, Masuda. She sat in the middle of the richly decorated room, surrounded by her seven children. Wine-colored tapestries hung on the walls and the carpets were freshly washed and well tended. She wore a dress with elaborate beading and embroidery running through the fabric. As someone who grew up making blankets and pillowcases, Sarah could appreciate the effort such handwork required. The crisp, loose-fitting gown looked new, not at all like the fading, threadbare dresses covered with old woolen shawls she was accustomed to seeing here in one of the most rural parts of the country. Masuda looked as if she wouldn't appear out of place in one of Afghanistan's heavily crowded and rapidly modernizing cities.

Sarah closed the doors to the room so none of the men could see inside, and began speaking in quiet tones, in hopes of calming everyone and persuading them that she would do all she could to keep them safe. She promised that no one would enter or be able to hear their conversation, and she begged the woman to speak freely. The children quieted down and Masuda began to tell her story.

This man you are looking for, she said, *invaded our home today. He began banging on our gate this afternoon and demanding that my husband let him in. My husband didn't answer for a while because he wanted the man to go away, but then the man shouted that he carried guns and explosives and that if my husband didn't allow him in our home he would simply blow up the door and kill everyone inside.*

The only sound in the room came from one of the older boys, who was sniffling loudly between bouts of tears.

Finally my husband had to let him in. What were we going to do otherwise? So he came into our house and demanded that we feed him. We prepared dinner for him—I made everything we had so that he would be full and then leave our house—and served him in the main house, because he insisted. But he wouldn't leave even after my husband pleaded with him to go. And then you came.

Sarah asked Wazhma to stand watch and left the room to confer with the Rangers. She and her fellow CSTs had heard this story of the "unknown intruder" frequently, and many times the facts proved it false. But tonight, Sarah thought, this woman's story added up. She learned that the Rangers had quickly identified Hamidullah by the bounty of guns, ammo, and grenades he wore strapped to his person. The only question was whether the other man present had been acting as his accomplice. Sarah conveyed to the Rangers everything she had learned from Masuda, explaining how the entire family had been held hostage for much of the day. Her account backed up the intel the Rangers had gathered, and it all led to the same conclusion: Masuda's husband had nothing to do with the insurgency and no connection to the would-be attacker. They just happened to live in the wrong place at the wrong time.

Sarah returned to the room with the tapestries to reassure the family that everything would be okay.

Finally relaxed for the first time that evening, Masuda stroked the arm of one of her sons, who was clutching a doll that Wazhma had given him. She described how a Taliban-allied network was running rampant throughout the region. Her husband made his money as a contractor for the Afghan government, which meant he earned coveted dollars that came from the Americans. This association with well-funded foreigners meant she lived with the constant fear that her home and family members would be a target. Sarah and Wazhma sat quietly speaking with her and the children until a soldier's voice crackled through the radio.

"CST, time to move!" As she filed out of the compound behind the Ranger unit in the courtyard Sarah saw Hamidullah. She thought of all her fellow soldiers who had been injured and killed in her two months on the ground at the hands of men like this one. Sarah and Wazhma then heard a voice come through Hamidullah's radio. It was now reaching very different listeners than the men on the other end of the connection expected.

"Where is Hamidullah?" the voice called out. Sarah knew enough rudimentary Pashto to understand.

Silence.

"Hamidullah, where are you?" came a second voice.

"He's not there," said a third man.

Finally one of the Afghan interpreters had had enough.

"Hey, Taliban: don't you worry about Hamidullah," the translator said, interrupting their conversation. "We got your guy."

The entire crew ran even faster than normal back to the helicopters, knowing they could still get blown up anytime on the way home. They called for air support to stand guard on the way out to protect them as they ran to the security of their lift back to their base. Sarah found the roaring of the bird's engines oddly comforting: a soothing white noise against which she could empty her thoughts.

Staring at the insurgent, Sarah wondered about the endlessness of it all, and the barbarity. If this man and his brethren had found the Americans before they captured him he would have beheaded them all and posted the video on YouTube for all the world to see. She had heard the voices of his fellow insurgents on the radio, men who no doubt were already forging plans for their next attack. She hoped Masuda and her children would stay safe.

In a few days, Sarah would turn twenty-four in this remote valley of Afghanistan. Her birthday would also mark the tenth anniversary of Operation Enduring Freedom, the official name for the military campaign that began in October 2001, weeks after the 9/11 attacks. Back in those dark days, Sarah sat with her father on the steps leading into their kitchen watching the TV blare news of the fight. She knew she would always remember the day America went to war, because in the middle of it her mother entered the room carrying a big yellow ice cream cake with a smiley face on it and belted out "Happy Birthday" to her girl. Now, ten years later, she was living in a spare outpost on the front lines of that very same war with a team that was tracking down insurgents. Instead of ice cream with her family she would share a hot chai and a CrossFit workout with her CST partner Lori. She wasn't complaining; she had chosen to be there. But life here was so different, and few back home could understand just how, or why.

She wondered where she would be next year. Would *she* make it to twenty-five? Sarah had told her mother little about what she was doing, but enough for her to understand its gravity and seriousness, and to be prepared in case something happened. Back in New York, Sarah's mother was composing a note for her daughter.

At 3:31 am they placed you, a purplish pink beautiful baby girl with dark hair on my belly. Daddy cut your cord and set you free to the outside world. What a magic, miraculous moment your birth was. As I was holding you and being wheeled to recovery, I was in awe of this new chapter of my life. I remember asking God to help me. I put you into His hands. Now more than ever, when I get scared or concerned about you, I think back to that moment. I think of God holding and keeping you safe because I can't. It gives me a sense of peace and calm.

You have made me the happiest mother on earth. Even though I can't give you a birthday hug, I know you can feel it in your heart as I can feel it in mine.

Continue to do the good work you have been doing on your missions. You are making a difference.

Back in Kandahar, Ashley too had just celebrated her birthday. She, Lane, and their bunkmate Meredith, who had first shown them around their rooms, had grabbed a couple of spoons and shared a Funfetti "cake in a jar" with frosting that Meredith's younger sister had sent from Illinois. Then they smoked a hookah in their room.

"It was definitely a memorable twenty-fourth," Ashley told the newly arrived Leda with a smile.

Having recovered in record time from the leg injury she had sustained in pre-mission training, Leda resumed her duties as officer in charge (OIC) in September, and traveled to Kandahar as part of her whirlwind tour of all the CST outposts. Her first order of business was to visit each one of her teams in person to make sure that everyone had what she needed.

By October, the CSTs had been in Afghanistan for almost three months and, as one officer commented, "the training wheels were off." It was a more seasoned group of soldiers, and Leda's role had shifted from helping them get ready for war to helping them succeed in it. While she had been back in the United States recuperating, she had tracked them closely by email and online and had coached some of them through the rough patches of integrating into their teams; now she was witnessing them in action, and she was gratified, if unsurprised, to learn about their successes.

Leda knew that some of the CSTs felt the burden of isolation at their remote outposts. They missed the camaraderie of the summer when they all lived together and could gather as a group for meals in the dining hall, joke around, or discuss tactics. To replace that physical camaraderie, Leda turned to technology: in addition to her weekly email report, the one that she sent to JSOC leaders that cataloged what they did, learned, and located each night, she created a second, internal-only version in which the CSTs shared moments only they would understand, from ordering Spanx bodywear so uniform bottoms slid on more easily to getting caught peeing or falling into a wadi (dry riverbed) while out on mission surrounded by a team of Ranger men. Leda also launched a series of regular video teleconferences for the CSTs so they could interact with one another while sharing the "best practices" they developed on the job as well as all the gory details of their battlefield mishaps. She knew that a key aspect of her job was to keep the team unified and morale high despite the physical distances between them.

Leda had long been a student of leadership strategies, studying everything from neurolinguistics to the work of Jim Collins and Tony Robbins. She viewed leadership in this kind of high-stress, high-intensity, high-performance environment as being all about caring for, supporting, and leading the whole person, not just his or her soldier self. The women, in turn, called on Leda for everything, small or large. When they hankered for Honey Nut Cheerios and the DFAC didn't have any, Leda delivered. And when a young male officer began making uninvited visits to Amber at her base, it was Leda she confided in. Amber never saw the man again.

They had never felt so taken care of in their lives.

Throughout August and September, Leda stayed in close touch with Ashley by email and phone. The North Carolina Guardswoman had always been special to Leda, ever since the first days at the Landmark Inn when Ashley had confided her fears that her quiet shyness might somehow hinder her potential. From the moment they met at Assessment and Selection Leda was confident this officer would come into her own at war, but she hoped that her breaking-in period wouldn't be any longer or more awkward than it had to be. Now she had come to Kandahar to see for herself how her younger friend and teammate was faring. And what she saw surprised her.

Leda's first inkling that Ashley was fitting in perfectly well came the morning she arrived. Standing in the barracks door she watched Ashley roll out of bed around noon, hair scraggly, T-shirt wrinkled, and black sweatpants bunched up around her shins. She looked like everyone else around her, drowning in her hoody and bleary-eyed from the rhythms of the nocturnal life that had become her new normal. She welcomed Leda with a warm embrace and in no time began describing in precise detail the previous night's mission.

Gone was the shy second lieutenant who had trouble addressing a group of Ranger men. In her place was an increasingly assertive, recently promoted first lieutenant who could comfortably and effectively communicate through an interpreter with Afghan women in the middle of a combat mission while searching for hidden insurgents and intel. Not only that: Ashley was eager to share with her OIC what she was learning each night and how it fit into the larger effort to end the war and make Afghanistan safer.

She's actually beaming, Leda thought as Ashley walked her through the evening's pre-mission brief. It seemed incredible to Leda that after just eight weeks Ashley's biggest concern was that her platoon leader would think she was too injured to go out that night. She had Band-Aids on her legs to cover rope-climbing burns earned at the gym. Leda assured her that no one would notice. "Those guys all have their own nicks to tend to," she said. "Keep the Band-Aids on and let your legs heal while they can."

More gratifying were the reports she was receiving from Rangers around camp who said Ashley had proven tactically efficient and increasingly adept at getting what was needed each night. Just as Jason had predicted, his wife's artless kindness and professionalism—boosted by Nadia's experience and guidance—had proven to be powerful in winning over both the men she worked with and the women and children she met each night.

Satisfied with what she saw and heard from the CST and the men she supported, Leda asked Ashley what her thoughts were about the future. With six months left in Afghanistan, Leda wanted all her soldiers to begin thinking about what they wanted to do next—and about how their OIC could help. Earlier that day she had put the same question to Anne, who replied that all she wanted was to keep doing CST missions as long as she could. Period.

But Ashley was contemplating a different future. She still wanted to become a physician's assistant (PA); the only question that remained was where she would go and what program would accept her. She also needed to find out where Jason would be stationed next and if he could remain at Fort Bragg, as she very much hoped, so she could try to find a job with JSOC after her deployment ended. Leda had once mentioned the possibility of finding a civilian role as a PA within the special operations community and after working with the Rangers, Ashley loved that idea even more. It had been a privilege to serve with special operations, and she also was keen to remain in the little house with the yellow kitchen in Fayetteville. She was already training for a marathon she planned to run in Ohio once her deployment was over. Leda sensed that the future was very much on her mind.

"There's one other thing," Ashley added.

"I think I want to be a mom," she said. Leda noticed the shift in tone from confident to nearly embarrassed as Ashley uttered the word *mom*. She guessed Ashley didn't want her hard-charging OIC to think less of her because she wanted to focus on family after this was all done.

"Ash, why are you hesitating? Were you nervous about telling me that?" Leda asked. "You want to be a mom? Of course I think that's great. Hell, yeah, I think that is terrific!"

Leda knew that Ashley had been poring over kinesiology books in the broom closet office whenever she wasn't on mission or asleep, and now said that if Ashley was serious about applying to physician's assistant school she could start her family and her studies at the same time and keep working within the special operations community. Leda mentioned several people she knew who would be helpful to Ashley as she thought through her job options and courses of study.

"Really? You think I could still contribute to this work and be a mom?" Ashley asked. She looked thrilled, and surprised.

"Definitely," Leda said. "You can do it all, Ash. You are going to be a phenomenal mom." Leda knew that the perception of special operations was of hard-fighting warriors who lived out of duffle bags and never saw their families. But many of the civilians who supported them had careers that were far more family-friendly. Leda wanted to make sure Ashley understood that she didn't have to deploy herself to support the men whose work she so respected. She could contribute in other ways *and* achieve her personal goals.

But for all her focus on a future family with Jason, Ashley still hadn't told her own family in Ohio exactly what she was doing in Afghanistan. Beyond her conversation with Josh on the fishing boat, Ashley had left them largely in the dark. Anne, who went out on her own missions every night, decided to approach her partner about the wisdom of that decision one early afternoon. Lane had moved a month earlier to another part of Afghanistan to work with another team, and it was now just the two of them in Kandahar.

"I know that you don't want to hear this," Anne began. Bad weather had kept the teams grounded and the two soldiers were running around the base before hunkering down for a CrossFit workout. "But you really might want to think about telling your family what you're doing. Or at least let Josh or Jason tell them about this job."

Anne knew how upset Mr. White would be; Ashley had told

her, only half in jest, that her dad would have taken Jason's baseball bat and broken her knees to stop her from leaving if he had understood the reality of her assignment. Anne didn't want to overstep her boundaries; the nature of their work created an almost instant bond, but they had only known each other for seven months, and Anne was now raising one of the most deeply personal questions a soldier faces. Still, it was one thing for Ashley to choose not to tell her mom and dad about her work before coming to Kandahar and understanding the daily realities of the role. It was another thing now that she knew the risks.

"This is a bad area; it's incredibly dangerous," Anne said. "It's not impossible to imagine that one of us might not make it home, or might go home without all our parts."

Ashley nodded, her eyes on her feet, pounding the pavement. "I know," she replied. "I know I should. I will."

Ashley spoke with her parents regularly, calling them faithfully every Sunday night, which was afternoon in Ohio. Her camp had a common area with computers and phones the soldiers could use to reach family and friends back home; it was one of the Army's strategies for boosting morale among the troops. Her parents would pass the phone back and forth, sitting in their comfy loungers facing the television in the ranch house in Marlboro. The conversations always began with Ashley peppering her parents with questions about everything and everyone in their hometown, and thanking her mom for the delicious cookies and for all the coffee and bread mixes. But whenever Bob or Debbie asked her about her work she swiftly changed the subject. As they understood it, she was part of some special team and she worked at a hospital in Kandahar. That was it.

Not long after her conversation with Anne, Ashley called her twin sister, Brittany. They had shared everything for twenty-four years and it felt strange now that thousands of miles separated them. They used email and Facebook to stay connected, but when they wanted to speak about something important—a situation they were going through or a challenge they wanted to tackle—Ashley would head to the common room and call her sister.

"Hello?" Brittany whispered into her handset. It was 2 a.m. in Ohio and she was just leaving a patient's room at the end of her shift as a neurology unit nurse at the local hospital. Brittany never took personal calls during her shift, but this was different; her sister was calling from Afghanistan. She popped into a patient's bathroom to answer her phone in a whisper; the sisters agreed to speak in an hour, when Brittany was on her way home and could have an uninterrupted conversation.

Later, Ashley thanked Brittany for sending her the photos from her first fitness and figure competition, a sport that combines female bodybuilding with gymnastics and emphasizes taut muscles rather than bulging, gigantic ones. Brittany had won the top spot her first time out. Ashley, of course, was unsurprised.

"You looked incredible!" Ashley said, and told her she showed the pictures to her Ranger buddies. "You have some serious admirers over here; they were all talking about you."

Sounding like the older sister she wasn't, she told Brittany how proud she was of her, and made her promise to keep up her fitness routines and do more shows.

Brittany promised, and described the rigors of her diet and workout regimen, which sounded nearly as strict and disciplined as Ashley's. The competitions required participants to be in razor-sharp shape and to perform choreographed routines to show off their finely toned physiques. Between her nursing job, her fitness and figure work, and preparations for a graduate program in leadership and management, Brittany was working around the clock, not unlike her sister.

Before she left for Afghanistan Ashley had mentioned to Brittany that she had won a competition of sorts, and had been selected for some elite assignment along with a group of extremely impressive women: some had served as FBI interrogators, others had gone to war three times already. Still others had won Bronze Star Medals for Valor. She had confessed then that she was intimidated by them. Now she talked to Brittany about her teammates with the fondness of the close friends and equals they had become. She told her about her conversation with Leda and how much support she had offered her. She felt certain about wanting to become a physician's assistant, she said, even though she wasn't sure she was "smart enough" for all the exams and advanced study that lay ahead. Brittany interrupted her sister and said she knew Ashley would be able to handle whatever came. "You always do, Ash, you just gut it out and work harder than everyone else. You'll ace the exams."

"You remind me so much of Leda, my OIC," Ashley said. "She's athletic and outgoing and beautiful just like you. And a huge cheerleader for all of us. I've been so lucky to have her support these last few months. You'll have to meet her when I get back."

Ashley paused.

"I can't wait to see you when I get back, sissy. Love you."

"Good night."

Brittany by now had reached her house. She would grab a few hours of rest, head over to lift weights at the gym, then make her way back to the hospital.

Brittany knew she would have to tell her parents about the call. She felt certain they'd want her to replay every moment of the almost normal conversation she had shared in the middle of a war with her best friend and closest confidante.

On the other side of the world, Ashley was off to the chow hall with Anne for her evening's "breakfast," then due in the briefing room to find out the details of her team's mission that night.

13

The Lies of War

★ ★ ★

A few hundred miles to Ashley's north not long afterward, Kate found herself in the middle of a hell of a night.

"Is there anyone inside?" Kate asked a middle-aged Afghan woman who was standing in the huddle of women and children to the left of the compound. "Anyone still in the house?" Her nineteen-year-old interpreter, an Afghan-American from the Bronx who went by the nickname "Angel," relayed the question.

The mission had started off a mess and gotten worse. Kate's team was seeking a fighter who had already evaded their grasp several times. This was the second compound they had targeted that evening and since it was his own home, they believed he was likely to be hiding out there.

Two women and several children streamed out of the house as soon as the American and Afghan forces arrived, but so far no one was talking. Kate's job was to protect the women she was speaking to while getting the information that would assist and protect the men with whom she served. *Quickly.*

The Afghan forces with her special ops team had taken the lead in tonight's mission. This was part of a broader push to have Afghan security forces lead their country's war as the Americans began their long-planned withdrawal. Several Afghan soldiers were now inside the compound hunting for the man their intel told them was a key Taliban fighter in the region.

"Is there anyone inside?" Kate repeated.

The Afghan woman's face remained expressionless. "She says there is no one in there," Angel told Kate.

Kate, Angel, and the two women stood about a dozen feet from the breach. Around them sat a cluster of children, ranging in age from infant to teenager. Kate kept thinking it didn't make sense. This guy *had* to be there. Then again, he had known enough to throw them off the trail earlier that night. Maybe he was just wasting their time some more.

And then, just a second later, came a deafening explosion, near enough to rattle the ground on which they stood.

"CST, get those women out of here."

Kate heard the command over the radio a moment after the explosion. Then came the *pop-pop-pop-pop* of gun fire in a stream of percussion.

"Get up, everyone, let's go, let's go!" Kate spoke the words in English quietly but firmly and seconds later she heard them again in Angel's Pashto translation. She pointed in the direction of a building that was fifty feet away, motioning Angel to move quickly. "Get them to that building to the right, at the corner!" Kate told her. They needed to get to the other side of the cement wall, just outside the compound. That should be far enough to keep them out of the firefight *and* within the line of sight so she could monitor what was happening and ensure that she and Angel didn't get left behind when the mission ended.

"Let's go, come on!" Angel said to the two women. She grabbed the hands of two children, one on each side, and took off running for the cover of the building. Meanwhile, the Afghan and American soldiers were returning the heavy fire that was coming from the compound. Kate and Angel had worked together long enough that the young terp knew to move everyone to shelter if shots erupted and things got hot. Kate took the rear to make sure no women or children got left behind in the chaos.

As she directed Angel, Kate scooped up a small baby, barefoot and crying. She threw the little guy over her left shoulder and took off running as the sound of gunfire grew louder behind her. Using her right arm she grabbed the hand of a small girl and drew her close to her body.

"Stay with me, stay with me!" Kate urged, hoping the child would trust and understand her movements even if she didn't understand her words.

Suddenly Kate felt the jagged terrain take hold of her left foot. She began tumbling forward as one of her boots got trapped in a deep hole she hadn't detected through the green film of her night-vision goggles.

The baby, Kate thought. Instinctively she held him tight against her chest as the momentum of her fall sent her spinning into a diving, forward roll. She released the little girl's hand just in time to keep her from falling, too.

A second later Kate lay on her back with the baby tucked up against her body armor. He hadn't moved despite the somersault and was now just looking at her wide-eyed and silent.

Kate felt the baby's warm breath on her neck, looked up at the twinkling stars above, and heard the rat-a-tat-tat of gunfire around her, now maybe three dozen feet away.

What the fuck is my job right now? she asked herself as she hugged the baby tight and again took the hand of the little girl who was standing nearby. This is crazy.

She jumped up, the two children in tow once more, and took off at a brisk trot for the building where Angel waited for her with the adult women and the other children.

"Do we have everyone?" Kate began counting all the women and children. They had indeed managed to move all of them to safety— even if she had eaten it in front of all of them on the way there.

Kate now looked at the middle-aged woman, the one who had told her there was no one inside. She had lied right to her face, sending the Afghan forces into a house where a shooter was lying in wait. The firefight Kate had heard—and shepherded the women and children away from —had been started by this woman's husband.

Now Kate heard over the radio that someone had been hit. She was about to start questioning the woman about who else was inside when an Afghan soldier ran over to where they stood.

"You lied!" the soldier screamed at the Afghan woman. "You said there was nobody in there!" He stood only a few feet from her and his fury poured forth in an avalanche of rage. "You just got two Afghans shot. You didn't get *Americans* hurt. You only killed Afghans. *Your own people.*"

The woman was not about to give him the satisfaction of tears, but her face now showed the emotion of someone who understood that her own husband, the man who started this gunfight, was unlikely to survive the night.

Kate found a secure corner of level ground for the little group, but the uneven terrain meant that flat space was in high demand. A medevac helicopter sent to tend to the wounded Afghan soldiers descended not far from where they sat. The women and children all pressed up tight against the building to give the medics space to run in and get the injured soldiers out of the building.

A few minutes later two stretchers passed within feet of where they all sat. One Afghan soldier lay silent and motionless as his brothers-in-arms carried him to the awaiting Chinook. The next stretcher passed by, even closer. Kate heard the moans of the second Afghan soldier, who was writhing from the agony of his wounds.

With nothing to do now but wait, Kate replayed in her mind that evening's mission. A few nights earlier another Afghan woman had told her immediately that the American and Afghan team had come to the wrong compound. Her information led them directly to the correct house, where they found the insurgent they sought.

Tonight the opposite had happened, with disastrous consequences.

As she stood with her team awaiting the helicopter that would carry them back to base, Kate kept thinking about the men on the stretcher and whether there was anything she could have done to protect them, and keep them alive. She respected their courage, their commitment to serving their country. And now one of them was dead.

At last she heard the *whoosh* of the arriving helicopter, an almost spiritual sound as the whirring rotors pierced the twilight's silence. In that moment of landing, they were all vulnerable to rocket-propelled grenades and small arms fire, and right on the verge of the adrenaline rush that came with running onto the bird as quickly as possible through a nearly blinding cyclone of kicked-up dust and dirt. In an instant she took off with Angel right behind her.

Kate didn't want to think every woman she met was covering for a hidden shooter. But she would never forget that night's lesson and the life it had cost.

III

Last Roll Call

14

The First Death

★ ★ ★

Hey, Nadia," Ashley said into her cell phone, "can you be back here in twenty minutes?"

Nadia was at a NATO-sponsored barbecue on the other side of Kandahar Airfield base and had been on the verge of biting into a juicy chicken kabob when the phone rang. It was around 10 p.m. and she was enjoying a lovely evening under sparkling stars, practicing her Spanish with an American soldier from New York over a traditional Afghan meal of rice, naan bread, and meat kebabs. It was a rare night off for her, and on such evenings she always took the opportunity to visit with the other interpreters or meet soldiers from another culture. She much preferred going out and talking with interesting people to sitting in her bunk and watching *How I Met Your Mother* or *The Office* on a laptop with the other girls. While Ashley and her teammates ate, slept, and dreamt their work, rarely leaving their section of the base, Nadia loved to explore the global village of men and women who had converged on Kandahar from every corner of the world.

"Um," she paused for a moment, "you know I am not actually cleared by the doctor to go out yet, right?"

Even as she said it Nadia wondered why she had bothered to object. If Ashley needed her to go, she knew she would make it work. After all, she had been working with Ashley the night she hurt her wrist a few weeks earlier. They had run off the helicopter just as they did each night, but a brownout had blinded them as dirt from the helicopter rotors proved more intense than usual. They couldn't see a thing ahead of them or behind. Just as they were sprinting away from the bird Nadia fell right into a ditch and landed on her right hand. She felt the searing pain before noticing that her entire hand was now facing backward. Ashley helped her get up and quickly return to formation; they still had several kilometers to walk. Tears of pain ran down Nadia's cheeks, but she set her jaw and didn't make a sound. She felt grateful that no one could see her in the pitch-black Kandahar night. It was bad enough that Ashley had stopped and helped her to her feet; she didn't want a soldier to catch her crying.

Once they reached their destination Ashley insisted that Nadia see the unit's medic. Only after he had given her a strong dose of Tylenol and a makeshift sling for her busted arm would Ashley let Nadia begin the night's searching and questioning. There had been a lot of women at the compound that evening and Ashley took notes for both of them as Nadia did the translation. Once it was all over, Nadia returned to base respecting Ashley even more than she already did.

Another girl would have been like, *forget it, carry on, when we get back to base we'll deal with your little injury,* she thought. The Afghan-American translators often said that the soldiers they worked with treated them like prostitutes, as if they had to get their money's worth every night. Ashley and her group were different. When it turned out the following day that Nadia had broken her wrist and would need to stay back and rest it for a while, neither Ashley nor Anne complained or gave her a hard time for taking the spill that removed her from action. But still, they were eager to get their terp back into circulation. She was one of the best—a coveted female translator fit enough to keep up with the CSTs and the Rangers—and it always helped to have her there. Nadia's competence and comfort in the local culture made them all feel safer.

Tonight, it looked like Nadia was going to get back to work, even if her cast had come off only a few days before and the doctor hadn't yet given her the official go-ahead. When Ashley asked her to meet her in twenty minutes, Nadia knew that without a doctor's sign-off no one would have questioned her had she said no. But Nadia was ready to do whatever she could for the CSTs, and especially Ashley, one of the most decent people she'd ever known. Heck, for Ashley I'd probably go out on crutches, she thought.

"Okay; no problem. It's fine, I can make it work," Nadia said into the battered cell phone she carried whenever she left the barracks. The war had created a boomlet in Afghanistan's mobile phone industry and phones were easy to get and cheap to use. "See you soon."

Ashley sounded glad to hear her answer. "It should be pretty routine, so don't worry." She explained that the helicopter would most likely land close to the objective that night. No five-mile marches, so no risk to Nadia's wrist. "It doesn't sound like it'll be a long one—we'll be back in no time."

Nadia ended the call, bid her new friends goodbye, and hurried back to her room, balancing a paper plate stacked with chicken kabobs she would share with Ashley and Anne once they got back. She brought enough leftovers to feed some of the guys, too. Surely everyone would be famished by the time they returned to base.

She ran into the ready room and in less than five minutes greeted Ashley, changed into her uniform, and headed out to the bird. Months into her new assignment, Nadia had long since shed her fashion scruples. Her hand-me-down gear hardly helped. Lane often commented on Nadia's lousy equipment—how it looked like it came straight from the landing at Normandy. "Your gear sucks, Nadia," Lane told her the first night they went out. "Let's try to get you some better stuff." The CSTs pitched in where they could: Ashley loaned Nadia a Crye combat top, which had the dual benefit of a snug fit and breathable fabric that helps wick away sweat. Of course, they still hadn't solved her night-vision goggle issue. After she finally got rid of the monocle she had been given a set of night optical devices, or NODs, to attach to her helmet. But the helmet was so old the

NODs wouldn't firmly clip onto it. "I guess your helmet is too ancient to have considered the possibility of night vision," Lane joked weeks earlier. While the nearly state-of-the-art NODs that Ashley and Anne wore attached solidly to their helmets, Nadia's jiggled and wiggled around on her head, which made her fiddle with them endlessly. She was still messing with them that night when Ashley met her near the barracks for the walk to an aging bus that would take them to the tarmac.

"Let's go," Ashley said. She smiled her familiar, reassuring grin. "You look nice!" Nadia still had her makeup on from the barbecue—eyeliner and a strongly defined eyebrow. There had been no time to remove it before heading out. Ashley walked her through the mission plan and briefed her on the intel so they could get what they needed as quickly and effectively as possible once they landed. Then the women boarded the helicopter as usual with the team's leaders, taking their seats toward the front. Nadia psyched herself up for her return to action following her injury, reminding herself how many successful missions she already had behind her. She had been vaguely reassured by Ashley's description of the objective back at the base, and also by the fact that the Rangers hadn't prayed as a team before they left. Nadia had observed that a group prayer always came on nights when the men believed they were facing an especially dangerous task. Otherwise, she knew that most of them prayed as she did, quietly and in their own way, as they headed out on the helicopter.

I hope we come back with something, she said to herself. She may have been a civilian, but she was committed to her part in the fight. On nights when they came up empty and failed to find the insurgents they sought, her ego suffered—she had let her team down. But on successful missions where she played a part in stopping someone before he hurt American soldiers and innocent Afghans, she felt like maybe it was all for a reason.

Her mother never accepted Nadia's desire to serve and remained miserable about her new job from the moment she learned about it to the day her daughter left for Kandahar. "The people are crazy there—even the insects are crazy," she had said, referring to the scorpions she vividly remembered from her childhood. "Don't go, I beg you." But Nadia went anyway. It wasn't long before Afghan women were cursing and spitting at her for working with the Americans, and Nadia realized that her mother might have been right. But she was there, and all she could do was work as hard as she could to do her part in stopping the insurgency. To resentful Afghans who cursed her with their ancient black magic, she simply suggested that their ill wishes would only come back at them. "You have to wish good for people," she would say, and that motto is what she tried to live up to. She always brought along money to help the neediest people she encountered, though she never felt she had brought enough, given the number of children all these women seemed to have. Nadia may have hardened a great deal since arriving in Afghanistan, but she knew she would never be able to forget the wretched poverty and the children who had so few opportunities. Later, when she got back to the humanitarian work she had originally planned on doing in Afghanistan, she would try to do her part to help build schools and maybe clinics. But for now she was on a helicopter preparing to land and begin another mission. She prayed silently for all of her teammates to stay safe.

A few moments later, with the helicopter safely landed, they were on a short run to the compound where a Taliban weapons maker was known to live. Nadia was right behind her CST. She hadn't noticed until that moment just how cut her teammate had become. Ashley and Anne sometimes asked Nadia if she wanted to join them in the gym and practice fast-roping, to which she would routinely smile and politely answer, "Heck, no." But she had been impressed by the gusto with which these soldiers attacked their workouts, and she saw now in Ashley's transformation that the dedication was clearly paying off. Nadia made a mental note to tell Ashley that she looked like G.I. Jane out there. Ashley may have been too modest to talk about herself, but Nadia didn't know a woman in the world who didn't want to hear how great she looked. Even if she was wearing Gore-Tex boots and body armor.

As Ashley had promised, the run hadn't been far, and Nadia was relieved it was over. But all of a sudden she saw the Rangers moving around quickly, not with their usual methodical precision. She stayed close to Ashley, as was their practice, and moved nearer to ask what was going on; Ashley was intently listening to her radio, something translators don't carry. Nadia waited in the tense darkness and watched as the men around her seemed to be moving in fast-forward.

She and Ashley stood on the side of the compound, close to one of the outer walls. The two moved closer to a footbridge that led to the house, then Ashley stopped to speak to Kristoffer Domeij, one of the senior Ranger leaders. His presence on the bird had also reassured Nadia; she knew from seeing him with his team around base, and Ashley said he was much loved by his guys, respected for what he'd seen and done over countless deployments. He was known for his competence and professionalism, but also for his sense of humor, smarts, and big heart. Nadia found his humanity reassuring. Ashley's roommate, artillery officer Tracey Mack, had learned a great deal from Domeij, who was always generous about sharing insights into the job of Joint Terminal Attack Controller (JTAC). His role as a JTAC was to direct combat aircraft that supported Ranger operations, from surveillance to lethal engagement. Kris was now on his fourteenth deployment, a number that filled Ashley with awe and had shocked Nadia when she first heard it. While Ashley stood next to him in quiet but animated conversation, Nadia began to grow antsy in the darkness.

Good Lord, let's pick up the pace, she thought. She felt uncharacteristically impatient; she knew that sometimes missions get jammed up in the fog of a fight and it can take a moment to get everyone back in formation. But there was too much talking already.

Just then all she wanted was to get the night's work done and to get back to her kabob.

She decided to use the time productively and turned around to look for more even ground so she could adjust her NODs and try to get a firm fit. They'll tell us where we need to be in a second, she figured.

Nadia walked a couple of feet toward a patch of grass. It had initially seemed close by, but when she reached the end of a gravelly pathway she realized she had misjudged the distance and the grass was a bit farther away than she had estimated. She turned back to check on Ashley and saw she was in the same place, still talking to the Ranger. She expected she'd be walking toward her in a moment, once they finished conferring about the mission details, so she decided not to stray far. What if she can't find me? Nadia thought. Let me just wait for her here.

She returned her attention to her aging NODs.

And then, from nowhere, came the thundering boom of explosions. It was as if the ground had turned itself upside down and begun shaking.

The blast propelled Nadia some dozen feet into the air and she came down hard, landing on her head, her face now buried in the dirt.

Ashley and Kris Domeij had been standing on a pressure plate that was attached to other plates in a system known as a daisy chain, which is rigged to create multiple explosions when someone steps onto one section. Chris Horns, a young private from Colorado serving his first deployment alongside the veteran Ranger, had also been caught by the blast. The whole grounds had been rigged to light up like a firecracker. But it had been the boot of another team member, stepping onto a plate in another part of the compound, that set off the daisy chain that tore through the night. He had badly injured his foot in the explosion but nevertheless heroically proceeded to clear the building, hobbling on his shattered foot to get people out of the way and prevent any further explosions that might harm anyone else on his team.

Just beyond the compound, Ashley lay still on the ground. She, too, had been sent airborne by the power of the explosion, and several Rangers were hovered over her, wrapping a tourniquet around one of her legs. There were others injured as well, including an Afghan translator. A medic soon ran to Ashley's side and began asking her questions.

"Where are you from?"

"The U.S.A.," Ashley replied.

"What state?"

"Ohio."

Minutes later she was loaded onto a helicopter headed for Kandahar Combat Support Hospital, the biggest on the base. While the helicopter flew through the night a medic worked to give Ashley the care she needed. He tried to stop the bleeding, checked her pulse and blood pressure, tried to keep fluids moving through her system. But her vital signs were dropping.

Nadia, still lying on the patch of grass, heard muted signs of chaos in the background around her, but it sounded miles away. A concussion from the blast had blunted her hearing, and she was struggling through the haze to get her bearings and figure out what had happened.

Her first question, once she was capable of a complete thought: Where's Ashley?

She was alone in the darkness, seemingly far from the others, and her fear was rising.

Oh, my God, they're not going to find me, Nadia thought as the ringing in her ears grew louder. It was pitch black, in the middle of the night, and there she was, lying in the dirt wearing camouflage. The fact that she was a civilian made her feel even more vulnerable, as if there were some invisible list of important military personnel and she was at the bottom of it.

I am never going to get out of here. The Taliban are going to find me here on this soil tomorrow and this village is going to have me for breakfast.

Just then a medic arrived. She hadn't been forgotten after all.

"Are you Nadia, the interpreter?" the medic asked. He rolled her over on her back, so she now faced the star-filled sky.

"Are you Nadia, the interpreter!?" he asked louder this time.

On his third try the sound finally broke through to Nadia's ears. *"Yes, yes!"* she cried.

An Afghan army soldier rushed over and asked what he could do to help; Nadia heard the medic tell him to grab the other end of the stretcher and help him transport her to the helicopter. Nadia knew she was injured, but couldn't tell where or how. Beyond a vague pain in her arm, she couldn't feel where the wound originated. She looked up and saw an injured Ranger and again wondered where her teammate was.

"Where's Ashley?" she asked again. Someone replied she was okay, and then a strong dose of some sort of painkiller took her out of the moment and away from her pain. All she was aware of was the rhythmic thudding sound of the helicopter's rotors.

Kandahar Combat Support Hospital began as a temporary facility run first by the Americans and then, starting in 2006, by Canadian forces. Constructed of plywood that presented a fire risk, the facility was full of dust; it had just eleven inpatient beds, mounted on trestles, the most basic lab facilities and a portable ultrasound machine. Over the next three years, under Canadian leadership, the hospital grew to roughly two dozen beds, three operating rooms, a blood bank, and ultramodern radiography and ultrasound capabilities. Among the staff were highly specialized neurosurgeons, orthopedic surgeons, a maxillofacial surgeon, and mental health experts. The hospital treated NATO patients, Afghan National Security Forces, and civilians, and by 2009 it boasted more than a 95 percent survival rate.

That same year the U.S. Navy assumed control of the combat hospital and its state-of-the-art capabilities grew even further; the expected increase in military operations in the area meant that the hospital had to be prepared for a potential rise in the number of injured reaching its doors. The hospital innovated in trauma care by developing a system in which a team of doctors, nurses, radiologists, surgeons, and staff gathered around each patient and worked together in an "assembly line-like" fashion to deal with their wounds. This strategy was so successful in Kandahar it was later applied to other crisis areas, including Haiti after the 2010 earthquake, and over time was introduced back home in NATO nations.

By the spring of 2010, a highly reinforced brick and mortar building designed by German engineers and built by a Turkish contractor under NATO supervision had replaced the original facility. It was designed to provide the most advanced care in Afghanistan, and opened just before the summer fighting season, which now included a bulked-up American force as a result of the December 2009 surge. The new combat hospital had a blood bank, imaging capabilities of every kind, and surgical, orthopedic, and critical care facilities; it looked like the kind of hospital you might find in the middle of a European city.

Even before the first patients began arriving that night, an advance call had warned the trauma team of the incoming injuries—including a number of "alphas," shorthand to signify the highest-priority soldiers with the most serious wounds. The hospital staff immediately fell into its own formation: trauma team members gathered to wait for the injured while the team leader coordinated care with nurses, medical technicians, anesthesiologists, and surgeons of various specialties who could be activated if needed. Radiologists often worked right there by the bedside, reading images from their patients in real time to help doctors and nurses make the best decisions in the critical minutes and moments they had available. The doctors and nurses stood in the quiet, cool trauma center and knew that their patient bays were about to turn into hell. Mass casualties like this remained a rarity, though since the surge began the hospital had seen a number of serious injuries, many of which resulted from IEDs. A medic stood with her elbows perched on an empty stretcher, staring straight ahead and waiting for the wounded.

When the helicopter landed the EVOC—Emergency Vehicle Operators Course—team was already on the tarmac, ready to move the incoming patients into armored ambulances. They rushed on board to tend to the injured. A nurse on the EVOC team for the first time that night reached a stretcher and then stopped.

There lying among the Ranger wounded was a female soldier.

The nurse tried to keep moving, tried to hide from her colleagues the look of shock she now wore as she and her combat team of EVOC professionals went about their finely synchronized movements, but this professional who had hardened herself to the many horrible things she had seen in this war now encountered something for which she was entirely unprepared: a beautiful young lieutenant on a stretcher fighting for her life.

Everyone in the hospital knew that women were out there on these operations, but they hadn't expected to see one so critically injured as to require their care. The stunned expression on the nurse's face made it clear that this was the first time she had attended to such a gravely injured female soldier.

The helicopter's smell—a mixture of fresh dirt, drying blood, helicopter fuel, and layers of human sweat from the many injured soldiers flying in all at once—was something the EVOC team would never forget. In moments the wounded were in the ambulances and speeding to the trauma bays.

"There's a female!" a medic shouted amid the chaos. Otherwise the choreography at the trauma center followed the usual script, as the ambulance's back doors flew open and a hive of staff burst into action. Ashley lay on the first set of stretchers and was lifted by blue-gloved men; for a moment, she was suspended in air between the black of the sky and the ambulance's glowing red brake lights as the staff placed her on a gurney. As she was rapidly wheeled into the trauma bay a Navy serviceman sidestepped along the gurney as it moved, pressing his hands to Ashley's chest to perform CPR. The blast had shredded parts of her uniform, but the two patches on her right arm remained intact. On top was an American flag. Below it, a rectangular patch with white letters against a black background that spelled out the letters *CST.*

Once inside the trauma team went to work with jaw-set silence. In each bay they drew IV lines, controlled bleeding, checked vitals, and took X-rays. They did everything they could do to find and maintain a heartbeat for each of the wounded. Under the harsh, bright hospital lights the extent of the soldiers' injuries became starkly clear. Ashley was pale from the loss of blood. The explosion had hit her just below the torso.

In the hospital that had been graveyard-still moments before the injured arrived, the desperate bustling of short-lived hope ruled the room. But the expressions of horror that ringed every face in the room betrayed the truth. There was no hope for the three most injured soldiers, including the female whose presence had so shaken the trauma team.

Doctors and nurses stood wordless before the line of blue curtains that separated each trauma bay. A nurse approached a large whiteboard that listed the status of every patient. Under the category "Injuries," she added three letters for each soldier: "IED." *Improvised explosive device.*

Behind one of the blue curtains Ashley lay in her uniform above a green woolen military blanket. The doctors and nurses had done everything they could to save her, but the concussive force of the blast had proved more potent than their healing powers and all the modern technology that surrounded them.

Ashley's heart had stopped. She was gone.

Anne was working in the Tactical Operations Center and speaking to a group of Rangers when she spotted something unusual in the hallway. People were huddled in animated conversation, not the usual, low-key, take-it-all-in-stride, Ranger kind of way.

She asked one of the Rangers what was going on.

"The platoon got hit," he answered.

Before she had a chance to react, another Ranger pulled her gently to the side.

"There are potential casualties," he said. "And it's possible that one of them is Ashley."

Anne nodded in reply, and in a moment she was gone, racing to retrieve the keys to a pickup truck she and Ashley had commandeered some weeks before to shuttle back and forth from the DFAC. They had a variety of cuisine choices on base, from Belgian to Indian, but Ashley always favored the East Asian dining facility. Earlier that same day she had enjoyed her usual—a grilled sandwich plus her favorite noodles, which she doused in a red, sweet chili sauce she loved.

"See you in a couple of hours," Anne had said to her partner as she walked out. Both women had expected to be on mission that night, but in the end Anne's team hadn't gone out. "We'll grab dinner when you get back." Dinner being breakfast, they often went for omelets. Ashley liked the veggie omelets in particular.

Just another night.

Now Anne was hurtling toward the combat hospital so she could be there when the soldiers started arriving—just in case it was Ashley. She hurried inside and followed the signs for the emergency room. When she bounded into the trauma center she found a scene of quietly managed chaos. So many doctors and nurses silently hurrying from one hospital bay to another, the only sounds coming from respirators and the occasional calling out of a patient's vital signs.

Anne spotted a senior Ranger in the hallway. She was about to ask about Ashley, but he spoke first.

"Do you want to say goodbye?" he asked.

He said no more, but handed her some of Ashley's things. Then, taking a few steps alongside her, he walked toward the bay where Ashley lay. The blue fabric curtain hung half open.

Anne struggled to process what she was seeing. Her teammate, her partner, her friend, was gone. They had worked out together the day before, had eaten breakfast together that very evening. The letters *IED* on the whiteboard coldly confirmed the fact, but Anne couldn't believe it.

Anne walked over to Ashley and closed the curtain behind her. She lowered herself into the chair next to her and took Ashley's hand, then embraced her friend. Then she took her by the hand once more and bowed her head.

"I am so sorry," she said. "Just so sorry I couldn't protect you. I am so sorry that I couldn't stop this from happening, Ashley."

Her teammate was still dressed in her battle clothes and her blond hair streamed out of its ponytail. Her face was smudged by dirt but looked peaceful.

Minutes passed and Anne sat there alone with her head bowed and her hand in her friend's. Finally, a chaplain came to say a final prayer and perform last rites. A young medic stood quietly behind the chaplain, ready to move Ashley's body from the room. He looked uncomfortable, and Anne knew his arrival was her cue to go, but she wanted them both out of there. She needed more time. But there was none. Slowly, she stood up and said goodbye for the final time.

A small crowd of men remained in the corridor paying their respects to their brothers-in-arms: Private First Class Christopher

Horns, one of their newest teammates, who had joined the Rangers earlier that year; and Sergeant First Class Kris Domeij, their much-loved leader. Next to them lay Ashley White. Three soldiers with such different stories from such different places: Santa Ana, California; Colorado Springs, Colorado; and Marlboro, Ohio. They had little in common other than their commitment to serving the United States. One was twenty-nine and on his fourteenth deployment; another was just twenty, serving his first. And one was a National Guard member who answered the call to join a new, all-female, all-Army special operations team. Now history would link them forever.

Just before 2 a.m., barely an hour after she arrived, Anne headed back to the parking lot and sat in the truck, staring ahead. She would not cry that night—she had too much to do. In fact, the tears would not come for months.

But the grief enveloped her immediately.

Already, the word was spreading among the CSTs.

"Hey, do you know Ashley White?" a Ranger poked his head into the small tent that Tristan shared with another CST at a base in another part of Afghanistan. The entire CST class—direct action members and those who served on village-stability operations—had been separated for two and a half months and were now spread around the country.

"Oh, yeah, is she here?" Tristan replied enthusiastically. Recently, some fellow CSTs from the VSO missions had come to visit; she was thrilled at the notion that Ashley was there.

"No, she is dead, she was just killed in action," he said.

"What?!" Tristan jumped to her feet. It was impossible, he couldn't be right. But an instant later she had a phone call in the TOC, and it brought confirmation of the terrible news. It was Leda; she said she needed to speak urgently with Tristan, but first wanted to be sure she was in a quiet place.

"I want to let you know that First Lieutenant Ashley White has expired," she said. She continued speaking, something about an explosion in Kandahar and Operation Enduring Freedom. But Tristan had stopped listening.

Cheese expires, milk expires, deli meat expires, Tristan thought. Beautiful twenty-four-year-olds don't.

She put down the phone and walked toward the door of the operations center. She was suddenly feeling claustrophobic, and had to get out of there. Her mind couldn't grasp what she now knew to be true. Heavy cloud cover had stopped them from going out on mission earlier that night, which is why the entire unit remained on base. But the clouds had passed, and now a crescent moon shone bright and clear. The stars formed a diamond-encrusted canopy overhead. Tristan stepped onto the three-hundred-meter gravel running track that circled the perimeter of her base and began running. Somehow the little track felt endless. Over and over, lap after lap, she pounded out the miles. On her iPod she played one song on a loop, Norah Jones's "The Long Way Home."

I'm so sorry, Ashley, she thought as she ran. Looking up at the sky, she couldn't help but think it was Ashley who had brought the stars out to offer her some comfort. That would be just like her to think only of other people at a moment like this.

Hundreds of miles away, in another part of the country, Sarah's XO took a rare step into the all-female hooch. He looked even more battle-exhausted than usual. Sarah was in her lightweight, half-cylinder-shaped tent known as a K-Span counting and sorting baby socks she had received from her old Girl Scout troop back home in New England to hand out to the kids she met on missions.

"Major Barrow needs to see you in the TOC."

He had a weird expression on his face, as if he had eaten lousy food or heard bad news.

"Did something happen?" she asked.

He nodded.

"In Kandahar," he said. Reading his expression, Sarah knew that something was very wrong.

"I know it is one of us," she muttered to herself as she walked quickly from her quarters to the Tactical Operations Center. "I just don't know who it is yet."

She entered the TOC to find Leda typing frantically on her laptop. In the hurry to get the CSTs out onto the battlefield—and perhaps in the belief that they would remain far from the front lines, since the combat ban remained in force—the women had never filled out their casualty packets with paperwork stating where they would be buried and listing all of their awards. As she typed, Leda was speaking on the phone to Anne, assembling biographical details that would accompany the news release announcing Ashley's death.

Sarah heard a snatch of Leda's side of the conversation—"and what year did she get that award?"—and knew someone had been killed.

"Who is it?" Sarah asked Lane, who was sitting next to Leda. Lane motioned toward the door and together they walked outside.

Between sobs, Lane replied, "Zhari district."

"IED explosion on mission."

"Ashley."

Throughout the night CSTs across Afghanistan learned about Ashley's death, struggled to believe it, and put off the pain of their own grief by making sure their teammates heard the news from Leda or a fellow CST. Each of them felt the need to keep her composure, not only for Ashley but for the program itself. No CST had ever died in battle before and the scrutiny would be high; they all understood this immediately. Keep it together, they counseled themselves, as the long night wore on.

Back at their base, Anne was navigating the maze of mundane administrative duties that a soldier's death unleashes. Cassie and her partner Isabel had been flown to Kandahar to help complete Ashley's casualty packet, beginning with her rank and the recent CAB award. They included her dates of service with the North Carolina Guard unit and at Fort Sam Houston, where she got her medical training. They all knew one another so well that it took hardly any time at all.

One of the Rangers brought Anne a few documents his unit used for their soldiers, and offered his condolences. When he left, Anne saw that a group of men from Ranger Regiment was in the hallway, crying for their friends and teammates. Loss had won a round that night.

In the small hours of the morning, the CSTs sat in their little broom closet office, a place that was filled with reminders of Ashley. It didn't feel real to any of them.

"Do you think they'll shut us down?" Cassie finally asked the question that was on everyone's mind. She knew that Ashley's death would propel the CST program into the public eye, and the real question was: how would the American public react when it learned that a woman had been present on a direct action, special operations combat mission? The American public knew more about military dogs and their handlers than it did about anything called a CST. A lot of people were going to want to know just how a group of women had ended up in the heart of the fight against the insurgency in Afghanistan.

"I have no idea," Anne answered. At that moment the only thing she knew for certain was that everything she and her teammates did from then on would define how their program looked to the outside world. Doing the job superbly was the most important thing they could do for Ashley. They were all soldiers, and death was part of their business. Ashley hadn't wanted any special treatment in life, and she certainly wouldn't have wanted it in death.

And still, no one knew how much information they could or should include about their mission, since the CST program had, from its very beginnings, navigated a fine line with regard to the combat ban. So Anne labored over every word; her eyes stung from fatigue and heartbreak as she stared at her computer screen and typed.

> *1st Lt. Ashley Irene White, 24, was born Sept. 3, 1987 and was a native of Alliance, Ohio. She was killed during combat operations in Kandahar Province, Afghanistan when the assault force she was supporting triggered an improvised explosive device.*
>
> *She was assigned to the 230th Brigade Support Battalion, 30th Heavy Brigade Combat Team, North Carolina National Guard, Goldsboro, N.C., and served as a member of the Cultural Support Team attached to a Joint Special Operations Task Force in Afghanistan.*
>
> *This was her first deployment to Afghanistan in support of the War on Terror.*

Anne's next duty was to pack up and inventory Ashley's room, standard procedure following a military death. She walked the football field's distance back to their barracks and entered the small bunk that had been Ashley's home for ten weeks. It had felt almost cozy when she crossed the hall from her room to visit Ashley earlier that day.

She unfolded an Army inventory form and began tallying:

> *Uniform tops*
> *Uniform bottoms*
> *Underwear*
> *Medical books*
> *Pairs of socks*

She counted them all and in a slow, neat hand wrote the number of each item on the form.

Among the books and pictures was a DVD, white instead of the usual silver and stamped in black cursive letters:

Our Wedding Portraits

The proofs of Ashley's wedding photos from that May had arrived recently. Ashley had promised to show Anne the pictures next time they had a free day.

Early the next morning hundreds from around Kandahar Airfield—soldiers, special operations commanders, staff, and dignitaries—gathered on the tarmac as the CSTs and Rangers prepared to send their friends and teammates home.

Bagpipes sounded the mournful notes of "Amazing Grace" over a loudspeaker as the ramp ceremony, a tradition marking the final send-off for a fallen soldier, began. The crowd stood around the three flag-draped aluminum cases on the earthen field. The base's flag flew at half-staff.

Cassie's CST partner Isabel and a group of Rangers volunteered to carry Ashley's transfer case down the airfield and onto the plane that would take her to Dover Air Force Base in Delaware, home to the military's largest mortuary and the traditional first stop on American soil for military personnel killed overseas. Cassie, as the most senior officer among them, led the ceremony, placing Ashley onto the cavernous C-17. She called for the soldiers to lower the silver case to the ground and, a few moments later, to present arms and salute their fallen comrade one final time.

But as she called for Isabel and the Rangers to return to their feet after lowering Ashley's casket, Cassie realized she had made a mistake: she had underestimated the sentiment of her Ranger colleagues. The men needed more time to bid their CST farewell, and two soldiers remained crouched next to Ashley's aluminum case for a few moments longer before rising to make their final salute.

Ashley's pallbearers filed off the plane and onto the tarmac just beneath its wing. Now that they had no work to occupy them Cassie and Isabel both felt the enormity of Ashley's death. Cassie heard sniffles all around her as she and her fellow soldiers tried to hold back their tears for Sergeant First Class Kris Domeij, Private First Class Christopher Horns, and First Lieutenant Ashley White. As he stood in formation behind her, one of the Rangers who had carried Ashley onto the plane patted Cassie on the arm.

"She was a great soldier," he whispered.

Throughout the ceremony Cassie, Anne, and Isabel each noted one heartening fact amid the terrible loss: Special Operations Command had made no distinction in death between Ashley—the enabler, the CST, the female—and the two Rangers who had died alongside her. The command treated them all equally: before the ceremony they placed Ranger coins on top of each casket, and afterward hung Ashley's photo on the wall of Ranger fallen, alongside pictures of Kristoffer Domeij and Christopher Horns.

It was small comfort, but one that would have made Ashley proud.

And then the plane soared into the sky.

Nadia awoke that morning in the combat hospital to find a collection of metal pins keeping her right arm attached to the rest of her body. She had nearly lost the limb, one of the medics told her; it had hung on only by tendons. After losing three soldiers that night, the doctors had been bound and determined to avoid an amputation. But that was a detail Nadia didn't yet know.

"Nice toenail polish," one of the hospital staff commented. He clearly hadn't seen red toes on any of his patients before. Nadia hadn't bothered to ask him for a mirror, but she did wonder what her makeup looked like after all that had happened. She was sure she was a mess.

She saw a bunch of Rangers milling around, visiting fellow soldiers who had been injured. She wondered when she was going to see Ashley. She was sure Ashley knew what had happened and could fill her in on the parts of the night she was now fighting to remember.

Then Anne appeared at her bedside. She looked tired, Nadia thought, like she hadn't slept. In truth she had been awake for well over twenty-four hours.

"Where's Ashley?" Nadia asked.

"She's not here," Anne said. She looked down while she spoke in a tone that had no emotion left in it. "She's gone. She didn't make it."

Nadia's mind sorted through shards of images from the night before: the tinfoil-covered leftovers, the rush to slip on Ashley's Crye combat shirt, the helicopter flight, Ashley talking to one of the Rangers, the patch of grass. The helicopter flight. Now Anne was standing at her side, telling her that Ashley was gone and the Rangers had lost two men.

Nadia's aging gear had been her saving grace. That short walk to find even footing to fiddle with her NODs had kept her from the brunt of the blast.

The IED had taken her friend and teammate and had nearly taken her own arm. Now it would take her off the battlefield. But the blast had not taken her memories.

She would think of Ashley every day.

15

A Grief Observed

★ ★ ★

The doorbell rang. And rang.

It took Jason a few minutes to realize that the strange sound that awakened him at the early hour of 6 a.m. was coming from his front door. It was a rental near Fort Sill in Lawton, where he was taking an officers' artillery training course. He wondered, who on earth even knew he had come to Oklahoma?

He fumbled his way to the door still in the T-shirt and shorts he was sleeping in.

Not that he had been sleeping well. Earlier that week he learned that he would indeed be returning to Fort Bragg, which meant he and Ashley could stay in Fayetteville and the ranch home she loved. Plus, Ashley could proceed with her goal to keep working with JSOC, this time as a civilian. They had both been thrilled. She had six months left in her deployment; he now knew where he'd be working and was moving forward in his own career. The couple had planned to discuss everything by phone Friday morning, but Ashley had sent a note in the middle of the night Thursday his time saying her team had gotten in too late for her to call. She knew Jason had an artillery exam that morning and didn't want to wake him. She wished him luck on the test and said she would call that night. He answered her email as soon as he woke up:

"Look, you are in Afghanistan. I don't care if it is 3:00 a.m. Just call me. I'll go late to formation and tell them my wife was calling from Afghanistan."

She promised to ring later that day. But Friday afternoon came and went, and Jason had to attend an officer promotion party. Then his friends persuaded him to join them at a haunted house to celebrate Halloween, only a week away. He joined them on the outing, but every two or three minutes glanced down at his phone to see if he had missed his wife.

"She's supposed to call," he told his buddy.

"Oh, dude, she knows it is Friday night here; I am sure she'll call you later."

But Jason left the haunted house without hearing from Ashley, and finally managed to drift off at 3 a.m. He slept with his Black-Berry just a few inches away, on the empty pillow next to him, so he could be sure to hear the phone when Ashley called.

Jason walked to the front door and looked through the peephole. All he could see was a uniform. He opened the front door a crack and saw three Army officers in dress blues standing on his doorstep: a battery commander, a first sergeant, and a chaplain.

"Captain Stumpf, we need to come in and talk to you," one of the men said.

"Let me put the dog out back," Jason answered. Ashley's Siberian husky Gunner barked at the strange men as Jason led him away by the collar. He left him in the yard, closed the gate, and returned to the front door.

I am going to Landstuhl, he thought. Ashley is hurt.

He ushered his visitors into the living room and remained standing in the doorway. His hand gripped the doorknob and he braced himself for whatever they had to say.

"Please sit down," the first sergeant urged Jason.

"No, thanks, I don't need to sit down," Jason answered. "Just tell me what is going on."

"We regret to inform you that First Lieutenant Ashley White-

Stumpf was killed in action," the battery commander began. Jason's ears hummed and his chest thumped so loudly he could barely hear what they were saying. He looked at his phone, wishing his wife would call and tell them how wrong they were.

The men kept talking. They didn't have many details yet, except that she had succumbed to wounds from an IED. They would give Jason time to collect himself and prepare for everything that lay ahead. They would return in a few hours.

They were very sorry for his loss.

Jason refused to let himself think. He went into Army officer mode and began doing what had to be done. It was the only way he would get through it.

But it was with a stab of dread that he realized the next thing he had to do was inform Bob and Debbie back in Ohio that Ashley had been killed. He feared they would see her photo on the news before he had been able to reach them, since officially her next of kin had been informed. He couldn't allow that to happen.

"What's wrong?" Debbie White asked immediately when she heard Jason's voice. She was in the middle of icing eight dozen cupcakes for a catering job when the phone rang.

"Oh, a pipe burst and it's leaking all over the kitchen and I'm not in my house so I don't know what to do," Jason lied. He just couldn't bear to tell Debbie; it wasn't his place. He tried to make his voice stronger, but he knew she knew something had happened.

"Where is Dad?" he asked. Debbie said he was at the shop. White Tool.

On the factory floor, Bob White heard the White Tool landline ringing. The clock read 8:32 a.m. and he wondered who the hell would be calling him Saturday morning; they weren't even open. He had just come in to check up on some recent orders of metal flagpole bases and streetlight fixtures.

"Who is it?" he asked as he grabbed the phone.

"Jason."

"Jason who?"

"It's your son-in-law, Dad."

"What's up?"

"Are you sitting down?"

"Just give it to me straight," Bob said. He had never been one for the soft sell.

"It's Ashley. She didn't make it," Jason said. His voice started to falter. "There was an explosion in Kandahar and she didn't make it back. I just got the news."

Jason listened, heartbroken, as Bob fired off a hot stream of expletives. He felt powerless to do anything to ease his father-in-law's agony.

Bob moved quickly to end the conversation.

"I gotta go home and tell Deb," he said. "I'll talk to you in a bit."

Bob would replay that moment in his mind every day that followed. That phone call would cut through his life and create a "before" and "after." He looked up once more at the clock, the same one that a teenage Ashley had used to mark her lunch hour and to see if her workday at White Tool had ended. . . .

Jason hung up the phone and buried his head in his hands. He had one more call to make. He knew that as hard as the last one had been, this one would be far worse.

"Brittany, you need to go home," he said when Ashley's twin answered her mobile.

"What's wrong?" she asked.

"It is bad. Ashley didn't—"

He got no further. He heard the phone drop as she cried out.

And then he called the only person other than Ashley he always turned to in crisis.

"Dad, Ashley didn't make it out," he blurted as soon as his father picked up the phone at his home near Pittsburgh.

"Well, isn't there another plane? She can just catch the next one, no?"

"No, Dad, she didn't miss her flight," Jason explained. "She was killed in action."

"What?" From his earlier conversation with his son, Jason's father knew a bit about what Ashley was doing, and that there had been potential risks. But he never entertained the idea that she wouldn't come home.

Ralph Stumpf started to cry, and the two men stayed on the phone in silent tears for long minutes.

Soon it was time for Jason to head to Dover Air Force Base to meet his wife for the last time.

Bob and Debbie White had their first clue about what Ashley had been doing in Afghanistan when they arrived at Delaware's Dover Air Force Base, the first stop on American soil for soldiers who die overseas. Dover's Port Mortuary is the Pentagon's largest, and the only such facility in the continental United States. Until just a few years earlier families of the fallen had to travel on their own dollar to witness the "dignified transfer" of their loved ones from the C-17 carrying them home. (The military did not use the word *ceremony* for such an event, because that would imply that it was an event in which family members needed to participate.) In 2009, under Secretary of Defense Robert Gates, the Pentagon changed the policy to allow public access to the media if the grieving family so desired and to pay for up to three family and friends to travel to Dover at government expense.

The first person to greet them upon arrival was a Ranger Regiment casualty assistance officer, whose job it was to support and assist family members when their loved one had died in service. But the Whites were unusual in that most times family members knew more or less what their loves ones had been doing. And usually the fallen weren't women.

Debbie did her best to stay quietly composed and keep everything—and everyone—together. She wanted to get her family through the next several days. Then she would deal with trying to figure out what Ashley was doing out there.

But Bob had a lot of questions. He was aware that Ashley was on some sort of a special team; this much he knew from Ashley and Brittany. But he had almost zero details beyond that. As far as he and Debbie had known, she was working at a hospital on a base, "setting up tents," as she had told them one time, and helping women and kids. The previous day the Whites had read a press release from Army Special Operations Command. It said Ashley "was assigned to the 230th Brigade Support Battalion, 30th Heavy Brigade Combat Team, North Carolina National Guard, Goldsboro, N.C.," and that she had been "attached" to a "joint special operations task force." It went on to say that she was an "enabler," and a member of something called "a Cultural Support Team." She had "played a crucial role as a member of a special operations strike force." It was a long way from setting up tents, and the Whites had been confused by the details of the job their daughter had been doing overseas.

The release ended by stating that Ashley's efforts "highlight[ed] both the importance and necessity of women on the battlefield today."

Bob had no idea what it all meant, and he was determined to get answers. He looked the Ranger in the eye and unleashed a barrage of questions.

What was my daughter doing with the Rangers?

Why was she with them on night raids?

What was she doing on these missions?

Was she helping women and kids? Was she working as a medic?

Finally, Bob wanted to know how Ashley died. He wanted to gather every bit of information he could about how that IED had found Ashley in the middle of the night in Kandahar.

The soldier tried to answer Bob's blizzard of questions, but some he simply couldn't. There was information he didn't possess, and there was intelligence he wasn't at liberty to share. Already he had crossed well beyond his job's usual boundaries: the casualty assistance officer program was created to help with funeral arrangements and honors, assist in processing of benefits, and make sure personal effects were returned. Facing a father who had just learned his daughter was the first-ever on her team to die in a special operations fight he hadn't even known she was part of was entirely new terrain. For everyone. But he fielded the questions as deftly and respectfully as he could.

Ashley was attached to a unit of Ranger Regiment serving in Kandahar, Afghanistan, Bob learned. Its main purpose was to reach out to women and children and to support the strike force's work of disrupting and destroying insurgent networks.

The Ranger explained that Ashley would be honored as a Ranger *enabler*, and he explained that enablers were teams of service members with specialized skills who supported special operators. Because her role was vital to Regiment, Bob heard him say, a Ranger would be with them in Ohio for the funeral and they would offer her every funeral honor. But there is a difference, the soldier tried to explain, between Rangers and the people who support them, or, in the military's terminology, *enable* them.

It was a difference that Bob, a civilian, was struggling mightily to understand. If women are out on the front lines marching with the Rangers every night, Bob asked, what is the difference? If they go out on missions and wear uniforms and carry weapons, and put themselves in danger to help the American military achieve its strategic goals, what is the difference?

If they are getting killed out there, what in the hell is the difference?

There was nothing the Ranger could say to satisfactorily explain Ashley's death to Bob. It was a reality he would simply have to accept. And there was another reality Bob would have to live with: his sense that if he hadn't given in on ROTC back at Kent, perhaps she would have stayed home. And he wouldn't be bringing her home to Ohio now. She could have become a physician's assistant, she could have started a family, she could maybe even have one day opened that bakery back in Ohio she and Debbie always talked about starting.

Now all of that was over. He and his wife had not only lost their Ashley, but generations of her to come.

Finally Jason signaled to the Ranger with a glance—apology, frustration, anger, confusion—and took Bob by the arm, slowly walking him into a room reserved for families. He tried to explain what Ashley had been doing, to explain what it meant to be part of this new team of women and how honored Ashley felt to serve with Ranger Regiment on counterterrorism missions. But Bob could not absorb it and at first couldn't understand why his son-in-law had kept Ashley's real mission secret. He knew that it was "classic Ashley"—as ever she had thought about others first and had wanted to keep her parents from worrying. He told Jason he understood why he did what he did, that it was what any good spouse would do: stay loyal to his wife's wishes.

But Bob and Debbie kept thinking that Ashley shouldn't have protected her parents. They should have been there protecting *her*.

16

The Man in the Arena

★ ★ ★

The night before Ashley's funeral hundreds who knew her and many her family had never seen before poured into her old high school gym to pay respects to their fallen soldier. They filed through in a line that lasted more than six hours and snaked all the way around the gym and out the door into the same hallways Ashley had walked as a senior six years earlier. Little children, aging women and men, parents whose children had grown up with Ashley and her siblings, they all came to pause at the table covered in red velvet upon which Ashley's Army medals were now displayed. Some, Leda included, made the sign of the cross as they stopped. Behind the velvet-covered table hung a banner with an empty military helmet and a rifle emblazoned with the words, "Lest they be forgotten."

Leda had barely slept since leaving Afghanistan three days earlier. As the officer in charge she had accompanied Ashley back to the United States on the C-17 and stayed awake watching over her throughout the trip to Dover via Ramstein. When she at last arrived at Dover she hurried to find Bob and Debbie and to introduce herself. She had heard so much about them from Ashley.

Leda told them what a beautiful friend Ashley had been to her. How dearly loved she was by her teammates. And how good she had been at her job. She told them how the Afghan women responded to her kindness and told her things that helped Americans and Afghans stay alive, how Ashley had been respected by the Rangers for her physical strength and professionalism, and how she had seen this all, firsthand, for herself during her trip to Kandahar in October.

She had expected to return to Afghanistan immediately after the ceremony for the fallen at Dover. She was desperate to get back to her soldiers, whose missions continued. But then Bob and Debbie had asked Leda to please accompany Ashley all the way home to Ohio. They needed her there, Bob said, to help them deal with this onslaught of military attention for which they had been unprepared. And to explain to their family and friends what Ashley had been doing there on the front lines in a job they hadn't even known existed.

Now the CST officer in charge sat among the imposing special operations leaders with rows of bars and medals on their uniforms in Ashley's high school gym where she had cheered for her brother, Josh, during so many basketball games. Leda looked on as the Rangers offered their funeral traditions to their female teammate. A young soldier in the Rangers' tan beret and dress green uniform stood at attention at Ashley's casket and did not move. Leda listened intently as one of the highest-ranking officers in the entire United States military stood to speak about her beloved friend.

The head of Army Special Operations Command, Lieutenant General John Mulholland, a highly regarded Green Beret and an architect of America's early successes in Afghanistan, came to present the Purple Heart, Bronze Star, and Combat Action Badge to Ashley's family. But before he did, he said, he wanted to explain just what the CSTs and their mission meant to him, to the Army, and to America. Just a few feet in front of him on folding chairs sat Bob and Debbie, working valiantly to hold together amid all the unexpected attention and their overnight baptism into the special operations community. Jason sat in his Army dress uniform next to Debbie.

"It is important that we do recognize that what Ashley was doing is something that a very small number, a very select group of women have raised their arms for," Mulholland said.

"They come from all across the United States and they come to

Fort Bragg because they have heard this call for women willing to do something unique in our country's history to serve alongside the Rangers, alongside our Special Forces that are the best warriors that our nation has.

"Make no mistake about it, these women are warriors; these are great women who have also provided enormous operational success to us on the battlefield by virtue of their being able to contact half of the population that we normally do not interact with.

"They absolutely have become part of our special operations family. They absolutely will write a new chapter in the role of women soldiers in the United States Army and our military and every single one of them have proven equal to the test."

As Leda listened to his speech, she was moved by Lieutenant General Mulholland's very public accounting of this program built for the shadows: who the women were, why the program existed, and where she and her sisters fit in America's fight against terrorism. Mulholland hadn't known Ashley personally, but her death had pushed all of the CSTs out of the shadows and into the public arena.

> I want you to have that sense of context for what it is that Ashley did. She and her sisters have set an entirely new mark on what it means to be a woman soldier in the United States Army, which is the finest army on the face of the earth. She will always be part of Army special operations, and we are extraordinarily proud of her and all of her sisters.

Next, Lieutenant General Mulholland presented Jason with Ashley's Purple Heart, "established by General George Washington at Newburgh, New York, August 7, 1782," in the name of the president of the United States of America. Jason stood to receive the award. Then came the Bronze Star. And the Combat Action Badge for which Lane and Anne had cheered Ashley on just a few months earlier.

Leda understood how rare it was for the head of the Army Special Operations Command to devote days from his schedule to honor a fallen lieutenant. She knew that Lieutenant General Mulholland attended Ranger funerals, but she didn't imagine he often attended memorial ceremonies for their enablers. For their part, Bob and Debbie knew nothing of the backstory of the CST program, or its politics; what they saw, and marveled at, was all these decorated, senior officers praising their daughter. They received a letter from Admiral William McRaven, the former JSOC leader and current SOCOM commander whose Request for Forces had turned the CST program from idea into reality.

"I didn't know Ashley personally, but I know what kind of woman she was. She was courageous beyond all measure," McRaven wrote. "She was patriotic. She had a sense of duty that could not be suppressed. She was full of energy and made everyone around her better. She was exactly the kind of woman we needed in the service of our country."

That her honor, her integrity, her humanity, her generosity had meant a great deal to many, her parents had imagined to be true. After all, it was Ashley. But even they were shocked the following day, Halloween 2011, to see the hundreds upon hundreds who turned out to line the main highway in Marlboro, Randolph, and nearby Alliance to her burial mass. Crowds of friends and strangers, Vietnam veterans and wounded warrior advocates, stood two- and three-deep to salute Ashley as she rode by. Boys and girls clasped their small hands in prayer and then waved goodbye.

Inside Ashley's funeral mass the wooden pews filled to capacity then overflowed with mourners. Her casket was carried down the same aisle she had walked as a bride only five months earlier.

Colonel Mark O'Donnell of the 75th Ranger Regiment picked up where Lieutenant General Mulholland had left off the previous evening and spoke to the crowd.

"From an intelligence standpoint what they provide by engaging women and children on the objective contributes immeasurably to our success," he said of the CSTs.

He read "The Man in the Arena" from President Theodore Roosevelt. The speech, given in April 1910, focused on the importance to democracy of holding all citizens to the highest of standards. The colonel noted that though the person described in this narrative was male, the words did indeed describe this *female* fallen soldier.

"The credit belongs to the man who is actually in the arena, whose face is marred by dust and sweat and blood; who strives valiantly; who errs, who comes short again and again," he quoted Roosevelt, "because there is no effort without error and shortcoming; but who does actually strive to do the deeds."

"On countless operations in which elite special operations strike forces targeted senior Taliban and al-Qaeda safe havens in which contact was likely, Ashley was frequently the only female on the objective," O'Donnell finished. "Think about this and the great courage that that took.

"She is the Man in the Arena," he said. "Ashley, rest in peace. Know that your Ranger brothers have mourned and now continue the fight, a fight that you have committed your life to."

Jason offered the final speech and talked of his wife's devotion, her patience, and her ability to listen to him "rant," whether he was deployed or she was. "I am not the ideal husband," he said. "She was the ideal wife."

Those days around Ashley's burial would come to be a blur for Bob and Debbie, but a few moments would puncture the fog of sorrow and the numbing motion of all the funeral preparations.

They would remember the horse-drawn black carriage that carried Ashley to her grave with hundreds marching behind and a bagpipe playing "Amazing Grace." They would remember Leda as she spoke at Ashley's funeral about her sister-in-arms and listed name after name of Ashley's fellow CSTs who sent their love and admiration and "their greater resolve" to continue their mission in Ashley's honor. Ten days earlier the Whites had never heard of these women; now they felt like members of their family. And they would remember the condolence card they received from the Rangers with whom Ashley served. "Having a woman come out with us was a new thing for all of us," wrote her weapons squad leader. "Being one of the first groups of CST, she really set a good impression not only on us, but also the higher leadership. I am sorry for your loss, but I want you to know that she was good at her job and a valuable member of this platoon."

And Debbie would never forget the stranger who approached her after the burial ceremony on the hill overlooking the church's playground. She stood taking a final moment alongside her daughter's pale gray casket, now covered in red roses left by those who had loved her.

"Mrs. White, I brought my daughter today because I wanted her to know what a hero was," the woman said, holding the hand of a little girl. "And I wanted her to know girls could be heroes, too."

That the Army had entered new terrain with Ashley's death had been clear from the outset, from how to announce it to the presence of Ranger leaders and Lieutenant General Mulholland's words at her funeral. It wasn't long before Jason began to see that the survivor community was breaking new ground, too. Gold Star Wives was the name of the group of widows/widowers whose spouses died while serving in the armed forces. And while the group worked hard to be inclusive, the name said it all. The soldier who came to talk to him about all the survivor programs the Army offered the bereaved had said as much, telling Jason that they faced such a small percentage of widowers, let alone dual military widowers, that they really didn't have that much in the way of support or grieving resources tailored to men. But the Army was there for Jason and would do whatever it took to take care of him, the officer had promised. Jason appreciated his candor. He was beginning to see how Ashley's death challenged the machinery of the United States military. And the society of which it was a part.

It began with offhand, thoughtless questions from fellow soldiers who asked him what his wife was doing there. Why had she gone to Afghanistan? Was he okay with her decision? And had he tried to stop her? At first he had answered patiently that he wouldn't and couldn't have done anything differently. He tried to explain to them who Ashley was and what motivated her to do this deployment. But he never felt he got through to people. And that became even clearer when an acquaintance asked him, if he could go back in time, would he do it again? Would he let her go? Or would he be a "real husband" now and look out for his wife? The question had infuriated him. And added to his pain. He wanted to answer that they had made this decision to join the program together. And that she wanted to contribute to her country, to do something she thought mattered, that belonged only to her, before they started their family. But he knew it was pointless. He only glared back in response. His wife had taught him to be the bigger man and he was trying to honor her memory and remain calm in the face of such ignorance. As his buddy told him, "You can't train stupid."

But it wasn't easy.

At night he would sit home alone with Ashley's dog, Gunner, on the couch he and Ashley used to share and mull over all the reasons why he had chosen to support his wife.

He always arrived at the same one: he wanted her to be happy. That was his job as a husband. He hadn't failed Ashley; he had kept his marriage vow to her.

And now he would have to learn to live without her.

But he wasn't yet ready to do that. Her *Glamour* and *Marie Claire* magazines remained where they sat in a wicker basket on the floor next to the couch, as did her collection of Minnie Mouses. He finished the to-do list she had stuck to the refrigerator the day she left for Pope Air Force Base. He kept her kitchen just as she had so carefully arranged it. But nothing was the same.

He reread the journal they had shared during his own time in Afghanistan and returned often to her notebook, the one in which he found the letter telling him about her CAB. And he thought about her looking down on him and urging him to keep going, not to give in to his despair.

As he told his buddy one night when he came over to see how Jason was doing, he would never regret anything that had happened. Even with all the pain.

"Ashley taught me so much," he said. "Some people are married fifty years and don't have what we did in the short time we were married."

That thought got him through each day.

17

Kandahar

★ ★ ★

Ma'am, are you okay?"

Tristan was sitting in a biplane run by a special operations contractor. Only one other passenger was on board: a warrant officer whose presence she had immediately tuned out the moment the plane was airborne. She was lost in her thoughts when the officer leaned over to check that she was properly strapped in. She had no idea what he was talking about—of course she was okay—and then she felt the plane perform aerial jumping jacks over the Hindu Kush, bobbing up and down in sharp vertical jerks just above the mountain range's jagged peaks.

Tristan hated to fly, but right now she was too nervous about her new assignment to care about the unsettling plunges of the bouncing plane.

She was heading from Bagram to Kandahar, that hotbed of house-born and vehicle-carried IEDs that had just claimed her friend's life, to replace Ashley. She wanted to feel gung ho about the job. She wanted to say that she felt bold and brave and ready to do honor to Ashley's memory. But in reality she felt nothing but worry. And fear.

We're about to crash, she thought, noting the irony, but here I am, more worried about what's about to happen on the ground in Kandahar.

At last the plane landed safely. The day was just turning to dusk;

it was dinnertime for most people, but it was midday for the Rangers and their enablers, and they had work to do. Anne met Tristan at the flight line and showed her around her new home.

"We're going out tonight," Anne said. "Let's get your gear ready and make sure you have all you need."

Tristan noted how calm and collected her new teammate was, and she tried to assume the same no-nonsense air, as if going back out on mission a few days after your partner was killed was just another day at the office. Tristan would have preferred a day to settle in. A day to get accustomed to her new environs, a day to quiet her fears. She figured Anne knew that but that Anne thought the best way to deal with Tristan's anxiety was to get her back to work. She knew Anne was right, but that didn't make it any easier.

A few days earlier special operations leaders had flown Tristan from her base to the memorial service in Kandahar in honor of Ashley, Kris Domeij, and Chris Horns. She arrived just in time to hear the wrenching ritual of the last roll call for the fallen.

"Lieutenant White," she heard boom over the loudspeaker.

"Lieutenant Ashley White."

"Lieutenant Ashley Irene White"

At last a voice answered.

"First Sergeant, she is no longer with us."

After the roll call they lined up before a photo of each of the soldiers alongside their boots and dog tags. Tristan knelt next to Ashley's picture and said goodbye.

A few minutes later it was over. Three soldiers gone. And now everyone back to work.

Before Tristan flew back to base that night Anne had taken her to dinner at the Asian DFAC, the same place where she and Ashley had enjoyed a meal together the night she died. Tristan pushed her lo mein noodles around her plate and listened as Anne talked drily about the threats, how IEDs lay everywhere, over the walls and throughout the orchards, and how she couldn't wait to get back out to find the men who had planted the device that killed their friend. While Anne spoke Tristan looked at the Buddha stickers on the dining facility's windows and listened to new-age meditation music from 1990s-style boom boxes. She couldn't think of any place less soothing and tranquil in all the world.

After the meal Tristan watched Anne head back to her room to suit up for that night's work. She felt awed by her teammate's stoicism and fearful of the risks she faced.

I am *so* glad I'm not based here, Tristan had thought as she and her CST partner flew out of Kandahar. It sounds horrible.

And then, two days after the memorial service, she was reassigned as Ashley's replacement in Kandahar. For the next six months, this frightening place filled with ghosts and IEDs and smelling of human excrement would be her home.

Tristan walked into her new room and froze.

Ashley's white ASICS sat there at the foot of her new bed.

She left the shoes there and moved toward the white wall locker to unpack her plastic bag of toiletries. There she found Ashley's travel-size Jergens lotions and some hair bands. There was also a candle in the scent "Puffy Clouds." How fitting, Tristan thought. She would safeguard it all as a reminder of her friend. And a warning to herself to never, ever get comfortable in this job.

Tristan entered the broom-closet-turned-office determined to pick any desk but the one that had been Ashley's. The moment she sat down and opened the desk drawer she realized she had chosen exactly wrong. Inside were Smart for Life protein bars in Green Tea flavor, which Tristan immediately recognized from their summer train-up. Ashley had selected them especially for their protein-to-carb ratio.

"It seems little bits of Ashley are everywhere," Tristan wrote in a letter home. She saw the bread maker in the corner already gathering dust from the Kandahar air and knew that no one would ever use it again. At least not while she was there.

With Anne's coaching she got her gear set up in the ready room—

every team had different protocols and ways of doing things—and went to introduce herself to the Rangers with whom she'd be working. Ashley's old team. They greeted her kindly, but stiffly. She was now officially "the replacement CST."

The first night Anne accompanied Tristan, to help her get her comfortable with her new team. At the outset Tristan thought only of IEDs; she knew that every step she took could be her last. But after a while she found her rhythm. She and Anne ended up searching and talking with dozens of women and children that night and divided the work between them. They had arrived by ground, in Stryker armored vehicles, and afterward, as they returned to base, Tristan felt a surge of relief. The new base, new teammates, new terrain, she would get used to them all. Being back in action had helped. Anne was right. She could move forward now.

But not everyone could. Tristan could tell how much respect the guys had for Ashley by the way they talked about her. One of the senior Rangers, a gruff guy whose deployments she imagined reached into double digits, approached her before the first mission. "Listen, please be really careful," he said. "No offense to you, but I can't deal with it one more time. Ashley was so young and she had so much to offer. I just can't go through that again."

Tristan realized how hard Ashley's death had been on these men. But she couldn't promise she wouldn't die and she didn't think the fact that they weren't used to women dying alongside them meant that she shouldn't be out there. She understood the risks going in. They were all soldiers, after all. These guys knew what that meant better than anyone.

Soon Tristan picked up a pen and began writing in her notebook.

Dad,

I'm writing this note; I guess in case something happens. I have witnessed second and third hand how much pain is associated with trying to pick up the pieces if the worst should happen. I'm not sure this letter will save you much pain, but it will at least save you the pain of searching for it.

Every night before I go to sleep I think of you guys. I think about all our times as a family. Summers in Vermont. Family softball games.

You always had a way of making us believe we could do anything. Whether it was making the softball team or becoming astronauts or just squeezing by in that math modeling class, you never doubted that any of us were capable of anything we set our hearts to. I could never tell you how much that has meant.

If something is to happen to me know that I wanted to do this job and that I placed myself in this position because I felt it was something I needed to do.

I'm grateful that I had such a wonderful family and that I had parents who were ever in my corner.

Love,

Tristan

As November and December wore on the CSTs kept going out each night and doing their jobs, though they all sensed that higher-ups were still trying to figure out what the first CST battlefield death meant for their work.

Back in Ohio at Ashley's funeral, one of the special operations leaders had asked Leda whether the women wanted to keep doing the job.

"Not one of us wants to stop doing this mission," Leda answered, reminding him that each of them had accepted the risks by signing on to work with the Rangers. "Nothing would dishonor Ashley's memory more."

He urged her to tell the CSTs to keep "serving with pride" and to make sure they knew the entire Special Operations Command stood behind them and wanted them to stay out there.

Leda returned to Afghanistan immediately after Ashley's service and shared that message. The CSTs needed to put their heads down and just keep doing their job better than ever, she said. Don't worry about anything else.

Around the same time, a special operations historian came through Kandahar to interview soldiers as part of his regular tour of bases across Afghanistan. When he sat down with Tristan, he asked how she felt when she learned of Ashley's death.

"Did it make you want to stop doing this job?"

"Just the opposite," she said. It made her more motivated to honor her friend and teammate's legacy.

Then the interviewer mentioned the chatter in Washington, D.C., and on military bases about ending the CST program with the war in Afghanistan. He asked Tristan how she saw the future of the program. "Should it be developed further or is it just a necessity born out of a specific conflict, because that's how we felt about the canine program during Vietnam."

Oh, great, now we're dogs! Tristan laughed to herself. But she told the historian that the program should not be dismantled, it should be expanded.

"They could really build out this job and get a whole lot more from the role if they wanted," she said. "Our team of CSTs will keep doing this mission as long as we can."

At last Christmas arrived. For Tristan, holidays had always been important; she wasn't going to let the fact that she was at war rob her of all her holiday cheer. She sketched a Christmas tree on a piece of scrap paper and taped it to the wall in her room, then put all the neatly wrapped packages from her family back in New England beneath it.

Things had gotten easier in the eight weeks since her arrival. At

November's end a new team of Rangers rotated in, and the platoon alongside whom Ashley had died finally got to go home after a deployment that had cost them so much and so many they loved. For this new Ranger crew, led by a fellow New England Patriots fan, Tristan was their first CST, and they had been open from the very start to her ideas and her suggestions for how she could contribute to their work. The more useful she felt she was, the better she got at the job, and the better she got at the job, the more they put her to work. Tristan and Kate instant-messaged regularly about how *nothing* that they would ever do afterward in the Army—short of Ranger school or Ranger selection opening to women one day—would ever compare to this mission.

Tristan would see Kate and all her teammates at Bagram the day after Christmas—the halfway point for their deployment. Leda had arranged the one-night, all-CST gathering; officially they had come to talk about their CST experience with their Afghan counterparts and to prepare Afghan women to do the CST job. Unofficially, Leda knew that the women needed to be around one another after Ashley's death and in light of all the questions about the program's future that were being raised.

Tristan snacked on muffins as she listened to Leda discuss ideas being floated among special operations leaders to make the CST teams a real MOS, or Military Occupational Specialty, rather than a temporary program. She wanted to pursue whatever MOS they managed to create, and told Leda and her teammates that she thought they should just be like all the other Ranger enablers, on the same training and deployment cycle of the guys with whom they served.

Then they began to swap stories.

"I actually thought Leda was calling to yell at us for fast-roping," Kimberly said about the call, the one she'd never forget. Official guidance had said that CSTs shouldn't fast-rope onto an objective given the injuries team members had sustained from it during PMT and in Afghanistan. Sliding quickly into a potentially hostile situation down a rope from a swaying bird wearing two pairs of gloves to prevent burns while holding steady all of your body weight plus fifty pounds of gear was dangerous work, and the Ranger leadership didn't want any more CSTs hurt. But after seeing them in action—both on their missions and with the Rangers—the SEALs Kimberly worked with decided she and her teammate Maddie could handle the assignment. They showed Kimberly, Maddie, and an Afghan army officer on their team how to climb up a thin, portable ladder and then come back down on the two-inch-thick rope that ranges from fifty to ninety feet in length that they had hung from the top of a building. They repeated the exercise twice without gear and twice in full kit. Next they practiced fast-roping out of an actual, hovering helicopter by day and at night to make certain they knew what they were doing. Still, Kimberly said, she and Maddie never thought they'd get to put the training to work given the debate about what was and wasn't allowed. Then one night they were flying to a mission when the SEALs announced they should all get ready to fast-rope in. Kimberly and Maddie had nudged each other there on the bird.

You gotta do this, Kimberly told herself in the moment, and not just for your sake but for all the other girls who can't. Don't go sliding down and don't land like a jerk and don't fall off the rope. Whatever you do don't get hurt. And don't you dare need a medevac to take you out of here tonight. Then she heard the command *Go*. Down, down, down she went. And then, suddenly, she felt the firm, cold earth beneath her. She balled her body up and did a combat roll away from the bird, just as the SEALs had taught, then leapt onto one knee to grab her weapon and pull security for everyone else. A moment later Maddie followed. With everyone safely descended from the bird, the team began moving toward the objective, just like any other night. But not before she and Maddie stopped to exchange a quick high-five. Kimberly saw one of the guys laugh silently from under his green night-vision halo and shake his head at the girls' display, as if to say, "You rookies."

Laughter greeted the end of Kimberly's story. Then Kate began.

One of the first nights out, she told her teammates, she and her platoon's first sergeant stood at the end of formation. Suddenly they heard the *pop-pop-pop* of fire and the sound of grenades on the radio and ran a hundred yards to take cover in a ditch alongside the road that was nearly as deep as Kate was tall. The guys up front started shooting at the insurgents firing upon them and her first sergeant put her up against the side of the ditch facing the back column and pointed. "That's your sector of fire," he had told her. "I was like, 'Fuck, yeah,'" Kate said. "That is the beauty of being a soldier. Right there in that moment with your rifle propped up against the dirt, knowing that even if you don't get to be the guy up at the front shooting, you have a sector that is yours and you know in your heart you will shoot any enemy that comes into it. That's how simple it is," she finished.

She had finally found her people, Kate said. Both her CSTs and the men she admired and was prepared to die for.

"I love you guys," Kate said. She confessed that after Ashley's death she now checked every night to see who was going out on mission and that they made it back okay. "You mean more to me than anything."

For Tristan the visit was the breath of fresh air that she needed. To see all her CST teammates and to know that everyone else was doing okay, too, did her heart good.

She flew once more from Bagram to Kandahar. This time the turbulence frightened her.

Tristan had just finished listening to the rundown of what they expected on the objective that night and now she was walking back to the ready room to make sure she had everything she needed for the evening's mission. On the wall just outside the briefing room hung photos of all those killed in action in Iraq and Afghanistan. Ashley's smiling face was next to Sergeant Domeij and Private Horns.

"Stay with me, Ashley," Tristan silently told her friend. "I think it's going to be a long night."

An hour later she was running off the Chinook and headed into what looked like the Afghan version of a trailer park, with homes all built close to one another. She and Anne, on a rare mission together, divided the labor: Anne searched the women while Tristan talked to them. It *was* going to be a long night; dozens of women and children were now standing in front of them.

Tristan flipped up her NODs and began talking to a pretty teenage girl with light green eyes and wearing a regal purple dress. She began asking her about what was happening in her neighborhood.

The night wind blew cold, and some of the other soldiers wore their puffy Army jackets. Being a New Englander long accustomed to running in twenty-degree weather, Tristan wore just a couple of layers—a waffle top, a shirt, and a vest—under her uniform.

Tristan noticed the girl looked nervous, as she bounced from one foot to another and looked over at her mother every time she spoke. When Tristan asked her once more what was happening in the house, quietly, the teenager started to talk. Yes, she said, the guy they were looking for was there in one of the houses. She didn't know anything more than that, but of that she was certain.

Just then Tristan heard the call over the radio:

"Nothing here," the Ranger said. "Let's move on."

"Platoon Sergeant, where are you?" Tristan spoke into her radio. "I just got something here. I think we should stay."

It was rare for her to push for more time, but the Rangers had encouraged her to speak up if she had something they actually needed to know; she was part of the team. Each night before mission she and her Ranger counterpart would exchange notes and talk about what they expected and what they were looking for as they sought to keep the pressure on the insurgent networks of Taliban and al-Qaeda guys operating around the area. Even out on the objective the Ranger and the CST would often huddle quickly to share anything critical they were learning and finding.

"Okay, we'll give you ten more minutes," he said; "see what you come up with."

While Anne spoke with the girl's mother, the teenager began telling Tristan about the men who often came around to the house, and some of the conversations she had heard.

Tristan wrote down as many details as she could. She grabbed her Ranger counterpart and he agreed: they would search the house once more, especially the back part of the compound where the animals lived.

Soon enough the Rangers unearthed more than a dozen, not yet connected, pressure-plate IEDs hidden in the ground. Even more immediately relevant to that evening's success, they learned from the insurgent singled out by the girl in the purple dress that IEDs set to detonate lay buried all along the path they were just about to walk to the next compound.

If they had moved on as planned, they would have stepped right onto them.

That night, after her trek over brambles and through wadis and back to the helicopter that would lift them home, Tristan went to listen to the post-mission brief and offer up a quick slide on what she had learned that night. On the way out she saluted her friend once more.

"Thanks, Ash."

April came at last. For the last few weeks Tristan and Anne had joined some of the operators on their camp in "tan ops," which entailed staying up long enough to catch the first rays of the potent

Kandahar sun. No one wanted to return home pale and wan. Or fat. Out went the Christmas cookies and care package M&Ms. No carbs. Only proteins, veggies, and energy drinks now.

Tristan couldn't believe they'd soon be going home. She dreamt about laying around aimlessly with no place to go and spending entire days reading celebrity gossip magazines and watching TV with her sisters and brother.

I'm going to miss this place, she thought. The guys she worked with, the missions she went on, the women and children she talked to each night, the children and their beautiful eyes. The moments of compassion and caring buried among the horrible moments of war. Even the smell of the poo pond.

On their way back to America all the CSTs would meet in Bagram for one last time as a team. They would fill out the last of their paperwork and find out for certain whether they could stay on as CSTs doing the job they now knew well, felt qualified for, and loved. Tristan missed Kate and Amber and Cassie and Sarah and Kimberly and all the other girls. She couldn't wait to hear their stories; she knew that as soon as they started to tell them it would feel as if they hadn't been apart for the last four months.

But before she boarded a plane out of Kandahar for the last time she would write one last letter.

We are leaving today.

Everything is packed and I have returned to my room for a few short moments. Just wanted to take one last look at the bed where I spent so many hours lying awake. Where I silently thanked God for returning me every night. I wanted to look one last time at Ashley's sneakers. Just waiting faithfully to be taken for a spin. I wanted to thank Ashley for the quiet strength she has given me over the last few months. I know we all have a lot of talking to Ashley to do in the next few weeks. I know watching KAF disappear will be hard. We will feel like we are leaving Ashley for good. But we are not leaving Ashley anywhere. Ashley will be with all of us, wherever we go, for the rest of our lives.

Goodbye little room.

Epilogue

On Memorial Day 2012, Lieutenant General John Mulholland stood before an assembly of grieving families to honor the Army special operations soldiers who had given everything to their country.

"It is important that we never forget that Ashley and her brothers-in-arms were truly exceptional people," he said during the annual ceremony held on the U.S. Army Special Operations Forces Memorial Plaza. "They had and always will have a value beyond measure; they are supremely competent in what they chose to do, were clearly committed to making a difference in the world in which they lived, and they unquestionably did so."

Bob and Debbie White, along with Jason and Ashley's siblings Brittany and Josh, sat among the audience on their folding chairs, holding red roses and listening as Ashley's name took its place on the Army Special Operations Command Memorial Wall alongside SFC Kris Domeij, PFC Chris Horns, and eight other Rangers killed in action in 2011. Ashley was the first CST whose name would be etched on a nameplate and join the granite memorial to the fallen.

Back at Bagram a month earlier, a number of the CSTs asked if they could extend their mission. But it was not to be. CST was a one-year deployment and now it was time for the soldiers to return to their home units. The next class awaited. More female soldiers had put their hands up to serve with the fighters of special operations and now it was their turn to deploy.

The problem was, returning to their pre-CST lives was the last thing many of the soldiers wanted.

Cassie couldn't fathom going home. She had been out regularly on missions with her strike force. She had cheered when her partner, Isabel, had been nominated by the Rangers for an IMPACT Award for finding explosives and other intel-related items that "would have been overlooked" in her absence. She even had the privilege of having one of the officers she served under inscribe her copy of Sebastian Junger's book *War* just before she left her base.

"You are a true warrior leader and your exploits in 'Leading the Way' for women in combat will be told one day," he wrote to Cassie. This officer had been one of the soldiers featured in the book she had carried with her to Afghanistan.

Next thing she knew, she found herself in an auditorium at Bagram listening to Kate explain to one of the generals who had come to offer his thanks to the CSTs that she and some of the others wanted to keep doing what they had been doing.

"Sir, with all due respect, you don't understand," Kate had dared to blurt out. Given the ban on women in direct action roles, "This is it for us. There is no place else for us to go. We have done nothing better and will do nothing better. And now we are being sent back to our units. *Nothing* else will compare to this."

When they returned to Fort Bragg, Cassie walked back into the Landmark Inn, this time without the hope and excitement of her last visit. How could she possibly go back to her old Army assignment and "normal life"? Whatever that was. The only people who understood her now were her fellow CSTs. They were as much her family as her family. Maybe more so.

Six more CST classes followed in the years that intervened. I recently had the privilege of spending an evening with a group of women from different years of the program, nearly all of whom had served the direct action mission. The connection they shared, even among those who hadn't before met, was obvious and immediate. What struck me that night was the same sense of intense friendship I felt the first time I met Ashley's teammates. They finished one another's sentences, served as each other's career counselors, divorce therapists, spiritual advisors, and baby shower hosts. It was clear the soldiers were bound by a bond that no one outside their small, invisible band of CSTs would ever truly understand. Leda's leadership, Ashley's loss, the mission they had loved and couldn't go back to, the fact that no one outside the group of soldiers and SEALs alongside whom they served knew what they had done and seen, all combined to create an unbreakable connection forged at war and cemented at home. They were all they had and they understood why.

In the years that followed Ashley White-Stumpf's death, being her parent became a full-time job for Bob and Debbie White. Ceremony after ceremony, memorial after memorial, they would sit in the audience and hear people honor and talk about Ashley. Sometimes they spoke as well. Each week they returned to her grave behind the church to clear the many mementos people had left her: kettle bells, silver charms, flowers, letters on lined notebook paper telling her she was their "motivation." Their mailbox filled with letters from people who knew her in Afghanistan, had met her in Ohio, or simply had read her story in the local newspaper. At Kent State a memorial scholarship and an annual run were established in Ashley's name. Her old high school hung her photo in a glass case. The North Carolina National Guard unveiled a granite memorial to her at the Goldsboro National Guard Armory. Her brother Josh gave a powerful speech at the Ohio Statehouse memorializing his sister and addressing the loss experienced by every family who loses a son or daughter at war. The Ohio legislature named part of Route 44 in Marlboro Township the 1st Lt. Ashley White-Stumpf Memorial Highway.

In January 2013 the ban on women in ground combat units officially ended. The rules had at last caught up with reality.

"A hundred and fifty-two women in uniform have died serving this nation in Iraq and Afghanistan. Female service members have faced the reality of combat, proven their willingness to fight and, yes, to die to defend their fellow Americans," said Secretary of Defense Leon Panetta at a news conference with Chairman of the Joint Chiefs Martin Dempsey. "Every time I visited the warzone, every time I've met with troops, reviewed military operations, and talked to wounded warriors, I've been impressed with the fact that everyone—everyone, men and women alike—everyone is committed to doing the job. They're fighting and they're dying together. And the time has come for our policies to recognize that reality."

Said Panetta, "If they are willing to put their lives on the line, then we ought to recognize that they deserve a chance to serve in any capacity they want."

Six months later, in June 2013, the Cultural Support Teams came up at a Pentagon news conference focused on integrating women into jobs that previously had been off-limits to them, including roles as special operators.

"Quite frankly, I was encouraged by just the physical performance of some of the young girls who aspire to go into the cultural support teams," said SOCOM's Major General Bennet Sacolick, who called the program a "huge success." He went on to say, "They very well may provide a foundation for ultimate integration."

By January 1, 2016, special operations command and each of the services will either fully open up all roles to women or explain the reasons why they will stay male-only. All exemptions will have to be approved by both the secretary of defense and the chairman of the Joint Chiefs.

On Veteran's Day 2013 First Lieutenant Ashley White-Stumpf marked another milestone: she became the first woman to have a tree dedicated to her on the Memorial Walk of Honor at the National Infantry Museum in Columbus, Georgia, just outside Fort Benning. Her fellow CSTs led by Amber and Lane raised the money for the tree and plaque in her honor. Then, almost exactly two years after

Ashley's death, a second CST, First Lieutenant Jennifer Moreno, an Army nurse, died in action in Kandahar Province alongside two Army Rangers and an Army criminal investigator. She would join Ashley on that Memorial Walk.

At that Veteran's Day ceremony on the grounds of the National Infantry Museum, members of CST-2 gathered before a square, gold-rimmed plaque whose first line read:

CST PAST, PRESENT, FUTURE

That mild November day beneath a blue-gray sky Bob and Debbie White sat next to the soldiers who had known and loved their daughter and who, by now, had become members of their own family.

Tristan took to the podium.

> When Ashley White-Stumpf became an angel she was at the apex of her life. She was a newlywed with an incredibly loving and supporting husband. She had just purchased her first home. She had a good job and an amazing family. And yet Ashley asked, "what can I do, how can I make a difference?"
>
> Think about that for a minute. How much better would this world be if every person, at the happiest, most fulfilled point in their life, thought not of themselves, but of the good they could do for things bigger than themselves?

It is a question for each of us.

Acknowledgments

For two years Bob and Debbie White have allowed me into their home, their lives, and their family. Their unending generosity and relentless determination to remember their daughter made it impossible for me ever to forget the stakes of this story. At a time when we seem as a country to have strayed from some of our most deeply held values: hard work, a commitment to merit, humility, sacrifice for the next generation, and the importance of serving others, the White family is a reminder of who we are at our best—and proof of the power of kindness and courage in action.

Ashley's husband, Jason, is an example of valor and grace in the face of grief. Those who knew Ashley at Kent State and afterward inevitably began conversations by mentioning the central role her husband had played in helping her to become who she was. Experiencing his commitment to honoring her legacy was both incredibly moving and an urgent reminder of why this story mattered.

Ashley's twin sister, Brittany, and her brother, Josh, and his wife, Kate, shared stories and memories and much more, and I am thankful for their openness in the face of such a monumentally difficult task. It is a kindness I have never taken lightly.

To everyone who serves America each day and each night, I hope these pages have done their small part to remind readers of the reality of your work, the value of your service, the costs of your sacrifice, and the importance of engaging with the wars you fight in America's name. I will be thankful always for the opportunity to shine a light on a world with which too few of us are familiar.

Getting to know the leaders who shaped the fight in Afghanistan has been a privilege and a pleasure, and I feel daily the weight of the responsibility of these stories. Thank you for allowing me to see the world as you do and for trusting me to share your stories with a country which must better understand what is asked of you, why you do it, and what that means for all of us. And to all the public affairs teams who shepherded my early calls, thank you for what you do and for your wisdom and care.

The soldiers in these pages share the unbreakable bonds of war. They are friends in battle and family for life. I knew the first time I heard Ashley's story that America had to meet them as well, and I am thankful for the opportunity and the great responsibility of this challenge.

And to the Afghan-Americans who served in this war and who helped to create this story and make it theirs, thank you for sharing your insight and your world.

So many people offered their views, their voices, and their memories to this project. I have worked to do justice to all that you have shared. To the ROTC leaders at Kent State, Ashley's friends from home, classmates from college, and fellow soldiers in North Carolina, thank you for making the time to help assemble this story.

Jim Gregory offered a gracious hand to help this story and incredibly valuable insight. Claire Russo, Matt Pottinger, Zoe Bedell, and a slew of others helped me to understand the origins of this program, and I am thankful for their wisdom. My Council on Foreign Relations colleague Janine Davidson, an Air Force pilot who flew C-17s and C-130s, offered valuable time and perspective, as did Susan Marquis and Linda Robinson of the RAND Corporation, author Dick Couch, Rebecca Patterson, and retired U.S. Navy Captain Lory Manning, who got me started with a reading list and a sense of history. Vice Admiral Lee Gunn offered his help and encouragement from the start. Jeremy Bash shared valuable wisdom and a big-picture perspective. Thank you to all.

My literary agent, Elyse Cheney, is the one you want next to you no matter the project; her tireless devotion to getting the shape and structure of this story right at the outset made all that followed far more manageable. Sam Freilich, Alex Jacobs, and Tyler Allen helped alongside. Jonathan Burnham at Harper believed in this story and pushed for it throughout. My wise and wonderful editor, Gail Winston, turned around the pages in record time, and each time the narrative returned stronger, sharper, and far more succinct. The incredibly capable Emily Cunningham made words flow and our production schedule manageable. Lisa Sharkey believed in *Dressmaker* from the outset and this book from the start, and I am thankful for all her support. Big thanks to our tireless publicity leader Tina Andreadis, marketing's Leah Wasielewski and Stephanie Cooper, and the sales team, including Doug Jones, Josh Marwell, and Kate Walker. To everyone at CFR, including Richard Haass, Jim Lindsay, Irina Faskianos, Hannah Chartoff, countless military fellows, and the indefatigable Lisa Shields, thanks for the encouragement throughout.

I am blessed with wonderfully talented—and generous—friends and colleagues. My assistant, Christy Morales, kept me on track and our research organized. Melissa Stack lent a spare office and Robin Wood Sailer and Tara Luizzi their spare rooms. Marketing mind Chris Villareal shared his wisdom and his creative talent, as did Gina Bianchini. Laurye Blackford helped to map out the book's launch from the start and offered invaluable advice and perspective all along the way. Willow Bay offered the very first set of notes for this book and the story was far stronger for them. Arash Ghadishah saw the power of this story at the same moment I did and was a consistent champion for this book. Lucy Helm, Anne Kornblut, Melinda Arons, Marc Adelman, Anna Soellner, Lee Gonzalez, Betsy Fischer Martin, Juleanna Glover, and Anna Robertson all supported this story in important ways. And you couldn't have a wiser friend or smarter sounding board than author and editor Annik LaFarge.

Family is at the heart of this story and I must thank my own. My mother-in-law is the best agent a writer could have and helped in countless ways. My aunt and my godmother, Gloria Rojas and Elaine Cameron, told me to keep going no matter what. Laurie

Sheets Forbes served as resident designer and Mark Cohen taught me a while back to never look for the easy path and that doing work that mattered was "supposed to be this hard."

And finally, thank you to my husband, a former Naval officer who talked with me at length about military culture and offered unwavering support for this story. He is at the center of making this and much else possible.

This book is for so many and a great number of people helped bring it to life. Telling this story has altered and moved me beyond anything I had imagined at the start. It is in the memory of all who have served and sacrificed that I say thanks to each of you reading these pages for being part of it.

Select Bibliography

America's Post–9/11 Wars

Bergen, Peter. *Manhunt: The Ten-Year Search for Bin Laden from 9/11 to Abbottabad.* New York: Broadway Paperbacks, 2012.

Bowden, Mark. *The Finish: The Killing of Osama Bin Laden.* New York: Atlantic Monthly Press, 2012.

Broadwell, Paula, and Vernon Loeb. *All In: The Education of General David Petraeus.* New York: Penguin Books, 2012.

Kaplan, Fred. *The Insurgents: David Petraeus and the Plot to Change the American Way of War.* New York: Simon & Schuster Paperbacks, 2013.

Mazzetti, Mark. *The Way of the Knife: The CIA, a Secret Army, and a War at the Ends of the Earth.* New York: Penguin Books, 2013.

McChrystal, Stanley. *My Share of the Task: A Memoir.* New York: Portfolio/Penguin, 2013.

The U.S. Army/Marine Corps Counterinsurgency Field Manual. Chicago: University of Chicago Press, 2007.

Special Operations

Bank, Aaron. *From OSS to Green Berets: The Birth of Special Forces.* Novato: Presidio Press, 1986.

Marquis, Susan L. *Unconventional Warfare: Rebuilding U.S. Special Operations Forces.* Washington: Brookings Institution, 1997.

Maurer, Kevin. *Gentlemen Bastards: On the Ground in Afghanistan with America's Elite Special Forces.* New York: Berkeley Caliber, 2012.

McRaven, William H. *Spec Ops: Case Studies in Special Operations Warfare: Theory and Practice.* Novato: Presidio Press, 1996.

Robinson, Linda. *Masters of Chaos: The Secret History of the Special Forces.* New York: PublicAffairs, 2004.

Weiss, Mitch, and Kevin Maurer. *No Way Out: A Story of Valor in the Mountains of Afghanistan.* New York: Berkeley Caliber, 2012.

The 75th Ranger Regiment

Black, Robert W. *Rangers in World War II.* New York: Presidio Press, 1992.

Bowden, Mark. *Black Hawk Down: A Story of Modern War.* New York: Grove Press, 1999.

Couch, Dick. *Sua Sponte: The Forging of the Modern American Ranger.* New York: Berkeley Caliber, 2012.

Jenkins, Leo. *Lest We Forget: An Army Ranger Medic's Story.* Leo Jenkins, 2013.

Lock, John D. *To Fight with Intrepidity . . . The Complete History of the U.S. Army Rangers, 1622 to Present.* 2nd ed. Tucson: Fenestra Books, 2001.

Posey, Edward L. *The US Army's First, Last, and Only All-Black Rangers: The 2nd Ranger Infantry Company (Airborne) in the Korean War, 1950–1951.* New York: Savas Beatie, 2009.

Women in the Military

Biank, Tanya. *Undaunted: The Real Story of America's Servicewomen in Today's Military.* New York: New American Library, 2013.

Blanton, DeAnn, and Lauren M. Cook. *They Fought Like Demons: Women Soldiers in the American Civil War.* Baton Rouge: Louisiana State University Press, 2002.

Holm, Jeanne. *Women in the Military: An Unfinished Revolution.* Novato: Presidio Press, 1992.

Williams, Kayla, and Michael E. Staub. *Love My Rifle More than You: Young and Female in the U.S. Army.* New York: W. W. Norton, 2005.

Wise, James E., Jr., and Scott Baron. *Women at War: Iraq, Afghanistan, and Other Conflicts.* Annapolis: Naval Institute Press, 2006.

Insights,
Interviews
& More . . .

Meet Gayle Tzemach Lemmon

GAYLE TZEMACH LEMMON is a Senior Fellow at the Council on Foreign Relations and a contributor to Atlantic Media's *Defense One*, writing on national security and foreign policy issues. In 2004 she left ABC News in Washington to earn her MBA at Harvard, where she began writing about entrepreneurs in conflict and post-conflict zones, including Afghanistan, Bosnia, and Rwanda. She is the bestselling author of *The Dressmaker of Khair Khana* and has written for *Newsweek*, the *Financial Times*, *International Herald Tribune*, *Christian Science Monitor*, CNN.com, and the *Daily Beast*, as well as the World Bank and Harvard Business School. Her 2015 TED Talk on *Ashley's War* has received more than one million views, and she appears frequently on broadcast outlets to discuss topics including U.S. foreign policy. You can find more of her work at www.gaylelemmon.com.

About the author

2

Cast of Characters

TEAM MEMBERS

Active-Duty Army

2nd Lt. Rigby Allen, intel officer,
    Ft. Huachuca, Arizona
Staff Sgt. Kimberly Blake, military police,
    Ft. Stewart, Georgia
Capt. Anne Jeremy, engineer, Ft. Carson,
    Colorado
1st Lt. Tristan Marsden, artillery officer,
    Ft. Sill, Oklahoma
1st Lt. Kate Raimann, military police,
    Ft. Benning, Columbus, Georgia
1st Lt. Cassie Spaulding, military police,
    Ft. Wainright, Alaska
1st Lt. Amber Treadmont, intel officer,
    Ft. Jackson, Columbia, South Carolina
1st Lt. Sarah Waldman, military police,
    U.S. Army Europe
2nd Lt. Rachel Washburn, intel officer,
    Ft. Huachuca, Arizona
2nd Lt. Isabel Wood, military police,
    U.S. Army Garrison, Yongsan,
    South Korea

National Guard and Reserve

Staff Sgt. Lane Mason, transportation
    corps, based in Nevada
Maj. Leda Reston, special operations,
    based in Washington, D.C.
2nd Lt. Ashley White, medical corps,
    based in North Carolina

An Update and "Where Are They Now?"

IN DECEMBER 2015, Secretary of Defense Ashton Carter announced that all combat roles would be open to women.

As long as they qualify and meet the standards, women will now be able to contribute to our mission in ways they could not before," Carter said. "They'll be able to serve as Army Rangers and Green Berets, Navy SEALs, Marine Corps infantry, Air Force parajumpers, and everything else that previously was open only to men. And even more importantly, our military will be better able to harness the skills and perspectives that talented women have to offer.

In a video released not long afterward, Gen. Joseph Votel, head of Special Operations Command, mentioned the role of the CSTs. "Since 2011 we have very effectively employed women as part of our Cultural Support Teams in Afghanistan where selected female servicemembers placed with our strike forces effectively doubled our access to the population."

* * * *

In the months following the publication of *Ashley's War* I have been moved beyond any expectation by readers' reactions. Fathers have written to request signed books for their daughters because they want them to dare big and do great things. Mothers of Rangers have written to say that *Ashley's War* gave them the most intimate look they had yet experienced of what America asked of their sons each night on the battlefield. Rangers wrote to say the book "reminded them of home." And young women just entering the military have written to say that Ashley, Lane, Leda, and all of the teammates featured in this story gave them the inspiration they needed to test and push themselves to the utmost in service to a cause greater than any one individual.

And so many who have never read a war story have written to say that although they didn't know anyone in the military and hadn't known what to expect when they picked up the book, they had loved meeting these young women and men. Having entered their world through the doorway of *Ashley's War*, they wanted to know more about what had happened to them since. "What happened to Nadia? To Jason? Where are the CSTs now?"

For years now women have served and died alongside Army Rangers and now they have the opportunity to access the Army's most prestigious leadership school. Since *Ashley's War* was published, Army Ranger School has opened to women and three women—all West Point grads—have earned the right to wear the prestigious Ranger tab. I headed down to Fort Benning to report on the school's first coed class and saw firsthand the gut and grit of all the aspiring Rangers battling their bodies and their minds to meet the tests before them. As columnist Chuck Williams wrote in Georgia's *Columbus Ledger-Enquirer*, "Ashley White paved the way for women in Ranger School." I agree. Just as Ashley and her teammates stood on the shoulders of those who came before them, they themselves led the way for all those who have and will come afterward.

And now, a look at where the participants in *Ashley's War* are today:

Nadia, Ashley's interpreter, was flown from Kandahar to a U.S. Army hospital in Germany for medical treatment. Eventually she returned home to recuperate. For more than eighteen months she suffered pain and faced mobility challenges with a right arm that barely functioned while she worked to rebuild her life from her parents' home in Orange County. Following a series of surgeries and a slew of medical setbacks, she is now working to move forward once more with her plans to study for a masters in international relations. She retains her ability to find the best in people.

Jason, Ashley's husband, continues to serve honorably in the U.S. Army and has deployed twice since her death.

Anne Jeremy, Ashley's partner, has left the active-duty military and is now in graduate school, as is Sarah Walden. Like most of her teammates, Tristan Marsden found that no other roles open to her ▶

About the book

matched the CST experience and she has left the Army to pursue entrepreneurial endeavors and graduate study. Cassie Spaulding remains in the military and is tackling new frontiers and challenges, as are Kate Raimann, Isabel Wood, Kimberly Blake, and Rigby Allen. Amber Treadmont and Lane Mason have both left active duty: Amber is in the Army Reserves and preparing for medical school. Lane is studying for a nursing degree, writing about her experiences as a soldier at war and as a survivor of sexual assault, and caring for her three young daughters. Leda Reston remains in the special operations community, along with several of the CSTs in this story.

Just after *Ashley's War* was published, one of Ashley's teammates who served with the Green Berets wrote to say: "I was always proud to have been a part of the program and would have been fine if no one else ever knew about us. However Ashley's death brought out something even more fierce and an absolute dedication to be the best we could be. Even though I have known others who have died and sacrificed their lives in the decade of war, her death truly broke my heart . . . a beautiful sister was lost.

"The world needed to know."

Indeed. ∽

Reading Group Guide
Discussion Questions for *Ashley's War*

1. What were your thoughts about women serving in the military before you read *Ashley's War*?

2. Given that First Lieutenant Ashley White was in some ways discouraged to join the military by her father, what went into her decision to do so anyway?

3. What were the reasons for the "combat exclusion prohibition" for women formalized in 1994?

4. U.S. Special Operations Commander Eric Olson says of the war in Afghanistan that U.S. forces had "to learn to think [their] way through this fight." What is an appropriate relationship between thinking and fighting, between intellect and force?

5. During the "100 hours of hell" assessment and selection phase, Rigby finds wisdom carved into a bathroom wall: "The mind is its own place. And itself can make a hell of heaven and a heaven of hell. Don't quit." What is the relationship between the mind and physical pain and suffering? How important is encouragement from others? And the experience of all those who have walked the same path before you?

6. What is the role of friendship in *Ashley's War*? ▶

7. Lieutenant Matt Pottinger, a journalist for the *Wall Street Journal* before becoming a Marine, combined "a reporter's instincts" with his training. What might a journalist and a soldier have in common?

8. What's significant about each of the three terms in Cultural Support Team?

9. Consider each of the women chosen to be part of the Cultural Support Team. What does each bring—in personality, skill, experience— to the group?

10. Cassie says at one point that "being female was a special burden in war." What does she mean? Is this a necessary part of war or could changes be made?

11. Often the women of the CST are referred to—even by each other—as "guys" or "girls," instead of women. Does this matter? How important is language in the push for opportunity?

12. Why is such extreme physical training so important to becoming and serving as a soldier in Special Ops?

13. What particular challenges face military couples?

14. Ashley worries at one point in the process that she is "a little bit too shy" to be a part of CST. Is extroversion an essential part of being a soldier? Of leading others? What are the essential elements of leadership?

15. There are many allusions to Hollywood films about war in the book. What role—positive or negative, for civilians or soldiers—do such films play in American culture?

16. Consider the role of the interpreters—"terps"—paired with soldiers and the CST. What are their particular challenges?

17. When Nadia, an interpreter from Orange County, California, returns home from combat, she feels totally disconnected from the celebrations and normal lives of her friends. What awareness should be expected from civilians who have never been near combat when their country is at war?

18. What elements of Ashley's performance as a Special Ops enabler win her over to the combat hardened male soldiers?

19. At Ashley's burial ceremony a woman brings her daughter so that she would know that "girls could be heroes, too." What is the nature of a hero? Who are other women that should be recognized as such? ∾

A Q&A with the Author and 1st Lt. Shaye Haver

1st Lt. Shaye Haver was one of the first women graduates of Army Ranger School.

1st Lt. Shaye Haver: *I love the way you described the feel of the room in the hotel when all the women first met. It reminded me of the first time I met the ladies with whom I would start Ranger School in 2015. Did they ever expand upon their feelings in that moment?*

Gayle Tzemach Lemmon: Yes, that moment at the Landmark Inn really marked the first time that they found their "family," the people who would become their friends for life. And for many it was the first time they had ever been around people just like themselves—who shared their desire to serve, to test themselves, to make a difference. And who were incredibly funny and cared about one another even as they competed against each other.

Haver: *The flyer for the CST program recruited women soldiers to become part of "history." When I volunteered for Ranger School, historical significance never crossed my mind. Why do you think the military decided to use the word "history" in the advertisement?*

Lemmon: I had the same question! They needed good people and wanted to attract soldiers who had always wanted to be part of special operations combat roles still officially off-limits to women—soldiers who wanted to be at the heart of the mission, testing themselves for their country alongside the best of the best. And that poster did its job: it grabbed the attention of so many women in *Ashley's War*—and changed their lives forever in the process.

Haver: *I had the honor of meeting some of the women in* Ashley's War. *Do you know if any of them will continue to seek combat opportunities as the military opens these roles to women?*

Lemmon: A few of the women in *Ashley's War* left the military while I was writing the story because a lot of jobs at that time remained closed to women and they felt that nothing would ever live up to the experience they had had serving together on combat missions alongside Rangers and SEALs. Several remain in the special operations community, and they are watching closely to see what opportunities to serve they can reach for as new roles open up to women.

Haver: *During Ranger school I had to learn a lot about tactics to which I had never before been exposed. I imagine these ladies had a similar experience, where they had to learn something and immediately be assessed on execution. What kind of feedback did the CSTs provide about their training after experiencing combat?*

Lemmon: No question those leading the program were "building a plane in mid-flight," and learning as they went about skills and knowledge the soldiers would need on the battlefield. These soldiers received six weeks of training to serve ▶

on missions alongside men who trained year-round and for years. But everyone understood this was war and the capability was needed right then and right away. So they learned on the job. And when they came back they offered feedback to their trainers—more tactical training, less classroom time for those on the Ranger mission.

Haver: *How have the women in* Ashley's War *committed to sharing their experiences with future generations of women in uniform?*

Lemmon: No one in *Ashley's War* thought they had done anything at all exceptional; they believed they had simply done their job and answered the call to serve. They spoke to me only because they wanted to make sure their friend wasn't forgotten. But I do know they were watching closely as you all made it to Ranger School and graduated and that they did feel that a part of what they accomplished was helping to lay the groundwork for all who followed. That is part of Ashley's legacy, the role she and her teammates played in paving the way for you and so many others. ◡

How to Get Involved with Veterans' Issues

Here are just a few suggestions:

First Lieutenant Ashley White-Stumpf
Scholarship Fund
http://ashleywhitestumpf.com/scholarship/

American Women Veterans
http://americanwomenveterans.org/home/

Bob Woodruff Foundation
http://bobwoodrufffoundation.org

Final Salute Inc.
www.finalsaluteinc.org

Fisher House Foundation
www.fisherhouse.org

Grace After Fire
www.graceafterfire.org

Iraq and Afghanistan Veterans of America
http://iava.org

National Military Family Association
www.militaryfamily.org

Onward Veterans
http://schultzfamilyfoundation.org

Ranger Scholarship Fund
www.rangersscholarshipfund.org

Special Operations Warrior Foundation
www.specialops.org

Tragedy Assistance Program for Survivors
(TAPS)
www.taps.org

Voices from War
http://voicesfromwar.org

Women in Military Service for America
Memorial Foundation
www.womensmemorial.org/About/
welcome.html

Words After War
www.wordsafterwar.org

Wounded Warrior Project
www.woundedwarriorproject.org ∽

Discover great authors, exclusive offers, and more at hc.com.

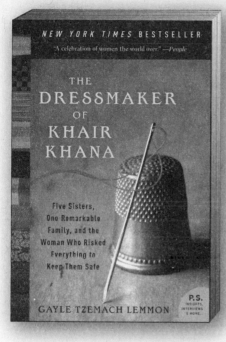